SEX AND THE MARRIED GIRL

STUDIES IN GENDER AND HISTORY

General Editors: Franca Iacovetta and Karen Dubinsky

Sex and the Married Girl

Heterosexual Marriage and the Body in Postwar Canada

HEATHER STANLEY

UNIVERSITY OF TORONTO PRESS
Toronto Buffalo London

© University of Toronto Press 2023
Toronto Buffalo London
utorontopress.com

ISBN 978-1-4875-0119-8 (cloth) ISBN 978-1-4875-1268-2 (EPUB)
ISBN 978-1-4875-2114-1 (paper) ISBN 978-1-4875-1267-5 (PDF)

Studies in Gender and History

___

Library and Archives Canada Cataloguing in Publication

Title: Sex and the married girl : heterosexual marriage and the body in postwar Canada / Heather Stanley.
Names: Stanley, Heather (Lecturer in history), author.
Series: Studies in gender and history ; 54.
Description: Series statement: Studies in gender and history ; 54 | Includes bibliographical references and index.
Identifiers: Canadiana (print) 20220396485 | Canadiana (ebook) 20220396515 | ISBN 9781487501198 (cloth) | ISBN 9781487521141 (paper) | ISBN 9781487512682 (EPUB) | ISBN 9781487512675 (PDF)
Subjects: LCSH: Married women – Sexual behavior – Canada – History – 20th century. | LCSH: Heterosexual women – Sexual behavior – Canada – History – 20th century. | LCSH: Sex in marriage – Canada – History – 20th century.
Classification: LCC HQ29 .S73 2023 | DDC 306.77086/55097109045 – dc23

___

We wish to acknowledge the land on which the University of Toronto Press operates. This land is the traditional territory of the Wendat, the Anishnaabeg, the Haudenosaunee, the Métis, and the Mississaugas of the Credit First Nation.

University of Toronto Press acknowledges the financial support of the Government of Canada, the Canada Council for the Arts, and the Ontario Arts Council, an agency of the Government of Ontario, for its publishing activities.

Canada Council for the Arts
Conseil des Arts du Canada

ONTARIO ARTS COUNCIL
CONSEIL DES ARTS DE L'ONTARIO
an Ontario government agency
un organisme du gouvernement de l'Ontario

Funded by the Government of Canada
Financé par le gouvernement du Canada

Canada

This book is dedicated with love to three generations of brave women:

Marion Bellamy (née Stewart)
Shirley Stanley (née Bellamy)
Alexis and Lucy Clapperton

Contents

List of Illustrations ix

List of Abbreviations xi

Acknowledgments xiii

1 Breaking Free from the "Nostalgia Trap": History and the Paradox of Female Sexuality in the Postwar World 3

2 Embodying Family Values: The *Canadian Medical Association Journal* and the Creation of the "Mother Body" 15

3 Sex, Marriage, and the "One-Flesh" Body: Married Sexuality in the Anglican, United, and Roman Catholic Denominations 47

4 Bringing Down Goliath: Oral Histories and the Engagement of Individual Bodies with the Ideal 87

5 Conclusion: Making Good (Sex) 137

Appendix: Interview Data 145

Notes 155

Bibliography 189

Index 207

Illustrations

1 Bonamine advertisement, *CMAJ*, 22 October 1960   27
2 Mornidine advertisement, *CMAJ*, 11 July 1959   28
3 Tace advertisement, *CMAJ*, 15 January 1955   30
4 Bellergal advertisement, *CMAJ*, 1 September 1962   31
5 Cartoon lampooning overbearing female patient, *CMAJ*, 15 July 1958   39

Abbreviations

AAC	Anglican Archives of Canada
CMAJ	*Canadian Medical Association Journal*
CPAJ	*Canadian Psychiatric Association Journal*
LAC	Library and Archives Canada
UCAC	United Church Archives of Canada
WAAF	*Women's Auxiliary Air Force*

Acknowledgments

Writing the acknowledgments for a first book, especially one that has been a part of my life for such an extended time, is a rare opportunity to reflect and take stock of the last ten-plus years. Writing and researching are often solitary endeavours, but my community of friends, mentors, family, colleagues, and students enlivened and emboldened this work and made the process of writing it bearable. This community has made this work so much more than it could ever be had I struggled unaccompanied on this journey.

As this work began as part of doctoral research, my first thanks go to my incredible mentor and doctoral supervisor, Dr. Valerie J. Korinek. Your support, teaching, and dry wit have been invaluable to the work in this book and in the shaping of the scholar I am today. I only hope that I can live up to your example of mentorship and feminist guidance. Thanks also to the members of my committee at the University of Saskatchewan for their consistent open-door policy and willingness to share their varied expertise. Appreciation also goes out to my friends and class cohort from that time: thanks for the ideas, laughs, and for your willingness to babysit my oldest daughter so that I could attempt to string two thoughts together.

Financially, this work was supported primarily by a SSHRC Doctoral Fellowship with revisions being completed while teaching at Memorial University of Newfoundland and Vancouver Island University. Short-term contracts that build in time for research are rare, and I have been extremely lucky to get two such employments that allowed me to do the necessary revisions on this manuscript as well as providing wonderful colleagues to work amongst. I am also grateful to my colleagues at the University of Lethbridge, who have supported me during what turned out to be a very unusual start to my employment: your encouragement and humour have been invaluable as I find my feet. I would also be remiss if I did not give grateful thanks to the many administrative assistants I have been privileged to work with over the years. Without your work none of our work would be possible. I am also grateful for the assistance of the archivists at each of the archives to which I was privileged to be granted access, especially those at the Anglican Archives of Canada and the United Church Archives of Canada, for their aid in finding obscure pamphlets, marriage manuals, and other publications.

Crucially, this work would also have not been possible without the wisdom and words of the eighteen women who bravely answered my advertisement asking for women who married between 1939 and 1966 to tell me about their lives and answer some "cheeky" questions. Ladies, you invited me into your homes, trusted me with your secrets and the intimate details of your lives, and made me laugh and cry with your stories. I hope I have done your words justice.

Working with Len Husband and the staff at the University of Toronto Press has been a lovely experience for me as a first-time author. I am also grateful for the feedback from the three anonymous reviewers who read the manuscript and helped to shepherd it in its journey from research to monograph. I am especially appreciative of the third reviewer, who stepped in after one of the other reviewers could not complete the process.

Finally, my family has been instrumental to the completion of this book. These few simple words of acknowledgment cannot hope to suffice in expressing the debt of gratitude I owe to each of you. Milt and Shirley Stanley, thank you for the foundational love of learning you instilled within me and your unwavering support for this and all other endeavours in my life. To my in-laws Carol and Jack, thanks for letting me come to your house and write and for providing me with endless cups of coffee and endless hours of childcare. To my extended family (on both sides!) thank you for championing me in this work and supporting me through this process. Jonathan Clapperton, you were the first person to hear the question that would become the central theme of this book, and your support of it, and me, has not waivered. You have read and re-read this work so many times and each time you helped make it stronger. You are always my first editor and my favourite collaborator. I am so glad I agreed to read over your term paper all those years ago. Finally, to my daughters Alexis and Lucy, this manuscript has been a background feature of your entire lives. (Perhaps sometimes it felt like an unwelcome interloper). But you were (and are) a constant source of inspiration and joy. Thank you for being you.

SEX AND THE MARRIED GIRL

Chapter One

Breaking Free from the "Nostalgia Trap": History and the Paradox of Female Sexuality in the Postwar World

The idea for this book came to me in 2008 while I was reading the original 1973 publication of the feminist health manual *Our Bodies, Ourselves*. For readers unfamiliar with this text, it was a work created by American feminist health activists designed to provide common-sense and accessible information about the female body – particularly the sexual and reproductive body. Alongside hand-drawn diagrams and information on how to talk to a male doctor so he would actually listen, the original authors shared stories – deep reflective pieces – about their own embodiment. Whether describing masturbation, sexual intercourse, abortion, or childbearing, these women expressed a combination of description of physical experience and the socially and culturally derived meanings of those experiences.[1] In that moment a thought struck me: "What did women in the 1950s think about their sexual and reproductive bodies?"

At that time for me, as for many others, the 1950s woman was a fantasy figure. Fueled by my own fascinated forays into late-night reruns of *Leave It to Beaver* and *The Donna Reed Show*, the 1950s housewife portrayed in those bucolic (and often boring) sitcoms seemed a historical anachronism; so content to be the perfect wife and mother, at times she seemed a disturbingly Stepfordesque figure, mindlessly vacuuming in her pearls and high heels. Even more contemporary renditions such as January Jones's performance as the deeply unhappy Betty Draper in AMC's *Mad Men* portrayed 1950s housewives and mothers as desperately striving for the image of domestic perfection even if it was a façade.

The character of the 1950s housewife/mother and the life she lived were also deeply political. For many conservatives of the time – for 2008 was the height of the Harper era – she was often cast as touchstone, a figure belonging to a mythical golden age: an oasis in history between the upheavals of war and the civil tensions of the social revolutions of the 1960s and 1970s where the complexities of modern existence had yet to invade the sanctuary of the heterosexual, monogamous, nuclear family unit. In this conservative fantasy, life was seemingly simpler, with social rules and roles that were clearly defined and easy to follow. Sex, sexuality, and gender roles were supposedly in congruence, and people were assumed to be generally happy fulfilling those roles for the good of their families and for society as a whole.

But who was the woman at the centre of this domestic fantasy, really? She was always attractive yet rarely directly sexualized, and her children, around whom her life and identity were supposed to revolve, were both physical evidence of her sexual normalcy and the centre of her gender role in society. Like most historical stereotypes, the image of a multitude of June Cleavers inhabiting endless rows of suburban housing in Canada and the United States (and, with important regional variations, in Australia, France, and Britain) contains a kernel of truth.[2] In part the cliché of the 1950s housewife stemmed from the deep concerns that social elites had about society and family in the immediate period following World War II and the need to rebuild Western society after half a century of war, disease, and economic depression.

In direct contrast to currently sentimentalized images of this time as an epitome of stability – a phenomenon American historian Stephanie Coontz calls "the nostalgia trap" – contemporary elites in Canada were deeply concerned that the postwar era was the beginning of a descent into social chaos and moral ruin.[3] In the wake of two world wars and the Great Depression, and spurred by fears of a postwar spike in divorce and the outside threat of communism, social leaders including government policymakers, the medical, psychological, and social work professions, social reformers, and leaders in the established churches looked to the heterosexual nuclear family as the bedrock on which to rebuild Western civilization and simultaneously worried it was too fragile to bear the weight.

The focus of many of these authorities, and the main unit of analysis in this book, was sex. Sex – making sure the right people had lots of it and the "wrong" people had none – was imbued with nigh-magical powers in the postwar era. The idea that if desirable Canadian bodies (those who were white, middle class, heterosexual, married, and monogamous) engaged in frequent and mutually satisfying intercourse marriages would remain healthy was discursively repeated over and over again. Furthermore, it was repeatedly asserted, through those healthy marriages desirable nuclear families and nuclear family values would remain strong and provide a bedrock of social stability on which to rebuild. The consistent repetition eventually made these statements seem common-sense truths.[4]

But how does a society police something that typically happened in private spaces far away from the elite leaders and organizations who were so relying on it?[5] The aforementioned social authorities worked, sometimes together, occasionally in conflict, to shape prescriptive discourses, which theorist Michel Foucault calls "organized systems of knowledge." Within these systems of knowledge, certain sexual behaviours, expressions, emotions, and sensations were deemed normal and productive for society while other experiences were either silenced, and therefore removed from social vocabularies, or relegated to the realms of abnormality to be shunned and "othered" in the community. To be "normal" therefore meant being allowed to participate fully in society, to be granted privacy when it was desired, and to be part of a dominant majority that was reflected and reinforced through media representation. Or, as sexuality historian Karen Dubinsky puts it, "to the normal go considerable spoils."[6] In this way the creators of prescriptive sexual discourses did not need to actively police each sexual interaction between each postwar married couple within Canada. The very creation of such binaries of normal/abnormal and the social rewards granted for normalcy made many Canadians police themselves and each other. As Gérard Bouchard demonstrates in his study of the sexual habits of married couples in Saguenay, strictures on the "macro" level of the state, the church, and other elites were often policed in the realm of the "micro," with communities and families providing additional and more immediate consequences for transgressions.[7] Feminist Foucauldian scholars such as Sandra Bartky have argued that though these discourses come from institutions such as the Christian churches or the biomedical establishment, they gain power over bodies, particularly women's bodies, by making society function as an ever-present panopticon. Society, including other women, remind women of the "rules" their bodies should follow to be given value or even seen as "normal." As Bartky explains using the ideals of feminine beauty and body weight as her example:

> The disciplinary power that inscribes femininity in the female body is everywhere and it is nowhere; the disciplinarian is everyone and yet no one in particular. Women regarded as overweight, for example, report that they are regularly admonished to diet, sometimes by people they scarcely know ... Here, "people" – friends and casual acquaintances alike – act to enforce prevailing standards of body size.[8]

In many cases the normal is not even explicitly defined. Rather, it is controlled and shaped by the social response to the abnormal, whose "grotesque" imagery is used to infer an ideal that does not have to be fully articulated to be understood. For example, many of the contours of postwar heterosexual normality were created by the pathologization of homosexuality, which was continuously constructed as a medical and moral sickness. Splitting sexual expression into the oversimplified binary of heterosexual (normal)/homosexual (abnormal) also served to silence other potential sexual expressions or identities. The combination of pathologizing and silencing certain ideas – removing them from people's social and linguistic vocabularies – is key to creating authoritative systems in which people become self-policing. If people cannot articulate possible alternatives, or are socially punished for doing so, their expression is necessarily limited.[9]

This book is an archaeology of one facet of postwar normalcy – the embodied sexual and gendered experiences of the wife and mother. In the twenty-year span covered by this work there was a great deal of elite discourse focused on the white, heterosexual, middle-class, married maternal body both to guide and shape her own experiences and also to influence postwar families as a whole. As this work will demonstrate, the maternal body, and the gender and sexual roles that were encompassed within it, became the lever through which the family, and eventually the state, could be moved and postwar society carefully shepherded into a new era.

This intense scrutiny and focus on creating ideals of embodied maternal womanhood had profound effects on how Canadian women lived their lives and understood their individual corporeality in the postwar era. Yet, as Foucault reminds us, no hegemonic discourse is ever complete, and sexually repressive discourses are actually extremely productive in that they mean people are consistently thinking, writing, and speaking about sex because of them.[10] So while this book begins as a deconstruction of normative discourses that sought to mould the sexual lives of heterosexual married women and give specific meanings to their experiences, it ends with oral histories from women who actually lived, married, and bore children during that time. Prescriptive discourses at best could only create "leaky hegemonies," and these women and their bodily experiences spoke back to elite organized systems of knowledge in myriad ways. Sometimes they reinforced the sexualized and gendered conventions placed on them, drew power from them, even disciplined other women's bodies because of them. Other times they subtly or outright defied such constructions of normal and in doing so created change.

This research was originally intended to focus solely on the sexual body in the hope of recovering embodied stories from the 1950s and 1960s similar to those found within *Our Bodies, Ourselves*; it soon became clear, however, that attempting to focus on sex and sexual embodiment in isolation was a historical fallacy for this period. Unlike those narrators from the 1970s whose era, combined with their experience in sexual activism, allowed them to interrogate different aspects of their womanhood with some degree of separation, this understanding was much more difficult in an age prior to the visibility and social action of marginalized groups such as the LGBTQ2+ communities. Indeed, as the project progressed it became clear that the separation of sex (the act of coitus and/or the biological division between male and female based on visual examination of genitalia) from sexuality (a person's sexual object choice or choices) and gender role (the social expectations of a person based on their assumed sex) was rarely expressed either within the authoritative discourses or by the women I interviewed, and that such a separation is a historical artefact in and of itself. Instead, in the immediate postwar era the idea that the triad of sex, sexuality, and gender role could be separated was either silenced or pathologized as abnormal. Each of the three facets of the triad reinforced each other, and certain aspects could be policed indirectly through each other. A woman who displayed physical evidence of her sexual normality by becoming pregnant was also assumed to be successfully fulfilling her female gender role as wife and mother and to be clearly demonstrating her normality in sexual object choice. Conversely, a woman not fulfilling her gender role by, for example, wanting to continue to work rather than staying at home with her children could have embodied experiences that urged her to reconsider her "deviant" path. Excessive nausea and vomiting during pregnancy were thought to be caused by "overly masculine" women who refused to accept that their biological roles as mothers equalled a social role as stay-at-home caregiver.

In making the postwar family, and in particular the mother, a focus of this analysis I join other works that have attempted to understand the enigma of gender and sexual roles during this modern "golden era." One of the first works to do so was Elaine Tyler May's *Homeward Bound: American Families in the Cold War Era* (1988), which began a larger debate within both Canadian and American historiographies over the question of agency and why women, many of whom had taken the opportunities offered by World War II to move beyond their gender roles, seemingly went back to those same "traditional" roles without much fuss. May's contention that two factors – an increasing focus on making sex pleasurable for women in marriage and increasingly abundant consumer goods – were consolation prizes that helped to explain women's willingness to return to domesticity has been criticized, and even turned into a straw argument, for minimizing the complexity of sexual expression both within and outside of marriage in the prewar and wartime era as well as the nuanced ways women reacted to the "return to domesticity" in the immediate postwar period. "Containment," as May termed it, was only part of the equation.

Scholars such as Joanne Meyerowitz in her edited collection *Not June Cleaver* and Canadian works, including Valerie J. Korinek's *Roughing It in the Suburbs*, Jennifer A. Stephen's "Balancing Equality for the Post-War Woman," and Veronica Strong-Boag's "Home Dreams: Women and the Suburban Experiment in Canada," have shown the many ways that postwar women could, and did, express dissatisfaction with the stereotypical housewife's lot.[11] From writing letters to women's magazines extolling the virtues of slovenly housekeeping to union activism to civil disobedience, many women protested and expanded the boundaries of social roles they found unattractive, unfulfilling, or untenable. Furthermore, certain populations found themselves wholly or partially disqualified from participating in the North American dream because that dream was predicated on a white ideal. Scholars such as Marlene Epp, Franca Iacovetta, and Joan Sangster remind us that immigrant, ethnic, and racialized women and families, though they were exhorted to emulate this white middle-class ideal, were also never allowed to fully enjoy the benefits of that normalcy by societies that only tolerated the mimicking of what was seen as inborn white perfection.[12]

This book joins these and several others that seek to add nuance to May's original and rather top-down concept of containment by unpacking the many ways that "normal" and "common-sense" idealizations were created in the postwar era, and how this normal was formed and reformed in ways that cannot be reduced to a simple binary of reward or punishment. For example, Doug Owram in his portrait of the baby boom generation *Born at the Right Time* demonstrates how the fabric of Canadian society wrapped itself around this new domestic fantasy, silencing and marginalizing those people who for myriad reasons would not, or could not, participate in "a world of children."[13] However, it was not just the sheer numbers of children born during the baby boom that gave this age its domestic flavour. Increasingly, as demonstrated by Mary Louise Adams in *The Trouble with Normal* and Mona Gleason in *Normalizing the Ideal*, children and teens were trained from a young age to see heterosexual marriage and adherence to postwar gender norms as achievements and badges of adult status, the benefits of which were considerable.[14] This book is a natural outgrowth of

Adams's and Gleason's. While they study how the new postwar normal was created for teenagers and children, the products of the boom, this work focuses on how similar normals were created for the adult women who were the producers of those children. These normals overlapped and informed each other as young women looked to their mothers as gendered and sexual role models, and adult women examined and often reinforced their own boundaries through intergenerational teaching and through engagement with discourses coming from their children's schools, pediatricians, and popular culture. There were also some important differences. For one, training and educating adults into normality came with an increased urgency as they were not malleable teens or children who could grow into their new roles. Adult women in particular needed to change immediately, in part to avoid warping the next generation. With this urgency also came greater responsibility. Failure or inability to conform was more likely to be seen as a deliberate act rather than a youthful error.

In *The Trouble with Normal* Adams echoes Foucault's assertions that heterosexuality and homosexuality define each other, and she warns of the dangers of attempting to research one side of that historically constructed binary without an awareness of the other. In congruence with this idea I draw heavily on the works of authors "queering" Canadian historiography, including Valerie J. Korinek, Cameron Duder, Patrizia Gentile, Gary Kinsman, Becki L. Ross, and El Chenier.[15] Their works, which have populated the Canadian postwar landscape with myriad sexual expressions and experiences and theoretical frameworks, have influenced my own.

One of the ways this book differs from much of Canadian gender and sexuality scholarship is that it is unselfconsciously focused on western Canada with a large portion of its evidence stemming from sources in British Columbia, Alberta, Saskatchewan, and Manitoba. However, it is not meant to be solely a regional history. This book is a Canadian history that seeks, in part, to add nuance to the preponderance of works in Canadian gender history that are written from a central Canadian and especially Ontario-focused source base. In congruence with the aforementioned scholarship, the evidence presented within this work illuminates the complexities of the dance between region and nation, with some discourses seeking to create (at least the surface appearance of) cross-country values while others drew additional authority by appealing to provincial peculiarities or an assumed western Canadian sense of self. In the case of the latter I have, when possible, highlighted these regional divergences and sought to explain them. Additionally, this work also follows the few Canadian gender historians, most prominently Jane Nicholas and Patrizia Gentile, who are bringing the body more clearly into the historiography and placing it at the centre of their research and analysis.[16]

In order to fully examine the relationship between sexual authoritative discourses and actual corporeal bodies, I join a growing body of scholarship that seeks to place corporeal bodies at the centre of historical examination.[17] Informed by Michel Foucault's observations on the institutional discipline of the body, embodied or "aesthesiological" histories examine how people experience their bodies differently across time and space and due to social differences such as culture and class.[18] Embodied history seeks to explain why, even though we know that the heart is a valved organ that circulates blood throughout our bodies, for many people a "heartbreaking" experience manifests itself as a physical pain in the chest.[19] In this way the boundaries between the body and the outside world are permeable, and that permeation goes both ways. The body sits on the nexis of the tangible and the discursive, and in the space between those two poles embodied experience is constantly being created.

In seeing the body as both discursive and corporeal I am taking a middle-ground position within a larger methodological debate on how to see the body within history. Unlike some studies that lend themselves to a more discourse-based perspective, such as the history of emotion or the philosophical understanding of dead bodies in war, or studies that focus on more concrete embodied experiences such as sense-based histories, sex, as a complex interaction between physical sensation and emotional and sociocultural understandings of desire, draws on both.[20] Sex is also historically specific. A practice that in one time is socially taboo and therefore causes disgust and physical revulsion may at other times produce the opposite effect. Simultaneously, sexual bodies can also act, and have acted, historically on their own with their biological reality working at cross purposes to the wants and needs of the person inhabiting them. In the postwar era certain markers of body normality, such as a woman's ability to achieve vaginal orgasm or bear children, were largely outside the control of personal will and were more accidents of physiology and circumstance. Infertile bodies, in particular, were coded with a great deal of meaning during the postwar period; some medical experts believed that infertile women lacked basic femininity or were even psychologically disturbed, which caused them to be unable to get pregnant or carry pregnancies to term. In this way it was the bodies, their inability to reproduce successfully, that created meaning for their inhabitants rather than the women making meaning for their own corpuses.

While individual sexual bodies are both discursive and corporeal, wholly discursive bodies have a significant presence in this research, as it also answers the call of scholars such as Carolyn J. Dean, Barbara Duden, and Moira Gatens to find the different historical ideal bodies that were created by elite discourses to police the very real corpuses mentioned above and to make those corporeal bodies serve the needs of the greater society.[21] Former Canadian prime minister Pierre Trudeau may have famously claimed that the state did not belong in the bedrooms of the nation, but sex and sexuality are not, and have never been, confined to the realm of the bedroom. Individual bodies may belong to their owners in an idealized legal sense, but they are also coerced to act as corporeal citizen bodies – part of the nationalized social body – and are tasked to aid in maintaining its strength and integrity.[22]

These ideal bodies, exemplars of perfection, were used to demonstrate the inadequacies and non-conformities of corporeal bodies and to exaggerate these deficiencies until they seemed abnormal and grotesque. Postwar bodies were supposed to attempt to live up to these ideals, to mimic their characteristics with various expectations of success based on their inherent advantages or disadvantages of class, race and ethnicity, sexuality, age, ability, and other facets of inborn conformity. However, even young, middle-class, white, heterosexual women were doomed to fail in their attempts at perfect orthodoxy. As theorist Moira Gatens demonstrates, real bodies can no more live up to a non-embodied ideal than an ideal body can encompass all of the experiences inherent in individual corporeality.[23] This disconnect between real bodies and ideal bodies created space for social change that could be enacted both by persons deliberately exploiting that space and by bodies themselves demonstrating the inability of ideals to fully police reality.

Where did these ideal bodies come from? As the extant historiography shows, postwar women were bombarded with ideal bodies and forms of sexual embodiment from a variety of angles, including government structures, popular culture from Canada and increasingly the United States, and their own families. In this work I have chosen to focus on two main centres of prescriptive discourse, the medical and the religious. Though this by no means covers the breadth of women's experiences these centres of discourse remain important, as much of postwar gender and sexual norms, those so prevalent that they were generally accepted as common-sense truths, drew on the authority of medical science, Christian morality, or both. The prevalence of medical authority over sex and familial relations is not surprising given that doctors enjoyed very high trust and social approval during this epoch. In contrast, some might question the pre-eminence given to religion and the dominant churches, as the 1950s and early 1960s marked a continued period of decline in church attendance and the rise in the number of people willing to publicly declare themselves to be atheists.[24] Yet even as overall church numbers declined, women, the focus of this study, still attended in higher numbers than men, and because of strict laws that limited the locations where weddings could take place and who could officiate them, most weddings still took place in the one of Canada's three dominant churches (Anglican, United, and Roman Catholic). Many pastors and most priests would not marry couples who had not gone through some kind of faith-based pre-marriage counselling or preparation, meaning Canadian couples often received church-based prescriptive discourse at the beginning of their married sexual lives. They frequently continued to encounter these discourses through the emergent welfare state and its associated social service programs due to the fact that professions such as social work evolved out of religious charity work and often employed or consulted clergy.[25] Perhaps most importantly, and as the following research attests, in the absence of a clear competing moral structure Judeo-Christian norms and mores for married sex seem to have held continued sway.

My archaeology of postwar sexual normals begins in chapter 2 with the medical community, using the *Canadian Medical Association Journal* as a primary archive. Taking a broad view of what constitutes heterosexual married health, it demonstrates the ways that general practitioners, as well as obstetrical and gynecological specialists, used a medicalized version of psychoanalysis to tie gender role expectations to biological illness in new ways. In doing so they made the body of the wife and mother their primary focus of diagnosis and treatment. Hers was a potentially dangerous body – able to cause a number of illnesses to her family, including homosexuality in her sons and gynecological complaints in her daughters. Her body was also perilously permeable in that the social and gendered transgressions of the entire family wrote themselves onto her maternal body, potentially making her mentally and physically ill.

Chapter 3 extends the analysis of chapter 2 by demonstrating new shifts in the ways that the dominant faith organizations understood the role of sex within marriage. All three denominations, Anglican, United, and Roman Catholic, increasingly drew on, and reframed, medical discourses to buttress their own doctrinal views. Each denomination also attempted to come to grips with ongoing changes to social understandings of sex and marriage. Sex within heterosexual marriage became increasingly viewed as positive and even sacred – a spiritually transcendent experience that melded the couple together and with

God. However, within the postwar period, the two Protestant denominations decentred children from the sexual act by advocating the "rational" use of contraceptives to ensure that marital coitus, with its sacramental benefits, could be enjoyed frequently without the stress of conceiving too many children. This support for equality in the bedroom did not automatically extend to supporting gender equality within the family, and the discourses of both the Anglican and the United churches reflect considerable ambiguity about the role of women in the postwar era. In contrast, the Roman Catholic Church in Canada maintained that married sex was only holy because each act held the potential for conception. This put its rhetoric at odds with the dominant medical views and arguments for sexual equality for men and women within marriage. The postwar Catholic Church was therefore put on the defensive and forced to use various strategies to cast its policies in a positive and modern light.

How effective were the religious and medical ideal bodies in policing actual corporeality? How did the discourses they created translate into often ephemeral social pressures to conform? How did actual women interpret and understand their own embodied sexual experiences, including losing their virginity, having sex with their husbands, or childbirth, and how did those embodied experiences interact with their perceived gender and sexual roles in postwar society? Chapter 4 seeks to answer these questions via eighteen in-depth oral histories conducted with women who lived and married during the postwar era. Though these women are not meant to be representative of all Canadian women, their narratives demonstrate the ways authoritative ideal bodies and corporeal bodies interacted on a day-to-day, moment-to-moment basis. While the women I interviewed ultimately benefitted in many ways from the social structure of the postwar era by fulfilling requirements as to heterosexuality, marriage, class, and race, they also weakened the dominance of postwar ideals by constantly exposing those ideals' impossible expectations. Occasionally it was the women's bodies that created these weaknesses; sexual response, infertility, ill health, and other factors defied the postwar promise that adhering to sex and gender roles ensured health and well-being for self and family.

Though medical and religious discourses produced incredibly similar ideal bodies in some ways – not surprising because they drew from and reinforced each other – the nuanced inconsistences between these dominant ideals did open up spaces for agency and manipulation of aspects of those archetypes. Chapter 5 explores these spaces and how some of the interviewed women took advantage of them. This chapter also looks at how other outside factors, such as geographical location, could pervert or weaken dominant messages to create unintentional change.

Sex and sexuality, particularly when housed within the married female body, were powerful forces in postwar Canadian society and therefore subject to the scrutiny of many. Yet the married housewife has hitherto remained isolated within the metaphorical suburbs of history. She has often been reduced to cliché, and her sexuality has only been made visible in the production of children to feed to the postwar baby boom. In the following pages female married sexual bodies take centre stage. Making that sexuality visible demonstrates the sexually charged nature of the postwar period, problematizing its image as both a bucolic paradise and an uncomplicated touchstone while establishing several surprising lines of continuity between this false oasis and the ideological upheavals on the horizon.[26]

Chapter Two

Embodying Family Values: The *Canadian Medical Association Journal* and the Creation of the "Mother Body"

"If the bedroom is not right, then every room in the house is wrong." Physicians should constantly bear this in mind when attempting to untangle marital difficulties which now appear to form such a high proportion of problems encountered in medical, gynaecological and general practice. Much time should be spent in listening to women with these difficulties and attempting to correct their emotional environment.[1]

So said gynecologist Dr. R.A.H. Kinch during a 1966 symposium on sexuality, family, and aging. For Kinch, as for many other medical men, the central building block of postwar reconstruction was the heterosexual married couple; "the bedroom" – a polite euphemism for married sexual coitus and sexuality – was both a useful diagnostic tool and a cure-all for many social and physical ailments related to the family. Significantly, Kinch notes that medical men should focus primarily on women who presented with any sexual difficulties. Though it is presumed that "the bedroom" would contain a heterosexual cisgendered duo, the medical gaze was overwhelmingly focused on the body of the wife and especially of the mother. The Canadian medical establishment, in congruence with postwar gender role expectations, persistently defined female bodies in relation to maternity. The role of mother included almost all female bodies; biological women were usually constructed as mothers, failed mothers, or wombs-in-waiting. Single women and girls were seen as future wives, and "wife" was seen as a temporary state before moving on to the ultimate embodied gendered role of wife *and* mother. So ingrained was the connection of women to heterosexual marriage and motherhood that the terms "wife" and "mother" were used interchangeably in many articles; authors were more likely to give clarification if the patient in question was in the liminal state of being a wife but not yet mother and let the reader assume than in all other cases wives were mothers unless otherwise specified. Motherhood was thus seen as a biological imperative for all normal women.

Fundamentally porous, the "mother body" provided a biological anchor to gender norms of the period. Using psychoanalysis as their primary method, medical men (and a few women) connected the fleshy body to the social body in new ways so that a postwar woman deviating from the narrow gender script of the time faced serious physical illness. However, it was not only the mother's gender role deviations that could manifest as physical symptoms. The mother body was made to be the handmaiden to the whole postwar family and, though a lack of proper femininity could make her children unwell in very specific circumstances, the family's deviancies were more commonly written on the maternal anatomy.

While the postwar use of psychoanalysis to anchor gender role adherence in the body was novel, it was also another permutation of a deep-rooted historical trend of medically embodied femininity and gender role expectations, as is well documented within the international historiography. Wendy Mitchinson, in her 1991 book *The Nature of Their Bodies: Women and Their Doctors in Victorian Canada*, provided the first sustained examination of how gender ideals for women influenced medical practice within the Canadian context. Arguing that medicine was anything but an objective science, Mitchinson tracked how the Victorian ideal of separate spheres was made a medical necessity for women's good health. She later refined and expanded this argument in subsequent works, including *Giving Birth in Canada 1900–1950* (2002) and *Bodily Failure: Medical Views of Women, 1900–1950* (2013), demonstrating that in the first half of the twentieth century medicine constructed the male body as the norm, and anything that happened to the female body, even natural processes such as menstruation and childbirth, was pathologized, predisposing the need for expert care.[2] Cheryl Krasnick Warsh's 2010 work *Prescribed Norms* expands on Mitchinson's work both temporally and geographically, demonstrating the role of both the American and Canadian medical establishments in imbuing female reproductive processes including menstruation, childbirth, and menopause with social meanings, with the authoritative medical gaze often reducing female bodily utility to those reproductive functions and processes.[3] Cynthia Commachio and Denyse Baillargeon have also added important regionally focused studies of childbirth to the Canadian canon that demonstrate the importance of the role of the citizen-mother and baby to the Canadian state and to Quebec's sense of itself, respectively.[4] This chapter builds and expands upon these works by demonstrating how psychoanalysis – an emergent therapy in postwar medical (rather than psychological) praxis – was increasingly used to continue the pathologizing of women's bodies by linking the feminine psyche to the female soma and creating a scientific schema where the body of the mother was a conduit and reflection of gender role adherence for the family as a whole.

This chapter investigates the creation and deployment of this "mother body" by making use of Canada's premier professional medical journal of the time, the *Canadian Medical Association Journal* (*CMAJ*). Rarely studied in its own right, the *CMAJ* consistently increased its reach through the postwar era, expanding from publishing once a month in 1946 to four times a month by 1966.[5] It also engaged in an aggressive marketing strategy after World War II that included distributing free copies to returning veteran medical officers in the immediate postwar years as well as to all medical missionaries and offering reduced rates for recent medical graduates. These measures produced results. For example, in 1950 the journal printed 148,270 copies; by 1958 that number had jumped to 389,351.[6] Though not the only source of medical knowledge in Canada, the *CMAJ* was the premier general-use medical magazine and therefore both a reflection of the hegemonic Canadian medical discourse and an engine of that hegemony.

Methodically, the *CMAJ* seems deceptively simple to break down and analyse; it has been digitally indexed and even keyword enabled in several places. However, the postwar period was a liminal time for many illnesses, particularly sexual and reproductive maladies. New names were created, symptom markers changed, and illnesses were split into ever-growing specialty definitions. This lexiconic fluidity required a much slower research process by which each issue had to be scrutinized focusing on titles (and abstracts when available) that had a potential connection to the married sexual body as well as content reflecting on the journal or medical profession in Canada. Though laborious, this process, combined with archival examination, allows for some general observations about the *CMAJ* as a whole. As with most professional journals, the *CMAJ* was a heavily managed source. Written and marketed solely for medical consumption, it both reflected trends within the community (as it was forced to remain relevant to its paying subscribers) and, due to careful editing, editorial work, and advertising, also served to curate the image of the medical profession as a group with a consistent ideology and praxis. Overall, the *CMAJ* trended towards the conservative. There were four editors during the period under review, all men and all well-established doctors. In addition to the doctors on the board of the Canadian Medical Association who oversaw the *CMAJ*, the editors gave the *Journal* an overwhelmingly male perspective focused on reflecting and promoting the prestige of Canadian doctors.

Conversely, the *CMAJ* was also a broad source. Though controlled by the editors, the journal was designed to reflect the plurality of Canadian practice; the majority of articles were published out of the large teaching and research hospitals in urban centres, but the voices of non-specialist general practitioners from small towns across the country were well represented in both published articles and letters to the editor. Rural or small-town doctors used the latter in particular as a venue for presenting their own experience to critique the conclusions of big-city specialists. As Wendy Mitchinson notes in her study *Fighting Fat*:

> Medical journals are rich sources for illuminating debates within medicine, the changing nature of treatments for any specific disease or condition, the problems that different treatments caused patients, and what was happening in the faculties of medicine throughout the country. Physicians who were members of those faculties and who also practised within hospitals were the elite of medicine, and many wrote articles that were published in the journals. That doesn't mean that general practitioners were ignored. Often the most interesting articles were written by those who were at the front line of taking care of Canadians in cities, towns, and rural areas. Such articles described the author's patients and their health concerns, and how the physician-author reacted to those patients. The reviews of work being done outside Canada and the reprinting of some articles published in other countries kept Canadian practitioners up to date and reminded them that they were members of a wider medical "fraternity" beyond Canada's borders.[7]

In short, prominent generalized journals like the *CMAJ* give the historian an important window into the macro and micro workings of the medical profession.

In its capacity as both a managed and a broad source the *CMAJ* overwhelmingly supported heterosexual middle-class social values and the normalized white body, often portraying ethnic and racialized bodies as problematic and inherently pathological. In the articles under review within this chapter, ethnic and racialized bodies were a rarity. Indigenous bodies are particularly noticeable by their almost complete absence, subtly disqualifying them from participating in postwar heterosexual married "normality" by their virtual erasure from articles discussing these topics.[8] Ethnic bodies, particularly from Eastern Europe, were also very rare but do appear on occasion, particularly as pathologized exemplars of women who could not conform to postwar gender norms. These were portrayed as brusque, mannish, and demanding, and their role in the *CMAJ* was to serve as a cautionary tale for Anglo-Saxon white women, who were to use their assumed racial/ethnic advantage to avoid such pitfalls and to continue the assumption that whiteness and gender role adherence (i.e., normality) went hand in hand.[9]

It may seem inconsequential that white heterosexual middle-class bodies were overly represented and normalized in the *CMAJ* given that they were generally over-represented and normalized throughout postwar Canada culture and media. However, the dominance of white bodies within the *CMAJ* had consequences far beyond the politics of representation. The medical othering of BIPOC bodies, whether specifically or by making the white body the default of health, necessarily compromises the treatment of non-white bodies because they are determined a priori to be abnormal.[10]

Science, especially medicine, has always reflected, reorganized, and recreated social norms. Prior to World War II much of this work was done through the practice of eugenics. After that war, though eugenics would still maintain a significant presence in Canadian medical practice, particularly in Alberta and to a lesser extent British Columbia, there was also a search for a new system – one that was not associated with the atrocities of Hitler and the defeated Nazis – through which social ideals could be confirmed by medical science. To be clear, the classism, racism, sexism, and heteronormativity associated with eugenic discourses of the interwar period did not disappear. In many cases eugenicist language and concepts were simply reframed and presented in new ways – one of these ways was through the embrasure (and often adulteration) of psychoanalytical principles, vocabularies, and practices.[11]

Despite early conservative pushback, psychoanalysis, with its newly accepted understanding of the mind-body connection, especially given the Freudian foci on sexuality, served the medical need to link the mind to the body and to concentrate illness within the sexual and gendered functions of postwar womanhood. Freud and other psychologists started developing the principles of psychoanalysis at the turn of the century, but their focus on the libido and sexual displacement were bars to the practice's early acceptance.[12] In Canada, despite some successes of psychoanalysis in dealing with post-traumatic stress in soldiers, many medical practitioners still expressed discomfort with its main principles immediately after World War II. In September 1947, H.O. Foucar wrote:

> The name of Freud occupies an important place in psychology ... He introduced the term psycho-analysis and replaced hypnosis by a method of

"free association." He stressed sex as the driving force and therefore the primitive emotion. That sex is important, no one can deny but to explain everything on that basis is no longer acceptable.[13]

He continued that Freud and his contemporaries saw sexual imagery everywhere, including the architecture of churches, which he deemed "fantastic and unnecessary and the figment of a warped mind."[14] N. Viner, who would write several articles promoting psychoanalysis for the *CMAJ*, admitted he had particular discomfort regarding infant sexuality, stating that he felt Freud dwelt on it with "excessive emphasis."[15]

Despite an uncertain start psychoanalysis found a comfortable home in Canadian healthcare; the *CMAJ* became one of its biggest boosters as editors increasingly published articles arguing that blending psychoanalytical principles with biomedical treatments was a new best practice that helped to fulfil emerging ideals of "whole patient" treatment (instead of merely focusing on diseased organs or illnesses).[16] In 1946 only two articles discussed psychoanalysis; ten years later twelve articles specifically focused on the "talking cure" while many others infused physical treatment with psychoanalytical discourses. In his 1947 address to the annual meeting of the Canadian Medical Association, reprinted in the *CMAJ*, prominent Toronto psychiatrist Dr. C.B. Farrar, while expressing some reservations about Freud, urged his colleagues to make use of "the oldest form of treatment" and employ "the 'scientifically directed' influence of one mind on another to promote health." Doing so, he argued, was a necessary measure since, in his estimation, 50 to 80 per cent of patients would have psychological features to their cases.[17] The rest of his address discussed the various ways that psychoanalytic treatment, a time-consuming practice, could be used within the limited time of a typical physical appointment.

Similarly, a 1960 editorial stressed the importance of general practitioners having some training in psychoanalysis to intervene in the everyday emotional problems that emerged in families before they became substantial enough to require a specialist's care. This shift towards acceptance of psychoanalysis was portrayed by some contributors as generational. The aforementioned Viner, along with many of his contemporaries, argued as early as 1946 that a paradigm shift in thinking about physical and mental illness was already underway. Viner argued that younger doctors, himself included, were excited about the new ideas of the mind-body connection even if other (usually older) doctors rejected psychosomatic ideas.[18] This does not explain why, while the contributors to the *CMAJ* confidently asserted the efficacy of psychoanalysis, contributors to professional psychological journals such as the

Canadian Psychiatric Association Journal (*CPAJ*) were much more pessimistic about their ability to cure the mental ills of Canada's populace. As Martin Roth, a prominent psychiatrist from Britain, noted during the 1959 McGill University conference on depression:

> It is sad to think that we are not yet in a position to give clear and conclusive answers to most of these problems ... Progress in relation to bread-and-butter questions of such great importance for the advance of psychiatry along other fronts is slow, partly at any rate because they lack the glamour that attaches to laboratory work or psychodynamic exploration.[19]

In his commentary on Roth's paper, Robert O. Jones concluded, "It would seem to me that we agree pretty well about what we know and still more about what we don't know and that most of us would agree that it has become obvious that the area which we don't know is by all odds the greatest."[20]

According to historian El Chenier, during the postwar period certain psychoanalysts committed to actively "selling" psychoanalysis to the medical establishment and to the public at large. Cross-referencing of the *CPAJ* with the *CMAJ* shows that several of these psychoanalysis "boosters" had articles printed within the *CMAJ* while the more cautious authors were less likely to be represented, creating an impression of overall psychoanalytic dominance and the efficacy of psychoanalytical approaches.[21]

By the 1950s most articles examining marriage, and many on other topics, used psychoanalytical language or concepts in some form. Concurrently, a shift within the pages of the *CMAJ* began to feminize the patient and, therefore, illness in general. At the beginning of the period under review the majority of submissions to the *CMAJ* dealing with psychological issues gendered all general patients male; if not referencing a specific patient in a specific case study, the medical community most often referred to hypothetical patients as "he" or "him." There was also a preponderance of male-specific psychological studies such as those examining the difficulty acclimatizing recently demobilized soldiers to civilian life. By 1966 non-specific patients were overwhelmingly gendered female, referred to as "her" or "she." This accords with the Foucauldian feminist argument espoused by Mitchinson and Warsh, that the medical establishment has long been engaged in creating the female body as inherently ill.[22] By pathologizing femininity the medical community significantly expanded its reach by medicalizing a host of issues in bodies previously deemed healthy. In other words, the medical profession was empowered "not only to distribute advice as to a healthy life but also to dictate the standards for the physical and moral relations of the individual and society in which [s]he lives."[23] Controlling such professional territory was crucial in the postwar era as socialized medicine was increasingly advocated both domestically and internationally, and doctors wanted to have the power to drive the direction of that program and the public's trust in doing so.[24]

The evidence of professional self-interest, however, does not mean that the contributors to the *CMAJ* were not authentically invested in postwar reconstruction of the family and society. Indeed, they extended their prescriptive discourse into their own lives. The *CMAJ* published several articles that focused on how a doctor, busy and displaying professionally mandated scientific detachment, could return home at the end of the day and fully engage with his own family. In a 1966 editorial the unnamed author worried that doctors "may be particularly prone to the excuse of overwork, a readily acceptable excuse in his profession," and that doctors whose profession demanded the "suppressing [of] his own emotional feelings [may be] unable to switch to a two-way and emotionally tinged communication system with his wife."[25] This distance had the potential to lead to familial crisis. It was critical that medical men, in their attempts to rebuild the postwar family, did not neglect their own. As prominent postwar authorities, doctors led the community by their own example as well as through the frame of "objective" treatment.

In many ways psychoanalysis was a perfect framework for postwar medical authority over the body. Psychoanalysis's focus on sexuality fit well with changing ideals about women's sexual drives, filling the vacuum left by the breakdown of Victorian and Edwardian images of the sexually passive woman.[26] This new sexual persona had to be contained, however, and so was only given legitimacy within heterosexual marriage. For the medical community, being able to express and enjoy sexual contact within marriage was deemed healthy and normal but to desire or to engage in sexuality outside of marriage was a prescription for ill health and situated one on the abnormal side of the spectrum. The psychoanalytical framework went even further. If a woman presented with symptoms tied to her reproductive system such as painful periods or pain during sex and there was no immediate and obvious physical explanation, doctors were encouraged by the psychoanalytical framework to investigate her background for psychological markers of gender role deviance such as dissatisfaction with being a housewife or crimes against postwar moral femininity, such as a premarital affair.

This change can clearly be viewed by comparing two published studies of dyspareunia, one in 1946 and one in 1955. In the first study the author, Dr. MacFarlane, argued there was almost always a physical reason for a woman to experience pain during sexual intercourse and that he never considered psychological causes except in extreme cases where the female patient was so visibly mentally disturbed as to already be institutionalized. In contrast, in 1955 the reporting physician, Dr. M. Bruser, foregrounded a psychological explanation despite the fact that he was engaged in demonstrating the links between endometriosis (a physical condition with clear biological causes) and dyspareunia.[27] He noted:

> It cannot be demonstrated statistically, but the impression was that many of these girls were of a "neurotic" temperament. It is guess work whether this is an accidental association or whether a connection exists; for example, is there a state of nervous tension engendered by repeated or constant pain, or apprehension concerning the next menstruation or the next act of coitus, or the cumulative effect of failure as a wife, both on account of pain and possibly infertility.[28]

By foregrounding the psychological explanation, Bruser was able to connect the physical pain that his patients felt to their assumed deficiencies as wives, in particular their potential inability to be mothers, and extend his medical authority over them; he was not only treating the finite physical condition, he was also asserting his authority over their mental state, extending the potential treatment indefinitely. Whether Bruser did so deliberately to increase his practice or was merely responding to the dominant discourses within his profession is impossible to know. It remains true, however, that the assumed connection between the reproductive system and the mind was so strong that even though Bruser had no compelling data, statistical or otherwise, for his psychological explanation, there were no published challenges to his conclusions in subsequent issues. The lack of set parameters in diagnosing psychological complaints, especially during the time under review, allowed for its broad application. This was in stark contrast to biological explanations, which needed at least the appearance of physical evidence.[29]

According to psychoanalytical principles, psychosexual issues, even if they occurred within the patient's distant past, could fester and cause the patient to experience physical symptoms due to the concept of displacement.[30] The body – a woman's biology – was inseparable from her ability to fulfil postwar gender norms. The connection between the mind and body also worked both ways. Women's bodies, especially their reproductive systems, were a danger, liable to dysfunction causing psychological pain and disrupting proper gendered family roles. Menarche, menstruation, and menopause were seen as arduous for both the female mind and body and were constructed as times of trouble in need of careful medical oversight and management to mitigate, if not prevent, harm. Because of the assumed union of the reproductive biology and gender roles, medical men believed that in such times of trouble the strain could be diminished by practising prescribed gender roles as vigorously as possible.[31]

The connection of the mother body to her postwar gender roles occurred long before women actually became mothers. As soon as women were of reproductive age their femininity was monitored as assumed mothers-in-waiting. In a 1958 article describing a study of premenstrual tension syndrome (PTS), psychiatrists J.N. Fortin, E.D. Wittkower, and F. Kalz directly linked the symptoms of PTS to their patients' supposed inability to embrace their femininity and adjust to their feminine role. In the study they compared women who did not have PTS (the control group) to women who experienced symptoms such as "tension, irritability, depression, anxiety ... swelling of the abdomen and limbs, itching, thirst, and various tendencies to migraine, asthma and epilepsy."[32] They concluded that PTS was often a response to guilt over sexuality and resentment at being a woman:

> The control group demonstrated a better acceptance of the feminine role and of the inevitable restrictions imposed on a girl; a reaction of pride to the menarche with emphasis on the positive aspects of femininity; a dependant relationship to the mother with fewer hostile features; and a better sexual adjustment. Their tensions, both internal and external, were dealt with more successfully.[33]

In contrast, those in the experimental group who had PTS were described as unable to embrace their femininity, resentful of their mothers, and envious of boys' freedom from both social and biological restrictions; a crucial part of women's embodied gender normality was the acceptance of their sex's second-class status. Lack of acceptance was mentally and physically pathological. The PTS example also demonstrates the ways that the mother body's deficiencies were seen to be "inherited" by their children. In the article the reporting physicians were careful to note that girls suffering from PTS not only had strained relationships with their mothers but also that they came from homes where marital discord between their parents was a common feature. This, according to the authors, demonstrated the mothers' inability to fulfil their feminine roles and was a contributing factor to their daughters' difficulty accepting gender role boundaries and an ancillary cause of their physical pain.[34]

In psychoanalysis, a woman's psychosexual development – her move from girlhood through the physical and emotional changes of puberty – was deemed complete only when she became pregnant. Motherhood was the culmination of her biological and psychological maturity. As Daniel Cappon, working in the Department of Psychiatry at the University of Toronto, stated, "pregnancy crowns a female psychosexual evolution ... Though ambivalence may exist, there is triumph of life over death, of motherhood over self-preservation, of motherliness over sexuality, of passivity and submissiveness over aggression and of femininity over masculinity."[35] He went on to argue that the proper motivation for a woman to get pregnant was not only to show love and gratitude to her husband – by providing biological proof of their healthy heterosexual relationship and his virility – but also "to prove [her] womanhood."[36] That is, by having a baby a woman could provide the world with physical verification of her normality, fulfil her gender role, and generally demonstrate the viability of her marriage and her own psychosexual maturity.

Finding the healthy pregnant body (or any healthy body at all) in the pages of the *CMAJ* is difficult; by definition, the majority of bodies contained therein were pathologized. The ideal pregnant body can be constructed primarily by inverting the described characteristics of the abnormal body; in almost all cases where the pregnant body was pathologized as abnormal, the women involved were portrayed as either unmarried – their pregnancies the result of taboo illicit sex – or at the very least were engaged in improper gender relations with their husbands. Dr. Gordon W. Preuter, in his trials of the anti-nauseate trifluouperazine, dismissed the cases where the drug proved ineffective by claiming, "Most of the failures occurred in very young patients (16–19 years of age) who because they were unmarried or had been forced into marriage were undergoing unusual emotional stress."[37] Extreme, drug-resistant nausea was also blamed on gender role deviation in a case presented by a Dr. M. Straker, psychiatrist, who noted on the woman's case file that not only was the pregnancy unplanned and unwanted (though the woman was married), she also had "marked fears of conception, of motherhood, of femininity," and despite her condition expressed her desire to continue with her career. Straker presented her case as one with a happy ending, however, as he proudly reported she "recovered" her sensibility after the birth of her child, demonstrating "warm reaction to child (boy). Gave up work and took up motherhood with enthusiasm."[38] Clearly the patient recovered from both her nausea and her maternal deviations.

The most obviously expressed image of the pregnant woman as an ultra-feminine ideal did not appear in the *CMAJ* articles or editorials but within the advertising. Advertising is an interesting piece of the larger *CMAJ* discourse puzzle, as it was the only sustained content not directly produced by medical men. Due to its narrow focus on its targeted medical audience, its advertising differed greatly from traditional public marketing. During this period advertisements in the *CMAJ* tended to be text-heavy rather than visually based and often mimicked the style of medical reports focusing on impressing their medical readers with clinical trial results, the economy of a product, or that product's usefulness in raising a practitioner's prestige. However, certain products, usually those focused on the domestic sphere and recommended for use by women and/or children, tended to have more images; these domestic images demonstrated the importance of gender roles. The very success of these advertisements, their consistency in portraying these gender ideas, denotes some level of internalization of these themes by the medical establishment. As Wendy Mitchinson puts it, advertisements in the *CMAJ* were "dialogues" between the product manufacturers and doctors where they "tried to develop a comfort zone through the expression of shared values between the drug companies and the physicians."[39] If the *CMAJ* advertisements had not resonated with doctors the advertisers would have changed tactics to better engage their audience.

Both Pfizer, maker of Bonamine, and Searle & Co., maker of Mornidine, used the image of the happy pregnant mother making breakfast to market their anti-morning-sickness drugs[40] (see images 1 and 2). In both advertisements the women are blissfully making a large breakfast of bacon and eggs. The background of the Bonamine advertisement includes her husband and school-age son waiting for their meal. Neither woman is visibly pregnant, though both wear lovely feminine nightgowns and are young (though not too young – between twenty and thirty) and demonstrate a conventional "prettiness" that is feminine but not overly sexualized. Their domestic setting is made clear by the text as well as the image. The Bonamine tagline reads, "This with Bonamine started last night for morning sickness." The tagline of the Mornidine advertisement reads, "Now she can make breakfast again." Image and text worked together to demonstrate that through the use of these drugs the women were able to return to their domestic roles and concomitant social good health. In both cases the pharmaceutical companies were not promoting their products to doctors to cure nausea per se – these symptoms are clearly ancillary. The message they were selling to physicians was that their drugs could be used to bring the

Image 1. Pfizer advertisement from the *Canadian Medical Association Journal* (22 October 1960, p. 26) for their anti-nauseate drug Bonamine.

mother back into her prescribed gender role, which, especially in the case of the Bonamine advertisement, would have a positive effect on the whole family. Such imagery also supported the medical ideal that while the mother body was fragile, so long as a woman had the right motivations – to return to her roles as domestic manager – medicine could effect a cure with a minimum of fuss.

If pregnancy was the apex of a woman's biological link to her gender role and femininity, the most dangerous time for her was when that biological link was severed. Menopause, with its final separation of the female body from its childbearing potentiality, was pathologized as a time that could cause extreme mental and physical strain on women.

Image 2. Searle & Co. advertisement from the *Canadian Medical Association Journal* (11 July 1959, p. 59) for their anti-nauseate drug Mornidine.

However, as with the anti-nausea drugs described above, the treatment of menopause's physical characteristics such as fatigue, pelvic pain, or night sweats were decidedly secondary considerations, if they were mentioned at all. A 1965 article titled "Ovarian Failure and the Menopause" noted the need of menopausal women for

> affection and understanding, yet often those needs are frustrated by a maturing and independent family and a busy, sometimes, indifferent husband. Essentially, the anxieties of these women reflect an emotional vacuum which a short time ago was filled with the dreams and hopes of youth.[41]

The term "ovarian failure," suggesting fault and malfunction rather than a natural change, combined with the image of a woman no longer needed as a mother – the one role she was socially allowed to excel at – presented menopause as a dire situation both biologically and socially. The author of the aforementioned article, Dr. Donald C. McEwan, used Primarin, an estrogen therapy, to treat women in this "emotional vacuum" and reported their families' reactions to their treatment as proof of their cure. Mrs. S.'s husband was "fascinated" and urged her to continue the treatment. Mrs. P.M.'s husband felt "her progress has been remarkable," and Mrs. H. was "able to manage her problems without concern to her family or herself."[42] In each of these "cures" the women were placed back into their feminine role as wives and mothers despite menopause severing the biological link to their motherhood. Tace, another drug meant to alleviate the symptoms of menopause, also capitalized on this idea with an advertisement that showed the patient before, sitting alone in her chair, and after, still in the chair but surrounded by her loving children and husband (see image 3). One advertising campaign for Bellergal portrayed a doctor taking a middle-aged woman by the hand in the middle of a giant, fractured female symbol; the caption reads, "Lead your patient through the difficult years." In this advertisement the female symbol serves as a gateway between the assured femininity (literally drawn in the image of the symbol) that is connected to biological reproductive capabilities and the unknown territory that the woman will occupy when she leaves the female (metaphorically) behind (image 4).

Even the famous Dr. Marion Hilliard highlighted menopause as a time of trouble when women might feel abandoned by a working husband and grown children. Hilliard, who appears in this chapter and in the next, needs contextualization as she occupies a singular place in Canadian women's health history. A prominent obstetrician-gynecologist, she wrote two books as well as a series of popular medical columns in *Chatelaine*.[43] Her advice to women often had an underlying feminist message and, unlike other doctors of the time, her cure for bored housewives and mothers was to step out of the domestic role rather than into it – usually by finding employment. Yet even Hilliard's message to menopausal women was at best ambivalent. Though she proposed that menopausal women take advantage of their new freedom to go and find a fulfilling non-domestic pastime such as paid employment or volunteer work, she still conflated gender roles, biology, and sexuality in a narrative of failure and social role loss:

> Sexual desire does not disappear entirely and may have sudden upsurges, so it becomes capricious and unnerving to a loving sensitive wife. To a wife, who has been loyal and dutiful only, a complete rejection may take

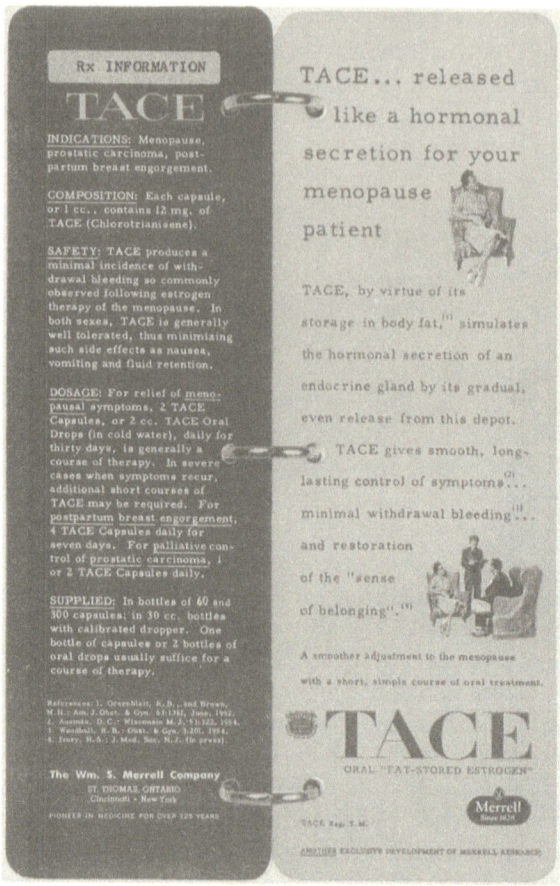

Image 3. Merrell advertisement from the *Canadian Medical Association Journal* (15 January 1955, p. 37) for Tace, an oral "fat-stored estrogen" hormonal secretion drug.

its place. When the very centre of the family is under siege like this, wise counsel is necessary.[44]

Hilliard affirms the role of the wife/mother body as "centre" of the family, predicting dire consequences for all members without a doctor's "wise council." Further, there is a clear value judgment implicit in the contrast between the "loving sensitive wife" and the lesser, problematic wife who engages in sex only to please her husband. For Hilliard the latter marriage is clearly already in a precarious position.

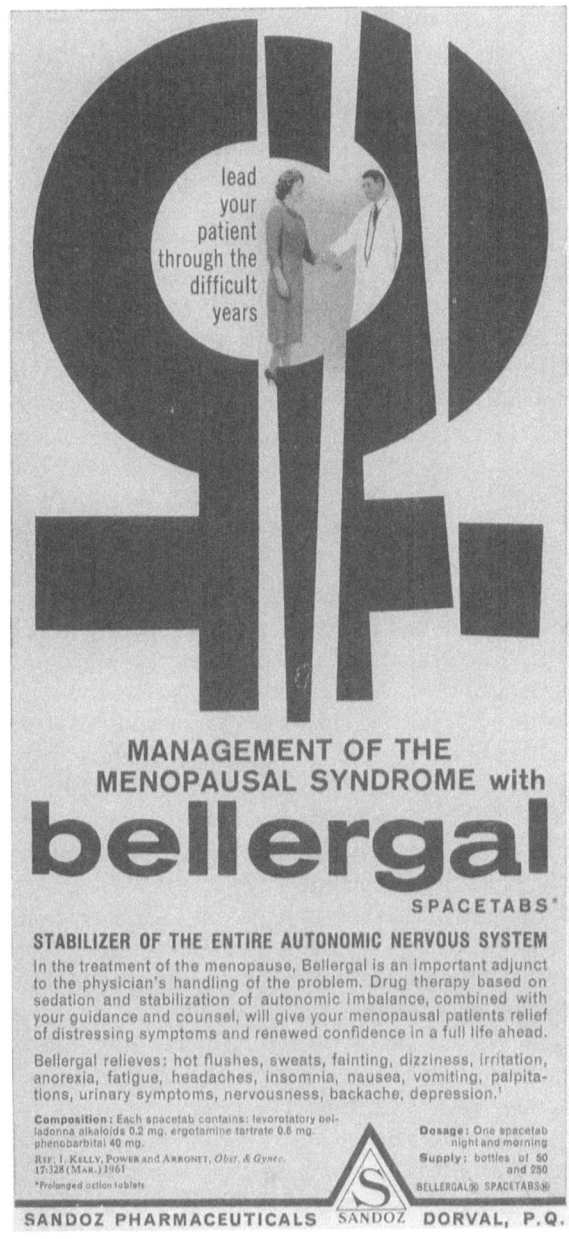

Image 4. Sandoz Pharmaceuticals advertisement from the *Canadian Medical Association Journal* (1 September 1962, p. 26) for Bellergal for "Management of the Menopausal Syndrome."

Hilliard presents an intriguing paradox within this period and in this context. Her own life as highly successful physician, surgeon, and chief of staff of the Women's College Hospital, Toronto, as well as her publicly single status, which hid the fact that she was a closeted lesbian in a long-term relationship, mark her as subversive and defiant of postwar domestic gender norms. Her advice was also very reminiscent of other second-wave feminists such as Betty Friedan who warned housewives and mothers that a solely domestic life would never be fulfilling. At the same time, as this and other articles demonstrate, Hilliard was trained and invested in promulgating the medical ideal of problematizing women's sexuality and reproductive functions. Her subversion of dominant medical systems of knowledge was thus a matter of degree rather than outright defiance and operated largely within the parameters set by that knowledge system. The fact that many of the women interviewed in chapter 4 of this book used similar strategies of subversion from within to negotiate their roles within their marriages suggests both the pervasiveness of postwar gender norms and one way that many women chose to negotiate them.

Menopause, though pathologized, was still considered a natural process. However, concerns about gender role and biology were highlighted even more in cases variously described as intersexuality, pseudo/hermaphroditism, and/or the congenital absence of the vagina. Despite the statistical rarity of such conditions a large number of articles were written on their treatment, indicating fear of anybody whose gender and biology could not be easily aligned.[45] In a 1956 editorial the unnamed author stressed the importance of quickly assigning a gender to any intersex child born, and that the child should always be raised as one gender and never told about the uncertainty of their sex: "Parents and physician should make up their minds about the infant's sex early (within the first few weeks) and stick to their decision so that a gender role is clearly defined and consistently maintained from the beginning."[46] Connecting a biological sex to a socialized gender as soon as possible and maintaining that connection was the surest way to normalize the child.[47]

In some cases intersex women also had short or missing vaginal canals, and there were several reports on different methods to "build" them a vagina in these cases. These articles tended to stress the normality of these women in their adherence to feminine gender roles and usually mentioned that the surgery was a precursor to an upcoming marriage.[48] Dr. L.T. Barclay, who had performed a number of such reconstructions, pointed out: "all of the three patients whom I have treated for atresia of the vagina were young women, attractive and with well-developed secondary sex characteristics." In the same article he gave an update on an earlier patient, a nurse, noting that "three years later [after the operation she] has an apparently normal vagina and [was] to be married soon, which is probably good evidence of normal sexual instincts."[49] Normal sexuality thus equaled a desire for heterosexual marriage and confirmed that the treatment – the implantation of a vagina as biological marker of femininity – was successful in helping the patient embody her social femininity. The latter was confirmed by the doctor's assertions that she was feminine and his careful notation of her properly womanly job as a nurse.[50]

What is most striking about the above discourses is the frequency of their engagement with "femininity," making an essentially non-medical term part of the diagnostic and treatment lexicon. For contributors to the *CMAJ* the label of "feminine" encompassed a woman whose gender and sexual roles were in congruence with her biology – the more congruent, the more feminine – with the pregnant woman the apex of femininity reaffirming the biological and social viability of the heterosexual nuclear family. The femininity of the mother body was also tied to particular ideals of beauty that were attractive yet wholesome and not overly sexualized. Accordingly, femininity became a medical synonym for female normality and this necessarily affected the way that female bodies were treated in the postwar era.

In her role as the keystone of the family, the mother body did more than just embody femininity, sexuality, and gender role normalcy; her body reflected, belonged to, and affected the wider family. One of the ways that the mother body's communal nature was constructed was through discourses on the limitation or promotion of fertility. Much scholarship has been expended on the efforts of second-wave feminists to create a society where a woman had complete control over her own body, primarily identified by a woman's right to control her fertility through access to abortion and birth control "on demand."[51] For postwar contributors to the *CMAJ*, limiting and promoting fertility was the communal "right" of a couple. Thus, the interwar period was a time of transition between the Victorian and Edwardian era, where upon marriage a woman's body was absorbed into that of her husband, effectively erasing her embodied personhood, and the developments of second-wave feminism where anything happening within a woman's body was deemed (ideally) solely her legal and social concern.

Contributors to the *CMAJ* portrayed birth control as overwhelmingly positive, so long as it was limited to married couples. Good sex for married couples was constructed as proof that the marriage was strong and normal and was also envisaged as having a prophylactic effect in that it could protect that marriage in times of trouble. Unwanted pregnancy was viewed as an unfortunate side effect to be mitigated if possible. Contributors noted that "complete continence in a happily married couple can be reasonably looked upon as an impossibility"[52] and "fear of pregnancy produce[s] much human misery, ill-health, marital tension and unhappiness."[53] As early as 1948 the *CMAJ* published a cycle chart, created by a British medical man, which "enables a married woman, to some extent, to regulate her married life in an intelligent manner without having to worry over the possibility of an unwanted pregnancy."[54] In 1962, seven years before the advertisement and sale of contraceptives would be officially decriminalized, the *CMAJ*'s board of directors made the decision to accept advertisements for contraception within its pages in part in recognition of birth control's social efficacy for married couples and to assert that it was the medical community – not the legal one – that should have authority over such substances.[55]

It was clear that birth control was only a positive force if the fertility it limited was the communal property of a couple – only then would it serve to remove the anxiety from married sex and not create additional stressors by changing the ideal postwar family dynamic. Contributors to the *CMAJ* repeatedly emphasized that birth control, even if the method could be engaged in without the spouse knowing (as with the Pill), had to be a family decision. The husband and wife would agree to use birth control, and any doctor aiding them to get birth control should ensure this was the case; failure to do so was to deprive a male of his right within a marriage to use his wife's body to produce progeny.[56]

At this time many new methods of birth control that limited female fertility were under review, and the communal ownership of the mother body was underscored by the fact that almost all reports of clinical trials of these methods – such as the Pill or various forms of intrauterine devices (IUDs) – had a special section for the husband's opinion of the method and his overall comfort in engaging in that type of contraception. Though the body under investigation was the female one, the patient under review was an amalgamation of, and owned by, both husband and wife. For example, in a 1965 trial of oral contraceptives for married women, the questionnaire included "Husband's opinion of the method," with a good deal of space left for his answer.[57] In a 1966 study on IUDs the authors noted:

> The husband of one woman suffered a penile hematoma after being "stabbed" by the tail of the device. The woman's coil was removed because of alleged excessive vaginal bleeding and cramps. We were unable to determine whether she actually had these symptoms or whether her husband had insisted that the coil be removed.[58]

The tone of the article made it clear that a husband would be completely within his rights to demand that his wife alter her contraceptive practice to maximize his enjoyment of her body even if that shift inconvienced her or potentially negatively affected her sexual pleasure.

Historian Christabelle Sethna, in studying the rise of acceptance of birth control in Western society, has argued that it was the threat of overpopulation from "undesirable" countries in the developing world that finally made certain methods of fertility control, such as the Pill, generally acceptable.[59] Evidence within the *CMAJ* suggests that this explanation is only part of the equation. Contributors to the *CMAJ* did view birth control as a measure to police and limit racialized and classed bodies deemed unable to control themselves. Nevertheless, they also viewed birth control as a practical reward for heterosexual married couples who, by right of their acceptance of the normality of heterosexual married unions, were allowed to engage in as much sexual activity within the confines of marriage as they desired, free from unwanted pregnancy. It was expected that couples would use birth control wisely and space their children to maximize those children's development and to prevent pregnancies for which they could not provide. Within the pages of the *CMAJ*, birth control and heterosexual couples reinforced the authority of each other. Married, monogamous, heterosexual couples were deemed legitimate and rational, and therefore birth control was associated with the normality of heterosexual union instead of the sexual excess epitomized by the sexually active single female body. Medical contributors to the *CMAJ* decried any couple (or woman) who used birth control to avoid having children entirely, even expanding the familial control over the mother body by citing a child's right to siblings![60] Family planning was a family affair. Framing birth control usage within the mother body rather than the dangerous single female body was crucial to its respectability.

The view that a woman's fertility, her general reproductive ability, was framed as communal property by medical contributors is strengthened when considered in context with issues of infertility, abortion, and sterilization. Couples dealing with infertility had few options in the immediate postwar period; the technological and biological innovations that would bring about the first "test tube babies" were still at least twenty years in the future.[61] The primary therapy, artificial insemination by donor (AID), involved using an apparatus to introduce semen directly into the mouth of the uterus.[62] AID was extremely controversial. When infertility was caused by a husband's inability to deliver sperm into his wife's vagina, for reasons such as a previous penile injury that prevented effective ejaculation, the procedure was deemed acceptable;

articles talking about AID with a husband as donor made this clear using the designation "AID (husband)," rather than "AID (donor)." However, a minority of physicians suggested AID could be used with donor sperm in situations where a husband's sperm itself was the problem, such as in cases of low motility.[63] The resulting backlash within the *CMAJ* to this idea both augments the image of the mother body as communally owned and complicates the picture of the postwar era as child focused. In his 1962 address to the meeting of the Canadian General Medical Association, legal advisor and Queen's Council G.P.R. Tallin warned doctors that allowing AID (donor) would usher in the end of marriage and gender relations as they knew it.

> In view of Aldous Huxely's "Brave New World" it is possible to conceive that present ideas of marriage may become obsolete. Ideas of equal rights for men and women, and of non-discrimination on grounds of sex, accompanied by the discovery of new techniques may lead to an alternating system under which Joseph and Georgina will function as husband and wife respectively in the odd numbered years and under the names of Josephine and George as wife and husband respectively in the even numbered years. This system would eliminate all complaints about a man-dominated world. Of course, Huxley has gone one step further and abolished husband and wives altogether. Children in his world are fathered by a spermatozoa bank and delivered from a test-tube. This of course is merely a scientific extension of artificial insemination.[64]

Though deliberately hyperbolic, Tallin was serious in his warning that by facilitating AID (donor) doctors were in fact aiding moral and legal adultery. Put simply, AID (donor) voided the marital contract by removing the husband's input in communal conception. In another example, an editorial on AID (donor) by an unnamed author used much the same language, warning that if AID (donor) "became widespread, it might well destroy family life as the basis of human society."[65] The unnamed editorialist further argued that donor insemination would have to be extended to unmarried women or men, thus negating the viability of the nuclear family. He concluded his editorial by comparing donors to prostitutes and characterizing the doctors who performed the donor insemination as pimps. The great irony is that, within the *CMAJ*, couples who could not conceive were urged to adopt; it was better to accept into the family a child with no biological ties to either parent than one who had ties to one parent and one person outside of that union.[66]

Compounding the above irony was the pathologization of women who wished to have their doctor facilitate AID (donor). Despite the focus on pregnancy and motherhood as the combined culmination of a woman's psychosexual development, desiring AID (donor) was not seen as a logical expectation for women living in the face of such social constructs but whose husbands were infertile. In their article "Psychiatric Aspects of Artificial Insemination (Donor)," psychiatrists W.W. Watters and J. Sousa-Poza cited case studies arguing that women who pushed for AID (donor) did so not out of a desire for motherhood but as a means of punishing their husbands for their infertility.[67] The doctors claimed that such women, though they claimed their primary desire was to experience biological embodied motherhood, were more concerned about the prestige of being pregnant and soon lost interest in their children after those children were no longer dependent on them. The women cited in these case studies were described as overly domineering, nagging, and particularly unfeminine; their lack of femininity and their desire to demonstrate authority within the marriage were seen as further proof of their disturbed psyches.[68]

Moving fertility out of the communal mother body and into the hands of women was also one of the reasons cited for why abortion should remain taboo. While on the surface medical discourse focused on changing seemingly draconian Canadian abortion laws, doctors were primarily interested in increasing medical oversight and control over abortion procedures in order to better protect themselves from criminal prosecution.[69] In the postwar era a woman could obtain a legal abortion only if a doctor deemed it medically necessary to preserve her life. The preservation of life remained an ambiguous categorization, as some women were able to secure abortions by claiming the pregnancy threatened their mental health. Unsuccessful applicants in this process were often pathologized to an even greater degree than women seeking AID (donor), though both were condemned for their desire to be in control of their own fertility. Indeed, several articles suggested that any woman desiring an abortion was mentally ill as her mothering instinct had become somehow disrupted, the connection between her biology and embodied femininity faulty. In a 1963 letter to the editor Dr. C.P. Harrison argued that women who wanted to be rid of a pregnancy were divorced from their inherent feminine desire to protect and preserve their offspring: "surely Nazi Germany lives in memory as an example. Sacrifice the weak to the strong is the cry – a strange travesty of motherlove."[70]

It was assumed that any woman seeking an abortion was doing so secretly, without her husband's knowledge or even possibly to hide another crime such as an affair. Trying to abort a fetus and move fertility out of communal control was constructed as an act of hatred towards a husband and often signalled the disorder of gender roles within that particular family. According to Dr. Zarfas, an Ontario physician who conducted a study on women seeking therapeutic abortions (many of whom he denied), almost all those seeking terminations were overly masculine. He described one patient, a German immigrant, as an "aggressive, demanding, intolerant woman who hated her husband."[71]

In all the above cases the women patients involved were described as gender role deviants whose masculine demeanour and authority over their husbands were cited as contributing factors to their illnesses and as evidence that they were ill. The contributors thus drew a direct correlation between loss of femininity, gender role inversion, and the removal of fertility control from the communal mother body. This image of the pathological, unfeminine, and overbearing personality was sometimes imposed on Eastern European immigrant female bodies, as they were deemed less likely to fulfil white Canadian ideals of womanhood; fears of postwar immigration likely also played a factor.[72] The overbearing woman, often portrayed as older and having lost some of her natural femininity and sexuality, became such a fixture within the Canadian medical zeitgeist that she was featured in several advertisements and lampooned as a stock character in the *CMAJ*'s recurring cartoon[73] (image 5).

The tie of biological fertility to the communal mother body was so strong that it influenced situations where both the male and female partner were pushing for the same medical procedure, as occurred in many cases of sterilization: doctors frequently refused to undertake a sterilization operation even if the couple wanted it. *CMAJ* doctors noted that while a married couple may agree that they had borne the number of children they desired, the possibility of widowerhood or widowhood was too great a risk. A second husband or wife might want children, and sterilization of either partner should be avoided because it would put this (purely hypothetical) future marriage in jeopardy.[74] There was also some concern that even if the marriage remained intact the doctor could be sued if either of the couple changed their minds. Even when sterilization was a consequence of a required operation such as a hysterectomy, articles stressed the importance of gaining the consent of both husband and wife. A 1948 editorial reprinted the words of Justice Kelly, a trial judge, after a legal case debating the ethics of consent, about how sterilization sat on the axes of marriage's social and legal functions.

> As the relationship between a husband and wife is not only confidential, but is of the most intimate nature and is attended upon with such far-reaching consequences ... anything that might be done which interferes with such a

Image 5. A cartoon featuring the difficult older female patient – a reoccurring character – from the *Canadian Medical Association Journal* (15 July 1958, p. 35).

sacred relationship and its consequences should be undertaken only with the consent of both parties ... Our laws recognize the mutual responsibility between husband and wife and we have actions in our courts claiming the nullity of marriage based on sterility of one or other of life partners. It, therefore, follows that any operation performed upon the wife which would interfere with the intimate relationship and its responsibilities and consequences should be authorized or consented to by both parties.[75]

In this quotation, perhaps more than any other, the right of a couple to the wife's fertility is spelled out: any changes to the mother body, even to preserve its own integrity and viability, must be "authorized or consented to by both parties."

This hyper-concern for consent – even to the point of obtaining permission from both the husband and the wife and even in cases where the operation was life-saving – provides a stunning contrast to the ongoing forced sterilizations of the "feeble-minded" and "mentally defective" women (and some men) that were ongoing, particularly in Alberta, during this time. Women such as Leilani Muir, whose fallopian tubes were deliberately severed during what was supposed to be a routine appendectomy while she was detained within Alberta's Provincial Training School for Mental Defectives, were sterilized without their consent and in many cases, including Muir's, without their knowledge. These operations, which sometimes were conducted with the permission of family members, were "justified" by the argument that the mentally disabled or "slow" could not handle the burden of parenthood, to limit the spread of defective genetics into the population, and in many cases to save the government money.[76] In her 2013 work *Facing Eugenics* historian Erika Dyck notes the importance of considering how sterilization with consent – usually of middle-class couples for medical reasons or fertility control – and eugenics-based sterilization have to be considered together because they are two sides of the same coin.[77] By juxtaposing her work with the cases above we can see that gendered familial control over female fertility could extend beyond the husband-wife dyad in some cases; Muir's stepfather had given blanket permission for Muir to be sterilized upon her entry into the training school.[78] It also demonstrates that fertility and the rights and responsibilities of social citizenship were intimately intertwined in the postwar era. Doctors' reluctance to sterilize healthy middle-class white couples even for medical reasons denotes those couples' rights and responsibilities to contribute desirable offspring to the social reconstruction of postwar Canada. In contrast, the fertility of those deemed undesirable members of society, including so-called mental defectives, particularly if they were Indigenous or Métis, was truncated without seemingly any ethical, social, or legal concerns by the parties involved.[79]

The communal nature of the mother body went far beyond questions over familial ownership of her fertility. At its core the mother body served as a metonym for the family as a whole, reflecting their gendered transgressions as well as being the medium through which they could (in some cases) be cured. In essence, the mother body had to bend and change itself to suit the needs of family members and was the primary interceder in correcting familial gender imbalances.

Maintaining the family's adherence to gender standards was often a balancing act. In a 1960 study entitled "Impact of Sudden Severe Disablement of the Father upon the Family," doctors R. Castro de la Mata,

G. Gringas, and E.D. Wittkower of the Allan Memorial Institute of Psychiatry in Quebec examined the treatment of eight families in which the father had suffered a sudden and acute illness or debilitating accident. They focused on who within his family aided (or hindered) his mental and physical recovery. From the beginning of the article the authors invoked the mother body, noting:

> When a person marries, he and his wife enter marriage with a series of conscious and unconscious needs which they expect to be fulfilled through interaction with each other. This produces a highly dynamic play of adjustment and readjustment to maintain a good level of equilibrium and successful functioning of the family as a unit.[80]

Despite the seemingly neutral gender pronouns, the rest of the article makes clear that it is the wife who must "adjust and readjust" to "maintain equilibrium." These adjustments – to maintain the patriarchal organization of the family – were advocated even when they put the wider family in jeopardy or went against the fundamental principles of psychoanalysis that the authors purported to promote. For example, after the father in Family A broke his back while working as a window cleaner the family maintained their "clear-cut and well integrated" family status. The authors noted:

> Although the older members of the family realized that the father's injury was serious and that the consequences might be grave, they adopted the attitude of "all will be well in the end." In fact, the family was so convinced that the father would recover eventually that the idea of her looking for a job never crossed the mother's mind.[81]

Castro de la Mata, Gringras, and Wittkower praised this course of action despite the fact that the family was barely scraping by financially, noting that such an attitude resulted in "the father's position being strengthened," an important factor in his medically unexpected full recovery. They argued that "by virtue of collective denial, a sense of tragedy had by-passed the family."[82] Not only did the doctors in the article value the family's financial survival below the father's gender role maintenance, they praised the family for ignoring the issue despite the fact that unearthing and overcoming the truth beneath denial is a central tenant of psychoanalysis. They likewise praised Mrs. C., whose husband suffered a leg injury in a car accident that rendered him temporarily helpless, as his other leg had been amputated in childhood. Mrs. C. took a job only during this time and quit as soon as Mr. C. was able to return to work. More importantly, she worked to maintain his status as the head of the household even when she was forced to take on aspects of the breadwinner role. As they noted: "she rose to the occasion with remarkable understanding, skill and tact. [She said,] 'We have to let him feel that we are dependent on him.'"[83]

In contrast, Mrs. B. was heavily censured for her inability to navigate her role and utilize her body to protect the family's well-being and maintain her husband's gendered dignity. Due to the permanency of her husband's disablement, caused by a series of strokes, Mrs. B took a full-time job. "The parent's roles have undergone a reversal: the mother goes to work while the father stays at home, prepares the meals and depends on his wife in many ways. This change has gravely affected the whole family. With some justification, the father feels cast aside."[84] In an attempt to regain his masculinity, they note, Mr. B. had begun to beat his wife and children. The subtext of this case, when taken in context with that of Mrs. A. and Mrs. C., is that Mrs. B. was somehow deficient in her handling the situation, and even that the ensuing familial destruction, including domestic violence, was her fault. Indeed, the problem is not that she got a job – other women in the study were forced to work as well – but that she allowed her husband to accept her feminine duties such as preparing meals. A better course of action, which would have aided in the entire family's happiness, would have been to take a job while still engaging in her subordinate homemaker role as other wives had done, shouldering the mentally and physically exhausting burden of the "double day." Doing so, combined with a deference to his dominant position as the head of the family despite his inability as a breadwinner, was deemed the "cure" for such disruptions.

In supporting the gender role bifurcation of the family, the medical profession was not engaging in any different or extraordinary discourse. What was unique, however, was the medical profession's ability to medicalize those gender roles, and with the notable exception of homosexual men, gendered illness remained overwhelmingly centred on the mother body. Male bodies, like those who were suddenly disabled in the Montreal study noted above, who were unable or unwilling to fulfil their role as breadwinner may have been frowned upon and suffered a loss of self-esteem, but there were no cases where a failure in heterosexual masculinity equalled a biological illness. Significantly, these men did not become impotent or suffer any pain regarding their reproductive abilities or systems as a result of their contravention of gender roles. Mr. B., though he beat his wife and children, was not particularly pathologized; indeed, the article gives him so much sympathy as to place most of the blame with Mrs. B., who should have better managed the situation.

When heterosexual men failed in masculinity, it was usually their female counterpart who had their husband's failed manliness written on their own female body. In a 1952 article on postpartum psychosis Dr. F.E. McNair, of the Crease Clinic of Psychological Medicine in Essondale, BC, presented two cases in which he directly attributed the wives' psychosis to their husbands' inability to fulfil their masculine role. According to him, the first patient, Mrs. J.G., suffered from postpartum psychosis, which was both caused and then exacerbated by her husband's inability to be a "man." McNair noted in the case records that "while pregnant she routed a thug's attack on herself and her husband."[85] Later, "as her illness developed momentum her husband became indecisive, did not assume responsibility and her elder sister took over." Another case study, Mrs. D.G., was the "war bride of a husband whose mother still dominated him."[86] In both cases the patient's husband was unable to fulfil the requirements of his gender role, whether through the application of physical force to protect his wife and unborn child or the ability to take control of the household, or even simply to govern the other women in his life. His inability forced his female counterpart into a more active role, causing, or at the very least contributing to, her illness. Interestingly, Robert Rutherdale in his study of postwar alcoholic fathers found a similar pathologizing of the wives of alcoholics. Wives who were overbearing and dominating were seen as a major factor in driving their husbands to drink. Women who chose to marry men already exhibiting tendencies to overdrinking were also pathologized as being intellectually and psychosexually immature.[87]

Again, this phenomenon did not merely involve a disinterested medical population foisting ideals on the public; cases occurred in doctors' own families. As noted earlier, there was general unease that medical men, required to be emotionally distant with their patients and burdened by overwork, would not be able to relate to their own families, especially their wives, in a mutually fulfilling way. As one American-based psychiatric study noted, "the doctor's professional role affords him unusual opportunities for dodging the solution of his marital problems." However, it would not be the doctor who suffered; as the study asserted, the doctors' wives, when compared to a control group, were *all* in psychiatric treatment and had much higher levels of narcotic, legal barbiturate, and amphetamine abuse as well as alcoholism.[88] Male doctors may have been unable to engage emotionally and sexually with their wives, but it was their wives who ultimately became the patients.[89]

The sole situation where male gender and sexual role abnormality was written on the male body rather than the female was in cases of homosexuality. In several articles homosexual bodies were described as more subject to venereal disease, which was not attributed to "risky" behaviours as characterized later AIDS discussions, but due to what was seen as their inborn weakness, again echoing eugenics discourses. Contributors to the *CMAJ* also suggested that homosexual men, especially those whose homosexuality was higher on the Kinsey spectrum, were in fact impotent.[90] For example, Samuel Laycock, a famous Canadian advice columnist, psychological educator, and eugenicist, noted that

> because some individuals whose interests are more homosexual than heterosexual are able to get married, have normal sex relations and beget children this does not mean that this adjustment is possible for the more pronounced homosexuals to whom heterosexual relations are not only repugnant but impossible.[91]

Given Laycock's past association with eugenics and his use of psychology to "sanitize" former eugenic ideals, the "impossible" in this passage suggests that beyond emotional repugnance, gay men could not physically beget children and that homosexuality was a personal biological threat as well as a social aberration.

Why were homosexual male bodies pathologized in this way while heterosexual male bodies were not? One likely reason is that homosexual men were perceived as existing outside or parallel to the nuclear family, and thus there was no wife/mother body to bear the embodied gender burden for him, opening the door for the pathologizing of his body. Further, while homosexual men's bodies were pathologized for their perceived gender/sexual role deviance and were in many ways constructed as the authors of their own downfall, even their bodies remained connected to the mother body. Mothers were usually blamed, at least in part, for "warping" their homosexual sons. For example, Dr. Marvin Wellman, a surgeon commander in the Royal Canadian Navy, reported on one homosexual patient who came from a home where the mother wanted to work and did not enjoy being a housewife and who, because she disliked her husband, focused her affections solely on her son. He concluded that this inappropriate focus precipitated the son's condition and made him effeminate in his mannerisms and appearance.[92]

The mother body was also brought to bear on cases of homosexuality as a "cure" for that affliction. Heterosexual marriage was used as a treatment for some cases of homosexuality as well as constituting public, ongoing proof that the treatment was successful. In Wellman's case his patient was pronounced cured when he demonstrated that "his marriage, *in which he is the dominant partner*, is successful."[93] Significantly not all homosexual men were thought to be curable in this way. "Feminized" homosexual men, who were deemed to have female-identified behaviours, were usually seen as lost causes.[94]

Heterosexual marriage and the maintenance of gender roles could also "cure" other sexual deviations. Two noted Toronto psychiatrists, Ian K. Bond and Harry C. Hutchinson, discussed a case of a man who was addicted to exposing himself to women. His condition went into spontaneous remission when he was courting his wife, as at that time his sexual impulses were channelled into a proper heterosexual conduit. However, after their marriage his wife, whom we only see glimpses of in the case history, became ill and bedridden with an ulcer, making her body unavailable to him, and his deviation returned. Like in the cases of homosexuality, his mother was blamed for making sex seem dirty to him, which, according to Freudian ideals, meant he retaliated by exposing himself. Using visualization techniques and inhibition therapy, the doctors claimed that they were able to reduce his sexual fantasies, and

> as his sexual fantasies diminished, exhibiting was involved in them to a much lesser degree. The patient was able to engage in mixed group activities without tension for the first time ... Sexually he became more virile and reported considerable enjoyment in his sex relations with his wife.[95]

Just as when he was courting his wife, his sexual impulses were once again channelled into a proper course, and thus by enjoying sex with his wife the patient was pronounced cured.[96]

These cases of homosexuality and sexual deviance demonstrate that the wife/mother not only reflected the gender role imbalances of the family but that sexual contact with her body, almost like the touch of a saint, could heal inappropriate postwar sexualities. The wives remain shadowy figures within the narrative and their voices are practically non-existent, reinforcing the idea that it is solely their bodies that effect the cure. This cure was deemed even more successful if their husbands were able to make them pregnant, thus adding a crucial biological component to the social remedy.

The mother body was a useful construct for medical professionals in the immediate postwar period, so much so that the editors of the *CMAJ* actively courted practitioners, particularly psychiatrists, who helped to create her. She served to legitimate postwar gender roles by grounding them in female biology, allowing doctors to write gendered discourses on the very flesh of their female patients. This was a very powerful position for medical men. They not only used Freudian psychoanalysis to place women's (and some men's) bodies in a situation where non-compliance with gendered prescriptions could make a person ill, they also, due to their almost complete domination of the medical marketplace, had a captive audience for their authoritative discourses. A sick woman looking for relief of symptoms had very few places to turn other than the medical authorities, and even women who were not ill encountered hegemonic medical ideals during times such as pregnancy. The postwar medical establishment thus wielded a power that was as pervasive as it was subtle. Indeed, not until the emergence of the women's health movement, which focused on empowering women to make informed choices about their own bodies, would society as a whole begin to realize the pervasive nature of medical ideals.[97] However, medical men (and a few women) were not part of some grand conspiracy to disenfranchise postwar women; there is evidence that medical authorities were expected to use many of the medical knowledge structures in their own lives, breaking down some of the barriers between the doctor and the patient.

Further, as demonstrated in chapter 5 of this book, these discourses could never hope to be fully hegemonic, but instead had to be negotiated within each individual doctor-patient relationship on a case-to-case and even moment-to-moment basis. Doctor-patient interactions also occurred in a wide variety of circumstances across Canada. Despite the idealized image of the institutional biomedical model suggested by the *CMAJ* of a seamlessly interconnected system where patients had full access to a general practitioner (who in turn had full access to all to the most modern diagnostic and treatment options and was backed up by researchers, hospitals, pharmacies, and other medical support systems) many Canadian patients and doctors, especially in rural communities, had no such access. These incongruities of experience created space for additional negotiations within and by the patient-doctor dyad. It should also be noted that at this time the psychology of sex was in its infancy and its practitioners were much better at defining postwar sexual issues than actually solving them. Reasserting the status quo was one of the few "treatments" that seemed to work, at least on the surface and in the short term.[98] These caveats aside, however, it is clear that postwar medical authorities used the mother body to create an imaginary body politic that, in many ways, made morality a medical issue and that enshrined non-medical entities such as "femininity" within diagnostic and treatment structures.

Chapter Three

Sex, Marriage, and the "One-Flesh" Body: Married Sexuality in the Anglican, United, and Roman Catholic Denominations

Bodies, especially sexual bodies, loom large in the church. Christianity has a long history of qualifying the usefulness of bodies based on sex and sexuality. In the Bible sexuality is used to demark miraculous events and demonstrate the hand of God in the everyday world. Aside from the virgin birth of Jesus Christ, the Bible, especially the Old Testament, abounds with examples of families made suddenly fertile, such as the nonagenarians Sarah and Abraham conceiving Isaac and the healing of Rebekah's barren womb. Catholic religious vocations require lifelong chastity. In early modern times the bodies of such religious had to be whole and without blemish, including the sexual organs, in order to take holy orders; impotence or bodily imperfection was often seen as evidence of sin and the general disfavour of God. In both the Catholic and Anglican faiths, proof that either the husband or wife had bodily or mental imperfections that prevented the completion of the penetrative sex act was one of the few grounds on which a marriage was subject to annulment.[1]

In the aftermath of the social upheavals of the first half of the twentieth century and what contemporaries viewed as profound shifts in the moral landscape, the three dominant postwar Canadian faiths – the Roman Catholic, Anglican, and United churches – attempted to instruct the faithful in a new, "modern" view of sexual morality. All three denominations presented sex, at least within the bounds of heterosexual marriage, as a positive, transformative force that would transmute two separate worldly bodies into a single, spiritual body that became "one flesh."[2] To encompass this idea all three denominations zeroed in on a passage from the Gospel of Mark: "But from the beginning of creation, God made them male and female. For this reason a man shall leave his father and mother and be joined to his wife, and the two shall become one flesh. So they are no longer two but one flesh" (Mark 10.6–8).

Though the denominations deployed this ideal of the one-flesh body for different purposes, together they helped make married sex a holy affair in which the couple could take pride and joy, rather than an activity tainted by shame or sin.

The previous chapter described how Canadian medical authorities used the female sexual body, on which the transgressions of gender could be written, to create dominant discourses about the sexual and gender roles engaged in by both men and women. While there was clearly a marked transference of discourse between Canadian medical and religious authorities, the latter did not completely adopt or adapt the medical ideals of female sexuality. Instead, the one-flesh body was deployed to discipline and explain postwar gender and sexual systems within and outside of marriage and to present sexual intercourse, gender roles, and heterosexuality as pieces of an interrelated and often unbreakable triad. All three denominations interpreted these texts to mean that the union of man and wife in marital coitus was a spiritual, even sacramental, event. In that moment of congress, man and woman were no longer separate entities. They became fused together, with God, in a holy occurrence that could not be duplicated in any other way, including meditation or prayer. This one-flesh body was both the ideal expression of spiritual sexual contact and contained within its doctrine the churches' particular gender and sexual mores. The spiritual one-flesh body defined which bodies were useful and productive and which were deviant. The discursive construction of the one-flesh body also provided prescriptions for individuals to move from a state of deviance to compliance within the various Christian faiths.

Historiographically, religious history in Canada has stagnated of late, locked into two dominant debates based on language and geography. In anglophone Canada the majority of works remain focused on supporting or refuting the secularization thesis, which argues that as dominant Protestant faiths waned in influence and lost their relevance for everyday Canadians, the churches reacted by engaging in increasingly secular pursuits, resulting in further lost spiritual ground.[3] The second debate centres on francophone Quebec, continuously asking whether the Roman Catholic Church in Quebec hindered or helped the creation of modern Quebec defined through the goals of the Quiet Revolution.[4] Both debates place religious history squarely in the realm of intellectual history. By focusing on the social understanding of religion I sidestep both debates, and the latter in particular because my analysis of the Roman Catholic Church centres on the anglophone Catholic west. Despite the image, perpetuated by the current bifurcation of religious scholarship, that Roman Catholicism was confined to Quebec and some small pockets in the Maritimes, the Prairie regions, especially Saskatchewan and Manitoba, boasted a strong Catholic population and infrastructure that was consistently augmented by "assimilated" European immigrants. Moreover, these Catholic communities developed a particularly western perspective on their faith that made them distinct from francophone Catholics. Authors such as Gilles Routhier have demonstrated that because francophone Catholicism has always been enmeshed in questions of national history and provincial politics, and due to the language barrier, anglophone Catholics and francophone Catholics ran largely parallel ministries that rarely directly intersected. Instead, English-speaking Catholics tended to meet and share resources with American Catholics, while French-speaking Catholics more often connected to Rome and Europe.[5] This book seeks to expand the limited history examining the contours of Catholic belief outside of the Quebec context.

The question of whether Protestant church discourses, secularized or not, remained relevant to postwar Canadians needs to be investigated in more depth. One of the main issues facing religious historians, particularly in the twentieth century, is the impossibility of measuring belief. According to the 1951 and 1961 censuses 79 per cent of Canadians identified as belonging to one of the main Christian denominations.[6] Yet declaring a faith to a census taker still leaves open the scope of belief and the degree of church attendance and participation in question, especially given the taboo of claiming "no religion" in the postwar social environment.[7] To supplement this data I rely on the testimonies of the women whose oral histories were collected within this book to speak to the reach of Christian discourse into postwar women's lives. Without exception all the women interviewed were exposed to the doctrines of at least one of the dominant faiths, particularly at the time of their weddings, as marriages in postwar Canada could only be conducted in a limited number of spaces and solemnized by specific people; church marriages remained the norm.[8] Coming into contact with these discourses specifically at the time of marriage means that the majority of Canadian women were likely to engage with the particular doctrines focused on marriage, gender, and sexuality, whether in the form of a pamphlet or course, a pre-marriage talk with their priest or minister, or even within the words of the vows they spoke. While the women interviewed in this work are not meant to be representative of all postwar Canadian women, we can assume, based on the experiences of the women interviewees, the census data, archival documents, and the secondary scholarship, that the majority of Canadian women who married during the baby boom were exposed to, and influenced by, some form of authoritative Church discourse regarding sexuality that they then had to decide to follow, modify, reject, or ignore.

The three church's postwar spiritual and sexual schemata of the one-flesh body marked a departure from early modern and Victorian schemas of sexuality. No longer was sexual activity within heterosexual monogamous marriage seen as (at best) a necessary evil that had to be curtailed so that individuals might focus their energy on God. Rather, the churches in the postwar period expended considerable effort assuring parishioners that marital coitus, if conducted within the guidelines set by the church, was legitimate and to be enjoyed by both partners. Far from being something that took energy away from one's communion with God, sanctioned marital coitus was, religious authorities argued, a type of spiritual union.

Though all three churches were united in their reification of sexuality within the body politic of the one-flesh body, this spirituality was conceptualized differently by the Roman Catholic and Protestant faiths. During this period the Catholic Church and the Protestant churches in Canada fundamentally disagreed over the doctrinal reasons that God ordained marriage and the sexual contact that would occur within it. The Roman Catholic Church maintained that the primary function of marriage and married sexuality was to create a family by having and raising children. The Catholic one-flesh body was an expression of obedience to the "natural law," which, if followed correctly, directed Catholics how to take only what was good or positive in natural processes such as sex. According to natural law, all marriages, barring infertility, were a step towards the creation of a family. Subverting the natural law in any way, including using artificial birth control, was subverting God; the bodies doing so would be classified as disordered and deviant. Marital sexual acts were holy because each act could potentially create a child. In embracing the potential of conception via coitus the couple was "showing their love for God by cooperating with Him in the creation of a new person to love Him eternally."[9] Other benefits, such as a feeling of intimacy and deepening of the love between the couple, were originally seen as ancillary, even unnecessary, though this view changed in dominant Catholic teachings as time passed.

Though the Anglican and United churches also argued for the importance of children to marriage and the significance of family in society, they viewed children as neither the primary reason for marriage nor the sole justification for marital intimacy. Admittedly, both the Anglican Church and the precursors to the United Church – the Methodist and Presbyterian faiths – had previously subscribed to the ideal of marriage as family crucible. Throughout the twentieth century, however, they increasingly moved away from that ideal.[10] As both churches would also come to support family planning during this period, effectively severing the potential of conception from most sexual acts, they had to look elsewhere for reasoning to make marital sex a sacramental act. However, outside of conception, no biblical or canonical sources could be cited in the creation of sex as sacramental. Ergo, the sacred character of Protestant marital sex remained undefined and amorphous during this period. While the Protestant denominations argued that the experience of the one-flesh body was still a mystical union with God, they attempted to merge this mysticism with emerging medical, psychological, and sociological norms of an ordered body, including the new psychiatric melding of body and social gender roles.[11]

The creation of both the Catholic and Protestant ideal one-flesh bodies also ordered the way in which these churches policed gender relations. All three denominations used the sexual coming together of man and woman – specifically how the two sets of genitalia fit together like puzzle pieces to create a whole – as a metaphor for, and biological evidence of, the correct complementary social roles of men and women. For Canada's Roman Catholic Church, which maintained its support for a patriarchal family structure, the one-flesh body was clear evidence of the different, complementary natures of men and women, and the rightness of the relationship of the man as socially/sexually active and penetrating, to the woman as socially/sexually passive and penetrated. However, for the Anglican and United churches, who recognized that the patriarchal structure was at odds with their new ideals of companionate and democratic marriage, the one-flesh body as metaphor was more complex.

All three denominations agreed that the postwar family in general, and marriages in particular, were in trouble. Church authorities were in agreement that two world wars and the Great Depression had combined to create a society lacking a moral compass, increasingly focused on the accumulation of consumer goods, and suffering from the many changes in gender roles brought on by nearly half a century of conflict. Societal decay was seen to be so great that two completely unrelated Anglican and United Church officials separately referenced Edward Gibbon's descriptions of the downfall of Rome in *Decline and Fall of the Roman Empire* in alluding to Canada's situation of the time.[12] Or, as the Most Reverend Francis A. Marrocco explained:

> I see ... categor[ies] of family life that would require a lot of "adhesive tape" treatment. By this I mean families in which patching up, readjustment and rehabilitation was urgently needed ... Many others, though

agreeing that we need counselling and rehabilitation services for family life in marriages that are sick, ailing and broken, have also been saying that an ounce of prevention is worth a pound of cure. Their voices continue to plead that if it is Christian to give first aid to injured marriages and impaired family life it is at least equally as Christian to work at reducing the causes of breakdown and decadence.[13]

Religious authorities were surprisingly pessimistic about their ability to aid those couples already in deep crisis – temporary and weak "adhesive tape treatment" was all they could offer. Instead, they turned their attention to future unions that they felt they could build up with stronger foundations. Further, they believed that fixing marriage would entail important trickle-down benefits for the family and society. Early intervention was key. The first union of a couple, assumed to be between two virgins, was regarded as a particularly potent joining that, if completed properly, would set the stage for an elevated spiritual sexual life.[14] Consequently, couples who engaged in coitus without the proper (i.e., Church-sanctioned) knowledge beforehand would be forever spiritually and emotionally handicapped and be capable of only ever experiencing a pale reflection of the one-flesh body.

The denominations' two primary concerns were that marriage, a serious and solemn occasion, had become overly romanticized, and that couples were entering the union without due consideration. This position was only strengthened when, immediately after the war, there was a (temporary) unprecedented spike in the country's divorce rate as some of those who had chosen to "marry in haste" divorced rather than "repenting at leisure."[15] The churches waged war on youthful, starry-eyed ideals of marriage, decrying such as the antithesis of lasting unions. As Elsie Robinson graphically put it in her article for the Catholic newspaper *Prairie Messenger*, "There is probably no institution on earth about which more sacrilegious tripe is written. This notion that matrimony consists of legalized romance is the silliest and most dangerous fallacy ever foisted on the human race. If marriage is romance, then the electric chair is a hot water bottle."[16] While several different "culprits" were blamed for such hasty unions, Hollywood was considered the most dangerous offender by far. Movies, and later television, according to religious authorities, created an image that made marriage merely the logical next step for people in love – the ending of the fairy tale – an attitude that prominent educator S.R. Laycock termed "romantic infantilism."[17]

The war on romance was a symptom of a larger concern by older religious authorities about the ability of youths on the brink of marriage to properly order their lives without expert aid. Preaching from the pulpit was no longer seen as adequate to address these concerns, and churches sought to expand their reach by creating and implementing new educational regimes focused on a variety of areas within family life. The two key branches of these regimes were always fixed on the interrelated matters of sexual education and marriage preparation. Educational efforts created a massive discursive archive containing letters, committee proceedings, conference proceedings, marriage courses, pamphlets, articles, and manuals – all demonstrating the prevalence of the one-flesh body ideology.[18] Such an archive can be unruly, as the variability of its sources can make one-to-one comparisons difficult. However, within each denomination's archive we can also see echoes of its internal structure, particularly the ways that coitus, heterosexuality, and gender roles were made to police and serve each other, and the ways this one-flesh body created and transmitted knowledges.

Unsurprisingly, the Roman Catholic Church had the most rigid structure, with doctrinal shifts and interpretations coming from senior levels of the church, including the pope in Rome, and being transmitted throughout the Catholic world in two primary ways.[19] First and foremost, the faithful would be educated and guided by their local priest, who in turn was guided by the rest of the hierarchy above him. The congregation could also be guided in living their lives by documents such as advice manuals and pamphlets, often translating the words of the pope into English, and by regional religious newspapers and periodicals. These periodicals had to be legitimized by Rome and frequently reprinted pieces from other Catholic periodicals and papers while maintaining a localized focus and content. I have made use of the *Prairie Messenger*, published out of St. Peter's Abbey in Muenster, Saskatchewan, to capture the perspective of western Catholics.

In contrast to the largely top-down organization of the Roman Catholic Church, the individual arms of the Anglican Church hold much more power. Canada is one of the provinces of the Church of England; each province is self-governing and creates and promotes its own educational materials. The head, or primate, of the Anglican Church – the name of the Church of England in Canada – makes the major distinctions about how doctrine will be presented in Canada. Doctrinal matters are also discussed and debated in the Lambeth Conference, held approximately every ten years by the Bishop of Canterbury in England. The minutes and reports of the Lambeth Conference are useful in determining the general doctrinal consensus of the international Church of England, though it should be noted that Lambeth decisions are meant as guiding documents and did not have the same weight as ecclesiastical law.

Interestingly, the Anglican Church, though it did have the lay Anglican magazine the *Anglican Journal*, did not use this vehicle to instruct its parishioners in matters of marriage and sexuality. Instead of more public pedagogical efforts, its archive contains educational materials focused on making each individual priest a better marriage counsellor. The one exception to this is *The Hallowing of the Union*, the main Canadian Anglican marriage manual, developed by the Diocese of Toronto and distributed throughout Canada via the Marriage Counselling Committee. *The Hallowing of the Union* directly modelled its structural organization, though not its content, on the modules from the existing marriage manual/correspondence course of the Roman Catholic Church in Canada, *This Is a Great Sacrament*, which was created at St. Paul's University.[20]

The United Church, a uniquely Canadian organization created in 1925 by the joining of the Presbyterian Church in Canada, the Methodist Church in Canada, the Congregational Churches of Canada, and the General Council of the Local Union Churches, had the most diffuse power base and the most eclectic archive. Church officials drew on, reprinted, and reformed doctrinal information from their international parent denominations as well as creating their own interpretations of the Bible and religious law. For much of the period they focused on fashioning educational materials to advise individual ministers, with their general periodical *The Observer* rarely commenting on sex and marriage. However, in 1959 the United Church of Canada entered into a publishing arrangement with the American Methodist Church, which published a magazine out of Nashville entitled *The Christian Home*. According to their agreement, the Methodist publishers would create a Canadian version of *The Christian Home* by adding Canadian content, including letters, to "American" articles and editorials already being produced. The publisher would then ship the "Canadian" version to Toronto where the Canadian United Church would distribute them. After its launch, the United Church in Canada pursued an aggressive marketing strategy to achieve maximum readership. Unlike the more general magazine *The Observer*, *The Christian Home* was designed for family lay readership and home devotion; it discussed married sexuality much more frequently. It also reprinted any relevant passages or articles from the *Observer* if they were thought to be of family interest.

Within each of these individual archives, the churches expressed their ideals of marriage as well as defined what made a good mate, how to date within the moral confines of the faith, how to enter marriage with due solemnity and consideration, and how to problem solve within the union, and offered sexual guidelines and meanings for marriage. It is important to note that these were managed archives expressing little disagreement and limited debate. In many cases, particularly with the Catholic Church, this is because only the final document would be published, keeping any dissension behind closed doors to create an image of uniform agreement. Of course, individual priests, ministers, or pastors could shift or reimagine official doctrine in their day-to-day interactions with their flocks. However, as these took place mainly in private it is difficult to create an account of how far individual priests, ministers, and pastors shifted the dominant doctrine to meet the needs of their parishioners. We can get some glimpses of these interactions in chapter 4, as some narrators did discuss private and family counselling within their churches, but they remain too infrequent to be generalizable.

It is also important to note that the Roman Catholic Church perceived marriage as a secondary embodied choice; Catholics were urged, above all, to accept a celibate religious vocation serving God as the superior form of sexual spiritual embodiment. Canadian Catholic discourses assert that celibate vocational bodies were not to be seen as asexual and that in fact, vocational bodies retained their holiness in part by their discipline of their sexual instincts to the service of God, which gave those bodies a special quality. The main Canadian Catholic marriage manual and correspondence course, *This Is a Great Sacrament*, made clear that married bodies were lesser bodies: "Marriage and virginity are not to be considered as being on the same footing, however. The celibate who willingly takes a vow of celibacy making it a fixed way of life, differs from the married person by the special renunciations which he makes with the help of supernatural love."[21] Only with divine aid could a person fully sublimate the sexual drives with which God had endowed humans to ensure the continuance of the species.

Only a select few who received a special calling directly from God were to take holy orders. Consequently, the sexual bodies of most Catholics would be controlled through channelling the sexual urge into the religiously appropriate realm of heterosexual monogamous marriage. For Canadian Roman Catholic authorities, the moment a man and a woman joined together in sexual congress created a new body of one flesh that became holy only if there was a potential for procreation. That is, the sexual act itself was not holy; the spiritual element was created in the joining because the couple were opening themselves up to the possibility of creating a new life with, and for, God. However, even if conception did not occur, the one-flesh body was still holy; by engaging in sexual congress the couple was allowing God, in that moment, to control their destiny by determining whether conception occurred. By that logic, to engage in contraception was to thwart God, and subverting the use of their bodies in this way had consequences. Couples who refused to have children would eventually become overwhelmed by their sexual passions, while those who had children would find their sexual joining became increasingly holy and personally satisfying over time. As *This is a Great Sacrament* stated:

> Nothing purifies the mutual love of a husband and wife as does the birth of children. It is very hard for a married couple to live a chaste life if they refuse to have children; on the other hand virtue is an easy matter for those who welcome the birth of children. The fires of passion of the early days change gradually until they become a steady, clear light, less tumultuous, but more soul satisfying, more harmonious and more intimately blended.[22]

In this way, the reward for giving up control of one's body to God was, in a sense, greater control over one's own body in the future; those who failed to do this would become increasingly steeped in sin and thus further and further alienated from God. The properly ordered Catholic body was always poised towards the ultimate prospect of salvation or damnation, and only disordered and deviant bodies acted without consideration of this future.

One of the signs by which couples could identify that they were using their bodies in the proper way was that the marital act would be pleasurable. Orgasm, to be experienced by both the male and female parties, was portrayed by several Catholic authorities as "part of His reward to them for the sacrifices they undertake in the sublime task of raising children for Him."[23] If one inverts this concept it becomes clear that couples who attempted to thwart God through the use of birth control, or couples who engaged in extramarital coitus, would not be able to achieve orgasm, making it the litmus test of marital success. This view of orgasm was a double-edged sword. It did confirm that women had a right to sexual pleasure; however, modern medicine has demonstrated the difficulty many women have in attaining orgasm through penetrative sexual acts alone, meaning that many couples would ultimately fail this test.

Tying all aspects of sex, including orgasm, to procreation had significant effects on anglophone Catholic sexual dogma. In many ways the one-flesh body was both the physical representation of male and female difference and the biological anchor for complementary gender roles – their triad was much more rigid in demarking the interrelatedness of sex, heterosexuality, and gender roles. In this, Canadian Catholic authorities were maintaining a Victorian sexual schema, albeit with a few minor doctrinal changes. Catholic women's ultimate destiny was motherhood, and their biological processes, as well as their feminine mentalities, pulled them towards maternity their entire lives. So strong was the rhetoric about the natural inclination of women to motherhood that religious leaders expressed great concern about "gap" women who had not received a religious calling but, for reasons such as a lack of marriageable men in the wake of the war, were unable to marry. As the unknown author of an article in the *Catholic Herald* stated:

> The normal woman wants to be of particular importance to one person; she wants a close human relationship; she wants to matter emotionally to someone. This means marriage and maternity, and there is no other way in which such satisfaction can be found. The life of the woman who is called neither to marriage nor religion must perforce at times be lonely.[24]

Women who found themselves in this undesirable situation were told to become "spiritual mothers," using their inherent maternal instincts to bring God's message to those in need. This ideal of "spiritual motherhood" was very different from what Michel Gauvreau described as advanced by the Quebecois Catholic Action marriage preparation manuals. According to Gauvreau, the concept of spiritual motherhood was used to empower all francophone Catholic women spiritually and politically. It seems the anglophone Catholic authorities adopted a much more conservative definition of the term, as it was made clear that spiritual motherhood was only to be practised by those with a religious vocation or who were unable to marry or procreate – fertile married women were expected to experience embodied reproductive motherhood.[25]

Unmarried women were assured that though they had been "call[ed] to love and serve God in loneliness ... He will give them the strength they need to endure their hardship."[26] Women who did marry but could not conceive were treated with a gentle pity and urged to adopt if possible and raise children for God in that capacity.[27] Only by adopting children could a barren couple have a fully Christian marriage and, more importantly, could a woman fulfil her biological role. Thus, the female body was deemed by the church as religious and celibate, maternal/maternal-in-waiting, or broken. There was no equivalent concern for men without wives. For Catholic men, fatherhood was only one way, and usually not the primary way, to serve God outside of a religious calling.

At the same time Catholic authorities, no doubt aware that their strongest adherents were usually women, strove to reassure women that they and men were equally worthy of salvation in the eyes of God, even though women were subject to a patriarchal system on earth. They attempted to placate female Catholics while simultaneously retaining their overall patriarchal structure by venerating motherhood. This discursive strategy had long been a part of their overall faith structure, as women had been encouraged for many years to idolize and pattern themselves after the Holy Mother, the Virgin Mary. In the postwar period this veneration of maternity allowed the Catholic Church to reify their image regarding women's rights; they portrayed themselves as the last line of defence protecting women's right to be mothers against the attacks of a modern society trying to force women to, in essence, become men. For example, in the statement of the Canadian Hierarchy on "the Family in Canada," Canadian Catholic officials noted that the pope had called for a living wage to be paid to all men so that women would not be forced to work outside the home due to economic necessity.[28] "Forcing" women to work outside the home was equated on one occasion with Mussolini's regime and, more movingly in the Cold War era, with the practices of communism.

> In Soviet Russia today, even more so in the so-called People's Republic of China, women can and do almost any work a man can. Yes, maybe it is not so bad and even good that some become trained professional people or skilled artisans. But what about the other end of the scale, such as ditch-digging and construction work, being part of a living chain carrying rock and earth by hand to build roads, runways, dams? So far, in these countries women still bear the children, as no alternative has yet been found. But even child-care is organized, to reduce to a minimum the loss of time on the job, through state nurseries or even more harshly in red China through the permanent wardship of the communes.[29]

Church authorities also expended a great deal of effort assuring housewives and mothers that their role was valued, interesting, and crucial to society.[30] Pope Pius XII both exalted the value of housewives and mothers and warned women that failing in these roles would negatively affect the rest of their family, especially their daughters:

> The daughter of the worldly woman, who sees all housekeeping left in the hands of paid help and her mother fussing around with frivolous occupations and futile amusements, will follow her example, will want to be emancipated as soon as possible and in the words of a very tragic phrase "to live her own life." How could she conceive a desire to become one day a true lady ... the mother of a happy, prosperous, worthy family?[31]

Women who satisfied their biological roles were the only ones who became both socially and physically "true ladies." Fulfilling the biological imperative to motherhood likewise had biological benefits, even being seen as a type of physical/spiritual anti-aging treatment. As J. Gerald Berry, archbishop of Halifax, noted in his sermon "Christian Family Apostolate," "Who has not seen the youthful look of a mother of a large family surrounded by her offspring?"[32]

According to religious discourse, Canadian Catholic women, though equal in their ability to find salvation, were naturally subservient to men. However, church officials normalized this by telling women that they, unlike men, had an inborn talent for compromise. According to *This Is a Great Sacrament*:

> This talent for adapting herself, a talent with which Providence has endowed her, imposes certain duties on her as a wife. It has been said that married people can be happy only if they meet each other half-way. It is a fact. But if one of the two should find it necessary to go more than halfway to ensure happiness, then it is up to the wife to do so, because it is much easier for her to adapt herself to her husband's ways than it is for him to adapt himself to hers. This applies to all circumstances relating to the home, food, way of living, tastes, etc.[33]

Catholic authorities suggested that any wife unable or unwilling to compromise was failing not only her marriage but also her God. Moreover, by stating that women had an innate ability to compromise, these authorities made abnormal any woman who chose to challenge conventions, whether within or outside of the home.

In an ideal situation, a husband's dominance over his wife would not cause friction in the marriage. Supposedly the husband, out of love, would naturally ask his wife's opinion on family matters, mitigating his own power but ultimately retaining control over final decisions. This was made especially clear in the answer key to the section in *This Is a Great Sacrament* on gender interrelations. The question: who was to rule in the household, the man or the woman? The correct answer: "Both, the man makes the decisions, the woman inspires these decisions."[34] It should be noted that the Catholic Church made sure there was no room for creative interpretation in answering such questions. Each section of *This Is a Great Sacrament* ended with a test, and the students taking the course had to correctly answer no less than 60 per cent of the questions before they could receive the next course module.

In marital personal relations the woman, deprived of an equal say in matters, was to use her inborn feminine tact to make her wishes known. More importantly, she was to keep her husband on the moral path, which, due to her feminine abilities, she could see more clearly than he. This was a message obviously derived from Victorian ideals of the woman as the feminine "angel in the home" and reflected tenets of Victorian anti-feminist ideology. *This Is a Great Sacrament* noted:

> The art of tactfulness that God has granted to woman imposes duties on her where her husband is concerned. She must be his guardian angel ... and very often, without letting him suspect it. She must circumvent him, sway him, influence him so that he will always remain on the right road – a woman's natural work if she is a loyal wife. But, and note it well, in her methods of doing this, there must be absolutely no trace of deceit.[35]

Women were placed in a role where passive-aggressive communication tactics were not only deemed necessary but actively promoted by the church. This facility to persuade was also the only thing that separated the husband's relationship with his wife from his with their children, as he was given dominion over both of the "two gentle beings, the mother and child."[36]

During the Victorian era medical science supported the same hierarchal structure of men and women as the Christian faith and supported the latter's authority over the body.[37] It is not surprising, then, that the Roman Catholic Church, finding its teachings at odds with the newly popularized medical system of sex ranking based on the mind-body connections of psychoanalysis, reverted to older scientific understandings that better supported its world views.

Remaining tied to the old scientific schemas of sex ordering alienated the Roman Catholic Church from the authority of more modern scientific concepts. Instead, the church's authoritative discourses were cobbled together from a bizarre and eclectic mix of Victorian and even early modern scientific and medical authorities. The starkest example of this occurs in *This Is a Great Sacrament* within the section "Male and Female Psychology." Students were provided with a table outlining the four basic "temperaments," which described the relative positive and negative traits of each and the likely combinations that would be found in a single person. Students were supposed to use the matrix to find their own personality type and that of their partners, then utilize that knowledge for conflict resolution. The four personality types were entitled "sanguine, nervous, bilious, and lymphatic." However, their described characteristics are clearly derived from, and correlate closely with, the early modern medical schema of the four humours: sanguine, choleric, melancholic, and phlegmatic. Though the schema is given the veneer of modernity by changing three of the names and claiming that these are "psychological concepts," it is obvious that this "new" system is actually an anti-modernist throwback to medical authority from a time when it better supported the Catholic patriarchal married structure.[38]

In their deviance from modern medical ideals, the Roman Catholic Church was very concerned about the possibility that parishioners might be receiving conflicting gender role and sexual role advice from their medical practitioners, thereby fracturing the triad of sex, sexuality and gender norms and robbing one or more of those elements of their power. In order to avoid this potential inconsistency, Catholic authorities continually emphasized the importance of Catholics only consulting a Catholic doctor.[39] When the dioceses of Saskatoon and Sault St. Marie sent out questionnaires about Catholic family life to their parishioners, both surveys asked whether the family went to a doctor who shared their faith, and if they sought out their priest or their family doctor for questions regarding marriage and sex. When less than half of the Saskatoon respondents confirmed that they had a Catholic doctor, church officials regarded this as cause for great concern.[40]

Using a Catholic doctor was particularly important regarding sexual issues within marriage because although medicine, as well as the Anglican and United churches, had established that women not only enjoyed sexual intercourse but also had an appetite for it as strong as men's, the Catholic Church remained tied to Victorian notions of female sexual passivity and quiescent desire. Even on their wedding night, when Catholic morality assumed both partners would be virgins, the male was described as taking an active role and warned not to let his stronger passions overwhelm his young and vulnerable wife. "More than one young bride has been rudely stirred and shocked by her loved one's brutality in the course of this first intimate union and … silent and bitter tears have dampened the pillow of many a young wife on her wedding night."[41] To avoid this tragic start to their married life, a husband

> should avoid all abruptness and haste. He should be patient in leading his wife, by gradual and progressive stages, to complete union. He will encourage her to desire these complete unions, and the pleasure she derives from them will be the measure of his success and the reward for his patient efforts. For this reason, he must be careful to indulge in no close intimacies without first having aroused a desire on her part for them. The wife should cooperate fully. Let her confide freely in the man she loves: their words of love and other manifestations of affection soon will overcome

her shyness; then, with nature's help, these will lead in the most normal manner to more and more perfect intimacy.[42]

It was the husband's job to awaken the latent passions in his wife – there is no thought that she might have passions that are equal to or even stronger than his, and it is clear that she will not be taking an active sexual role in arousing *him*. This has a direct correlation to Victorian marriage manuals and medical texts, which, according to historian Angus McLaren, "presented women not as passionless, but sexually dormant, needing to be aroused by a partner."[43] Then, and in the postwar period, the wife's role was to "cooperate fully," leaving her without control or ownership of her own sexual desire.

The use of the phrase "complete union" and later the plural form "unions" is interesting as it does leave an opening for alternative interpretations. Conservative Catholics might read the above as the Church's admonition that all sexual activity had to conclude with male ejaculation into the vagina. Acts that did not conclude this way precluded conception and thus were deemed incomplete and abnormal.[44] A more liberal reading, less focused on procreation and more focused on the couple themselves, would be that it was the husband's responsibility to provide his wife with an orgasm and, given the use of the plural, that he should if possible give her more than one. This interpretation was supported by a passage in *This Is a Great Sacrament* claiming that the highest level of the one-sex body was achieved when the couple experienced mutual orgasm: "it is highly desirable that both experience orgasm simultaneously. This point is important. We recall it to your attention without going into further detail."[45]

On a basic level the burden of the success of a couples' sexual relationship was the husband's responsibility. *This Is a Great Sacrament* did allow that the wife, if she had not achieved orgasm immediately after the husband did, could touch herself "to obtain this satisfaction" without committing a sin.[46] However, a few lines later the manual shames the husband for letting this situation occur, once again placing the burden of her sexual satisfaction on him. "It is a duty of love for the man to see to it that his wife experiences satisfaction in their marital intimacy, and that as far as possible it reach its climax at the time the male seed is discharged."[47] Thus, while church authorities allowed that a woman's obtaining her own satisfaction within specific parameters was not sinful, they also demanded that the husband take control over his wife's body and shamed him if he was incapable of doing so. Such ideals would have put immense pressure on the marital couple, especially during the early encounters in their relationship. Indeed, though church officials blamed Hollywood for creating unrealistic ideals for marriage, they replaced those ideals with standards that were equally difficult, if not more so, to attain.

Aside from burdening husbands with the responsibility for their wives' sexual enjoyment, there is a more sinister overtone to such a Victorian sexual schema. Women were warned that if they did not give in to their husband's request for sex, even if he was rough during intimacy, they might force him to commit either the sin of adultery or the lesser sin of masturbation.[48] As one marriage advice column stated in *The Prairie Messenger*:

> You must understand too that he loves like a man – with body desires that are always easily aroused by the sight and touch of you. You won't sadden him then with the reproach that he is too rough or coarse or a "beast." You will remember God's word to you both: "And they shall be two in one flesh." And though you might not feel like it yourself at different times, you will readily, cheerfully give yourself to him with great understanding of his more ardent nature. In that way, you may save yourself serious sin, you may save him sin, you may save his soul – that soul for which you are partially responsible since he gave it to you on your wedding day. That really would help a lot to make and keep him a good, God-loving husband.[49]

Giving husbands control over the entire sexual relationship placed great social pressure on wives to "cooperate fully" whether they wanted to or not. Canadian Catholics during this time were told by church leaders that to deny one partner sexual intercourse within marriage was actually a sin. "The spouse, who without sufficient and serious reason refuses intercourse, is guilty of mortal sin; such refusal robs the partner of his (her) just right to the use of the other spouse's body."[50] On the surface this statement seems gender neutral, but when combined with the surrounding discourse that makes clear the binary between the active male and the passive female, it is obvious that the male will always be the active initiator and the female the participant or receiver, albeit a usually willing one. "We have repeated over and over again that the male, more than the female, seeks carnal gratification ... The female, on the other hand, being receptive, awaits man's pleasure for her sexual satisfaction."[51] The reasons given for legitimate refusal were extremely narrow, including extreme intoxication and abuse of the sexual privilege by requesting sex too frequently, defined as "three or four times a night."[52] Sexual intercourse was also suggested as a way of solving disagreements as "at times, it is very useful to *demand* intimacy in order to bring about a reconciliation of husband and wife."[53] The husband, who was, as stated, the active partner, could command his sexual privileges of his wife in the midst of a heated debate. Exerting this privilege in the face of disagreement not only reminded his wife of his church-sanctioned dominance over their relationship and her body – an excellent way to conclude the argument in his favour – but also could be interpreted as allowing men to use more extreme sexual coercion, even marital rape, to control their wives. Like the other aspects of a Catholic marriage, the authoritative discourse on sex relied heavily on the beneficence of the men whom it empowered.

The Catholic Church, more so than any other discussed here, had an uneasy and complex relationship with medical science and the emerging social sciences during this period in Canada. Science was both a potent source of authority to tap and a dangerous challenge to some religious principles. As the Reverend Robert J. Dwyer noted, "There is a kind of magic in the modern mind in the word 'scientific.' It is a shibboleth of marvellous potency. Anything that is unscientific is ridiculous, and the meaning of science has been progressively restricted to a matter of apparatus and test-tubes."[54] Though in most cases Catholic authorities avoided scientific and medical ideas, they were not averse to deploying such authoritative discourses when doing so reinforced religious doctrine. When, however, Catholic authorities did use concepts made popular by postwar psychology, they remained clear about their superior authority. As Mr. Howard Fowler and Dr. H. Breault claimed during the discussion period of a 1959 Cana Conference (a type of marital spiritual retreat):

> A child will always model itself on some prototype, most normally its parents. The mother should be to the girl a real MODEL of womanhood, and the father should be to the boy a masculine transparency of God the Father – thus both parents are involved in bringing the child to maturity and to God ... Up to this decade Freudians and other psychologists did not realize the importance of fatherhood in the early years of the child's life. This left father's [sic] confused. Happily there is now a whole new concept being developed [concerning] the tremendously important role played by fatherhood at all levels of the child's existence.[55]

The above passage both utilizes psychology's postwar authority and undermines it by suggesting that the church had always recognized the importance of fatherhood; psychologists and psychoanalysts, though claiming to be pioneers in understanding the human psyche, were only recently coming to the same discovery.

This ambiguous relationship to science was characterized most clearly in the debate surrounding birth control. Up until the last few years before the publication of *Humane Vitae* officially banned birth control in 1968, western anglophone Catholic Church discourse remained strongly against birth control. It especially resisted the majority medical opinion that frequent intercourse without the burden of unwanted conception was beneficial to married couples and strengthened families. Maintaining that the primary purpose of marriage and married sexuality was procreation, the church decried those who supported birth control as contributing to Canadian moral decay – even equating birth control promoters to purveyors of pornography.[56] Catholic authorities argued that birth limitation was a symptom of society's move to place materialism via financial success and commercial acquisition above more important concerns such as family and spiritual well-being. In direct contrast to the Protestant denominations, who promoted family planning to suit a family's financial means, the Catholic Church portrayed those who wanted to limit their families to fit their budget as having a lack of faith in God to provide for them.[57] Further, users of artificial birth control were seen as lacking the proper "self-control" required of Catholics even in marriage; this control was crucial to Catholic understandings of the ordered body. In one *Prairie Messenger* article, Father John J. O'Connor wrote that married couples using artificial means of birth prevention degraded women, effectively making them take on the role of "paramour or mistress." Without the possibility of procreation to make the sex act spiritual, O'Conner asserted, women became slaves to men's basest lust.[58] O'Connor, like other Catholic authorities, thus used anti-birth control rhetoric to affirm that women would not desire sex without the arousal of a male or the potential for conception, while framing that discourse as being supportive of women's rights rather than limiting their embodied expression. Drawing on Catholic doctors and psychologists, Catholic authorities also warned their parishioners that birth control, especially the Pill, had dangerous physical side effects, including permanent infertility. Authorities argued that the use of contraceptives could cause deep psychological disturbances in both men and women, as they robbed the one-flesh body of its holiness and alienated the couple from God. Far from aiding married couples in becoming closer, as medical and Protestant authorities claimed, these physical and mental side effects threatened a couple's marriage as well as their overall health.[59]

The Catholic Church was especially embattled because Dr. John Rock, one of the creators of the Pill, was Catholic. Rock did not hesitate to tell the public that he was inspired to the discovery by the spectacle of poverty amongst working-class Catholics caused by having too many children.[60] This placed Catholic authorities in a difficult position, as the unnamed author of one 1962 editorial noted:

> Not a few Catholic couples wonder when the Church is going to approve contraception as the other religious groups have done already. A Catholic doctor who has helped to develop a contraceptive pill told reporters that he hopes that Catholics will be allowed to use it because many are now using less reliable methods! ... Catholics and the rest of the world can be very sure that the Church will uphold God's law regarding the primary purpose of marriage until the end of time. It is blasphemous to believe that the sacrament [of marriage] puts a blessing on blind and passionate sexual indulgence.[61]

Even though the rhythm method was technically allowed to Catholic couples wishing to try to limit their families, many Canadian anglophone Catholic authorities actually took pains to warn their parishioners that the rhythm system was permissible only under certain rare circumstances and had to be used with the right frame of mind. The rhythm system was not to be exercised to prevent the couple from having children entirely or to drastically limit the number of children. As the authors of *This Is a Great Sacrament* cautioned: "The biological phenomenon of sterile periods is absolutely normal in itself. The same may not be said of its 'clever' employment by married couples who use it with the intention of avoiding or controlling the birth of children." The emphasis on the word "clever" here is a clear linguistic link to the prideful "knowledge" that was a part of original sin where Adam and Eve ate of the forbidden tree. According to *This Is a Great Sacrament*, the rhythm system could only be used when it was necessary to avoid conception for the mother's health, and even then only after consultation with the couple's priest and a Catholic physician. Furthermore, additional emotional strictures applied:

> The first reaction of Christian hearts, reduced to the use (according to the conditions already explained) of the Rhythm System should be one of **regret**. Deep within their hearts should be a pang of sorrow at their being unable to bestow the boon of life on a new soul. This regret is a sign of the sincere and good faith of the husband and wife ... Unhappily, this *attitude of regret is rarely found* among those who practise this method of continence; in its place are found instead motives that are worthy of severe censure and rebuke, motives for which the guilty partners will have to answer to God.[62]

As with the use of artificial means such as the Pill, the marriage guide warned couples that always limiting intercourse to the times that the wife was infertile could have a negative effect on her mentally and physically. "According to nature's law, the marriage act is ordained to produce a fruit; if it always takes place at a time when nature is unfertile, it is to be feared and regrettable physical results will ensue, in discomfort, and an upset nervous condition in the woman, etc."[63] This sentiment is very similar to the Victorian medical concept of the "hungry womb," which was perceived to have a natural desire to be filled; if it remained empty, it could cause debilitating mental and physical symptoms.[64]

One of the greatest discursive weapons that advocates of birth control wielded was the threat of overpopulation. Fear was widespread, based on Malthusian predictions of population growth and in the wake of the privations of two world wars and the Great Depression, that prosperous Western nations would once again be cast into poverty as food and other commodities became scarce. Roman Catholic authorities had a variety of arguments to counter this claim. They noted that Canada, "where we have more square miles than we know what to do with" actually needed more people.[65] Such sparsely populated areas would be able to absorb a growing population, through both homegrown citizens and immigration, the latter from overpopulated areas, therefore balancing out the population of the earth as a whole. Occasionally they simply denied the accuracy of world population statistics. Most commonly, the Catholic Church expressed faith that science and scientists, through advances in bioengineering, crop production, and other discoveries, would counteract the predictions of worldwide famine. As Monsignor DeBlanc noted in an article for the *Prairie Messenger*, "It is interesting how scientists in this country dealing with food are always optimistic. They know we can produce almost anything we imagine."[66] DeBlanc and other Catholic authorities refused to recognize the paradox of their argument that science (in the form of birth control) was not the answer but that science (bioscience relating to food production) would save the day.

Of course, no authoritative discourse is completely hegemonic. Indeed, outside of the anglophone Canadian discourse, the postwar international Catholic Church was experiencing what would be, in hindsight, a period of openness and self-discovery, with appointed authorities such as bishops representing a variety of viewpoints along the spectrum from conservatism to extreme liberalism. In these international discourses, there was a distinct movement towards decentring the importance of procreation and making it equal, or even subordinate, to creating marital intimacy between couples. Though the western anglophone Catholic point of view tended towards conservatism, evidence of this international debate did occasionally creep into the discourse. For example, the *Prairie Messenger* reprinted the following passage from the *Catholic Herald*, without context, as a filler piece; reprinted here in its entirety, it expresses a view of married love that, though not romantic by today's standards, was fairly rare in anglophone Catholic discourse in that children are not mentioned at all.

> Love is built on giving[,] it inevitably implies sacrifice and suffering; learning to give every bit of ourselves to our marriage partner in complete trust, losing ourselves and finding ourselves anew in our husbands and wives; learning to mould ourselves to the needs of one another, if necessary giving up our special pleasures and little selfish habits to meet each other's requirements. Love is accepting each other completely as we really [are], loving the shortcomings as well as the strong points, the mistakes and the successes, the faults as well as the virtues, accepting it all and yet all the time forging and growing in love to the point where another fault is left behind, where another island of selfishness is covered by the sea of love that should ever be engulfing husband and wife.[67]

While there is no actual reference to Vatican II in such passages, it seems that the uncertainty about the primacy of procreation to sexuality and the general introspection caused by the church's role being debated made a rhetorical space for alternative visions of married sexuality to be expressed. This international Catholic openness to debate would be ended both by the publication of Pope Paul VI's encyclical *Humanae Vitae*, which followed the minority report and banned all artificial contraception, and by the subsequent papacy of John Paul II, who made a return to conservative orthodoxy one of his primary platforms.[68] Yet well-informed Catholic couples, engaged in the wider international literature, may have found the discourses prior to 1968 more in line with their own views and continued to use those definitions of married sexuality and love even after they were no longer expressed within the Catholic hierarchy.[69]

Unlike the Canadian Catholic discourse, which with few exceptions maintained a conservative focus on procreation as the centre of marriage, the Anglican Church during this period increasingly moved away from such ideals. This marked a shift from a former alliance with the conservatism of Catholicism to sharing more in the liberal ideology of the United Church. Both Protestant intuitions focused on placing the couple in and of themselves firmly at the centre of marriage and coitus.

Immediately after the war, the Anglican Church, like most religious institutions, was deeply concerned over the issue of rising divorce rates. More specifically, the church faced queries over whether divorced persons could remarry within the Anglican faith and the general position of divorcees within the Anglican ministry. Anglican Church authorities were deeply conflicted between their belief that marriage was meant to be for life and their assertion that only God could truly "judge" a person, especially as in their ministry they increasingly portrayed Jesus Christ as first and foremost loving and forgiving of sinners. This conflict was aptly demonstrated at the first postwar encyclical of the Anglican Church, held in 1948.[70] In its "Resolutions on the Church's Discipline in Marriage," the church upheld the prohibition of divorce mainly to preserve the family as the crucible in which children were formed.

> It [the Committee on the Church's Discipline in Marriage Questions] is convinced that maintenance of the Church's standard of discipline can alone meet the deepest needs of men; and it earnestly implores those whose marriage, perhaps through no fault of their own, is unhappy to remain steadfastly faithful to their marriage vows ... Inasmuch as easy divorce in Great Britain, the United States, and elsewhere, has gravely weakened the idea of the life-long nature of marriage, and has also brought untold suffering to children, this Conference urges that there is a strong case for the reconsideration by certain States of their divorce laws.[71]

The resolutions went on to assert that children with divorced parents were likely to be maladjusted and would inevitably be "forced to pay a life-long penalty for their parents' selfishness and sin."[72] However, the same document expressed concern about its own position, noting that many couples, through no fault of their own, were inadequately prepared by society to enter marriage. While the church could not condone divorce, neither could it cast aside those whose marriages had failed.

Church authorities also recognized that the emotional trauma caused by marital disintegration could be the spark that created a spiritual awakening in a person, reviving their faith or even bringing them to the church for the first time. Further, because of the Anglican Church's British roots and its ties to that country's legal system, there was particular concern about the "innocent party" in cases of divorce stemming from charges of adultery.[73] It was seen as supremely unfair to keep these persons from Holy Communion for something that was not their fault. This door, once opened, proved very difficult to close; the question of allowing communion to the adulterer, if they had truly repented of their sin, soon arose. Some church leaders blamed themselves and their institution, at least partially, for what was perceived as a current wave of societal decay. In its *Confidential Report on the Church's Discipline in Marriage Questions* the committee noted that the Church of England has not taught, with the necessary persistence, simplicity, and conviction, her divine doctrine of marriage, nor has she made known her attitude and policy to those who break her laws. She has allowed those who were married before her altars to exchange vows and assume responsibilities about which they have never been instructed; and in the perplexities and problems which so commonly ensued, she has too often left them without the spiritual direction and pastoral care of which they had desperate need.[74]

These factors combined to create a great deal of ambiguity in the Anglican Church's point of view regarding the purpose of marriage and its dissolvability.

It was not until the 1965 General Synod that divorce was officially recognized by the Anglican Church. However, the authoritative literature suggests that prior to this official acceptance many priests, left to their own devices and due to the lack of a clear prohibition, solemnized the second marriages of divorcees and allowed divorced persons to take communion. Unlike the much more clearly defined, and therefore stronger, authoritative discourse of the Roman Catholic Church, the Anglican Church's position on the purpose of marriage was fairly amorphous, though it was clearly moving away from the ideal that the primary purpose of marriage and marital sex was children. For example, in the 1958 Lambeth Conference it was stated that "the procreation of children is recognised as a primary purpose of the institution of marriage, though not the over-arching purpose of particular marriages. A contemporary understanding of the relation of sexuality to personality has begun to inform theological discourse."[75] Further, they noted that

> it has been common, in Christian theology, to mention the procreative function first, as if to say that it is the ruling purpose. So it is, in the sense that no marriage would be according to God's will which (where procreation is possible) did not bear fruit in children. But it is clearly not true that all other duties and relationships in marriage must be subordinate to the procreative one. Neither the Bible nor human experience supports that view. Where it has been held, the reason generally lay in a fear of misuse of the sexual relationship or in a false sense that there is, in any sexual relationship, an intrinsic evil.[76]

Over the span of ten years, having children had moved from being the reason to keep an unhappy marriage together to one that only had equal weight with securing the couple's own happiness. The purpose of the one-flesh body had become dual, though this duality would not last; by 1965 the focus on children was distinctly a second-place consideration. That year the church published *Marriage and Family Life 1: On Marriage in the Church (Canon and Commentary)*, which was intended to help acquaint the public with the church's new ideals of marriage. In it, authorities suggested that each couple wanting to be married in an Anglican ceremony make the following declaration to demonstrate they understood the true nature of Anglican marriage:

> We intend to strive thereafter to fulfil the purposes of marriage: the mutual fellowship, support and comfort of one another, the procreation (if it may be) and the nurture of children, and the creation of a relationship in which sexuality may serve personal fulfillment in a community of faithful love.[77]

Though procreation is mentioned, it is no longer an intrinsic part of the one-flesh body. Children are only mentioned as a possibility, and that possibility is not tied explicitly to a couple's ability to conceive, meaning choosing not to have children was an option. By decentring children within marriage and refocusing on the relationship of the couple themselves, the Anglican Church provided itself with an avenue to reverse its historical position on the prohibition of divorce. This did not mean that the church stopped being concerned about the welfare of its youngest parishioners. Indeed, some authorities argued that it was healthier for children to be from a home "broken" by divorce rather one where the mother and father were constantly in conflict and the home was "broken" in all but the legal sense.[78] However, marriage was no longer solely the vessel through which children were born and raised; marriage was foremost a union to meet the needs of a couple, and together they created the one-flesh body. Only if those interpersonal needs were met could the couple's relationship serve as a successful keystone to support the rest of the family, including children. This may seem a very subtle change – more a matter of semantics – since children were still seen as an important part of individual marriages. In reality, this new focus on the couple and the importance of their happiness to the strength of the entire family reverberated into all aspects of married life, not least of which was sex and sexuality.

The United Church, with the most liberal view of divorce of the denominations under consideration, maintained throughout the postwar period that the couple was the centre of marriage. This was likely due to the church's institutional youth, the fact that its policies were created during the relatively liberal 1920s, and its need to attract parishioners. As early as 1946 the United Church noted the ambiguity of Jesus's teachings on divorce. Not only was divorce allowed in the Old Testament, but the prohibition of modern divorce rested on a debate over whether Jesus's assertion that marriage was for life was an ideal or an absolute law. In the immediate postwar period, the United Church left questions about divorce to the individual couple and their minister; by the 1960s, it actively joined the lobby to relax Canada's divorce laws.[79]

Focusing on the couple rather than children as the purpose of marriage had consequences that went far beyond the possibility of church-sanctioned divorce. In decentring children, both the Anglican and the United churches had to find new discourses that emphasized the positivity and sacred quality of sexual intercourse without resorting to the Roman Catholic focus on the potential for procreation. Protestant churches were not satisfied with the argument that sexual relations between married couples deepened their personal love bond; they maintained it had a higher, spiritual quality. Unlike Roman Catholic discourses, the Protestant creation of sex as sacramental had no theological underpinnings and so was exceedingly vague, almost mystic. Nebulous references to the "communion of flesh and spirit," the "union of spirit with spirit," and "fulfilment of personalities" gave neither a reason why sex should be sacramental nor how that sacrament should feel when experienced.[80]

The Protestant one-flesh body became an almost magical event where man, woman, and God were fused together in a way beyond linguistic description, and ultimately only explainable in the most lyrical of terms. For example, in the main Canadian Anglican marriage manual *The Hallowing of the Union*, sex is described as

> a means of expressing love between partners and for the product of their sexual action, and for God who has given them the power and the privilege in participating in the creative activities of the universe. The sex act when engaged in in love can become the symbol of mutual respect, confidence, devotion and submission, not only to the participating partners but also to their offspring and to the divine purposes of God.[81]

In another particularly poetical example, United Church doctrine compared the sexual experience to the coming of Christ, "The Word became flesh in Christ, thereby manifesting the truth that the physical can be the vehicle of the spiritual." The passage continued: "Sex is a power which when sublimated to the Christian principle of chastity before marriage and fidelity within the marriage bond, can be morally creative in helping to build 'the more stately mansions of the soul,'" and affirmed that sex within a Christian marriage was "lifted above the merely temporal and physical level to one that is deeply religious."[82] While there is no evidence that the Protestant denominations deliberately used extravagant language to obscure the fact that there was no particular theological grounding to their new position on married sex as sacred, the use of such discourse did give the spiritual one-flesh body at least the semblance of religious doctrine.

Despite its lack of theological authority, the Protestant spiritual one-flesh body was as useful as the creation-centred one-flesh body was to the Roman Catholics. By making the one-flesh body a mystical, transformative, emotional, and physical experience, both Protestant denominations were able to argue for its containment within the bounds of matrimony. Couples engaging in premarital or extramarital sex would never be able to achieve the one-flesh body and would, by attempting to achieve it outside of matrimony, potentially ruin their future experiences of it – even if they had premarital sex while engaged and subsequently were married. As the authors of the "Report on the Family in Contemporary Society" at the 1958 Anglican Lambeth Conference argued:

> Pre-marital intercourse can never be right; it is selfish and sinful in its irreverence for the sanctity of both a man's and a woman's life; and it tends to make impossible the really happy fellowship that belongs to a marriage when the partners bring to each other a complete offering of selfhood unspoiled by any liaison. The full giving and receiving of a whole person which sexual intercourse expresses is only possible within the assurance and protection of the faithful, life-long promise of each to the other, "forsaking all others."[83]

In addition, the one-flesh body was viewed as being so powerful that attempting to achieve it outside of marriage was physically, emotionally, and spiritually dangerous.

> Sex is like fire. Take fire out of our modern civilization, and you would wreck it. Let it get out of hand through ignorance or carelessness, and it is devastating in its destruction. Fire supplies light, warmth, and power. Sex is tied up with the light of inspiration, the warmth of friendships and love, and supplies a kind of power in human relationships. Some people get their fingers burned playing with fire, and some burn to death. Sex, uncontrolled or mismanaged, can be just as devastating. So long as we understand the nature of fire and its possibility for constructive use and respect its powers of devastation, we may use it for the benefit of ourselves and others. Correspondingly, if we can secure a sufficient understanding of the part of sex in life, according to the plans of the Creator, and respect its powers of devastation, we may achieve the richness and abundance intended.[84]

Thus, even without the threat of conception out of wedlock the Protestant churches made extramarital sexuality both deviant and dangerous.

According to some scholars, the United Church sanctified marital sexual expression in an attempt to pacify women into maintaining their normative domestic gender roles; the situation when viewed more broadly, however, is more complex.[85] Both Protestant churches struggled to define their positions on the emerging changes in gender roles that simultaneously gave rise to a discourse encouraging women to be more than "just housewives" and yet undermined any support for women to engage in new occupations. Both the United and the Anglican churches recognized, in contrast to the Roman Catholic Church, that they could not continue endorsing a patriarchal family organization because such male dominance was increasingly incompatible with postwar societal shifts. Doing so was also incongruent with their continued promotion of the democratic, companionate marriage. In his advice to priests giving couples premarital instruction, Anglican minister Reverend George Luxton noted that it was a good idea to reassure the wife that the word "obey" in her marital vows was nothing more than an archaic holdover that would be deleted as soon as a new version of the Prayer Book was published. He wrote:

> While it is accepted that the man is the head of the house, the least said about it the better. When he finds it necessary to assert his legal authority, it is a sign of failure in the partnership ... We ought to be frank with the young women of the church on this score and do our utmost to expedite the remove of the word itself.[86]

The United Church likewise pledged its support of democratic familial relationships.

> Social science has thrown new light on the role of the male and the female in our society. A girl enters marriage today more equal than her mother did. Women today have more social, economic, and educational independence than formerly. Stable marriage is based on good human relations and good communications between equals.[87]

At the same time as they supported this newfound democracy and equality within marriage, both Protestant denominations were deeply concerned about what kind of social structure would replace the vacuum left by dismantling the patriarchal system and whether that new structure would contribute to the familial decay they felt was rampant in the postwar era. As Anglican canon W.E. Scott, later elevated to the

Primate of Canada, noted in his essay in *Scope*, an Anglican magazine for teens:

> We may come to recognize that the roles for male and female in our society have certain limitations, some of which we accept or reject. We may come to feel, for example, that some of these limitations are rather arbitrary and based mainly on prejudice or out-dated social situations. If men are not more or less capable or intelligent than women, is it only childbearing that prevents most women from pursuing careers? ... If those patterns of behavior and those sets of attitudes which once told us that we were either male or female are becoming less helpful, how do we discover what it means to be a male or female? Or, if we cannot pattern ourselves after mom and dad pretty much in the same way they did after their parents, then where do we look for guidance?[88]

Ultimately, Scott had no answer for his youthful parishioners because the Protestant churches were in a state of conflict over the new roles of men and women.

Nowhere was the ambivalence of the main Protestant denominations over Canadian women's changing role more apparent than in the United Church lay magazine *The Christian Home*, which continuously published articles that at one moment supported gender role choices for women but at the next tore them down. One of the most obvious examples of this occurred in the July 1961 issue, which began with the article "If You're a Working Mother, Be Prepared to Work Miracles," by Maxine Schweiker. On the surface the article is full of tips on how to successfully negotiate the "double day," such as buying drip-dry clothing for one's children to save time ironing (and still maintain appearances) and not worrying overmuch about volunteering for extra work with organizations such as the Parent-Teacher Association. Unsurprisingly, the author does not suggest the father should help his wife by cooking or cleaning – these are still female-signified activities.[89] Thus, the "saintly" wife, left alone to fulfil both a domestic and a work role, is forced to "work miracles." Working mothers were then further undermined by homemaker Emalene Sherman's following article, "Be Glad You're a Housewife." Sherman gleefully expounds about her rewarding and fulfilling life at home, free from the stresses outlined in the proceeding article. She concludes, "I would not return to the tensions of the office for twice the pay. The basic satisfactions for a woman are still in the bosom of her family."[90] The irony was that Sherman worked as a freelance writer, which she cleverly and explicitly classified as something she merely did in her spare time to mask her own potential deviance. However, even wives who did not go out to work but who sought some kind of fulfilment outside of the home were targeted as not being sufficiently family oriented. In the provocatively titled "Are You Faithful to Your Husband?," Anne C. Thomas coyly admitted she was not actually referring to extramarital affairs but instead was asking if modern women are really honouring their marriage vows.

> Don't you know women who live such busy, supercharged lives that you feel lazy by comparison? They are constantly on the go, filled to the brim with committees, activities and worthwhile organizations. They are always busy. And yet, have you ever known one of these women well enough to see what goes on behind the scenes at home? At some time or another, these persons become driven beyond their sheer mental and physical endurance. This usually happens at night and consequently in the presence of their husbands. Then, all the waters break loose and these efficient, indefatigable young wives become downright screaming shrews![91]

These articles together create an archive demonstrating that, while the United Church would accept women's taking on new roles, they could do so only as an addition to their role of wife, mother, and homemaker. Like war wives who worked outside of the home, these women were expected to take on a double day, completing fully both domestic and work tasks and, more significantly, take their identity and self-worth solely from the former. Additionally, this double day was thought to be beyond the physical and mental capacity of most women. This was likely true in many cases, as the discourse makes it clear that a mother's domestic tasks could never be assigned to any other member of the family.

The Christian Home warned women that if they failed to live up to postwar social standards they risked losing both their physical femininity and their marriage. In the article "When He Takes You for Granted," author Kay Hodell Chilcote warns women whose husbands seem distant or unengaged that the fault likely is with themselves. Chilcote suggested that in such a situation a wife carefully take an inventory of her "worthiness," all of which centred on gaining her husband's approval.

> Neatness? Good disposition? Interest in his work? A good listener? This is no time to cheat. No one is going to see this list but yourself, so force yourself to be scrupulously honest. If your waist measured twenty-four inches a few years ago, don't break the tape trying to equal that figure. Mark down the exact measurement today.[92]

This reference to waist measurement recalls women's role as a sexual ornament confirming her husband's status as well as suggesting that women who had gained weight since their wedding day had failed both their social and physical obligations to femininity. The fact that these articles were written by women and published in a church-sanctioned magazine gave their message a strong orthodox status.

The postwar gender role ambivalence found in *The Christian Home* was not unique. As Valerie J. Korinek demonstrates in *Roughing It in the Suburbs*, Canada's most popular women's magazine, *Chatelaine*, juxtaposed many similar articles in the fifties prior to the tenure of feminist Doris Anderson as editor in 1958, and even afterwards. As Korinek notes, in magazines like *Chatelaine* working women would be lauded in an editorial in one instance and then warned off in the next by articles and advertising promoting the punishing expectations of what was an extremely high minimum standard for housework, childcare, and food preparation.[93]

This similarity is significant because although *The Christian Home* did not publish critical letters or other reader feedback, it is possible to infer some potential reader responses based on Korinek's analysis of *Chatelaine*'s readership and how they navigated such mixed messages. Korinek's analysis shows fractures in the uptake of generalized discourses – particularly those predicated on an assumption, similar to *The Christian Home*, that the ideal reader was a member of a white, heterosexual, middle-class nuclear family with access to money for consumer goods.[94] This variety of response is unsurprising in a country as large and diverse as Canada and because the general ambivalence of the messages consistently created rhetorical space for readers to react against, creatively reinterpret, or deliberately misunderstand dominant or intended meanings.[95] We can see this process clearly in the reactions of rural and working-class women who noted the inapplicability of much of the household advice in *Chatelaine* due to their remoteness, lack of funds for "time-saving" appliances or prepared foods, or lack of time caused by farm work or necessary outside paid labour. Some readers attempted to modify the discourses to suit their needs while others rejected them outright.[96] Korinek also notes that both progressive articles focusing on expanded opportunities for women and those supporting more "traditional" housewife roles elicited positive as well as negative responses, suggesting that gender roles were in a state of flux.[97]

The main Protestant denominations were deeply ambivalent about changing gender roles at a time when parishioners were looking to them for answers. It was in this environment that the spiritual one-flesh body became useful as the only unambiguous answer that could be given to the congregation, as it allowed the churches to avoid making declarative statements about the new role of women, relying on sex and heterosexuality to speak for gender roles. The one-flesh body gave them the ability to concentrate on the creation of the whole, which was seen as more important (or at least less conflict ridden) than focusing on how the two component parts related to each other. As Reverend Frank Morgan noted in his brief to the United Church Commission on Christian Marriage and Divorce:

> Marriage partners differ in physical strength, intellectual ability, emotional maturity, spiritual understanding and physical anatomy. Partners were made by God to complement each other in these areas and neither sex is always dominant in any one area. Therefore, in an ideal marriage there is no such thing as obedience or equality because the former can exist only between a greater and a lesser and the latter only between two similars.[98]

This statement serves as a Band-Aid obscuring the fractured discourses mentioned above. Morgan is careful not to identify which are female or male strengths, but simply asserts that just as man and woman are made to fit together biologically, so too are they socially. More simply, Hazen G. Werner in his pamphlet "The Marks of a Christian Home" states, "Marriage is founded upon mutuality. There are to be no superiorities and no inferiorities. A man and wife are to be equal like two blades of the scissors, both important and necessary to each other."[99] The equality of two blades coming together horizontally (rather than vertically with one piece being dominant) is a clear departure from Roman Catholic metaphors, which maintained male superiority over female passivity in both sexual and social matters. The metaphor of the scissors also demonstrates the two churches' attempts to provide their parishioners with an answer that maintained men and women were equal in all things but, like the blades of scissors, opposites. Without both blades working properly in opposition as well as in tandem, the scissors – that is, marriages and society at large – could not function properly.

In promoting this metaphor of men and women as socially and sexually equal yet different, the Protestant churches had a distinct advantage over the Roman Catholic Church. The former were able to utilize the authoritative discourses of the medical, psychological, and sociological sciences that also supported the linking of sexual or biological roles and social and gender roles. Protestant authorities, like Roman Catholics, noted the "marvelous potency" of the label of science and applied it whenever possible. Linking their spiritual one-sex body to the medicalized body schema not only gave their discourse an extra veneer of authority, it also provided a more visible structure for the ordering of gender relations, as the one-flesh body itself lacked doctrinal support. Indeed, because they viewed the Bible as metaphorical Anglican and United Church authorities claimed that new developments such as the emerging social sciences could, and should, be used to interpret the Bible's message. As prominent Canadian Anglican legal authorities C.R. Fielding and H.R.S. Ryan put it:

> Anglicans are accustomed to learn not only from the New Testament as it has been interpreted in the past, but also from its interpretation by those to whom theological and moral authority is usually accorded today, for example the Lambeth Conference. In common with our contemporaries we are also accustomed to learn whatever we can that may illuminate the contemporary scene from researchers in law, medicine, and the social sciences. This last is particularly important if the Church is to keep its canon law and the procedures based on it in fruitful contact with the life of civil society as well as with the life of the Church.[100]

For Protestant leaders, the only place that natural law, which they defined as life lived without human interference into biological processes such as illness and contraception, could be practised was in the Garden of Eden prior to the Fall. Thus, unchecked human fecundity could only be practised in a world not facing issues such as poverty and want, both at home and in an international context.

The Protestant one-flesh body was spiritual but also fundamentally ordered. Natural processes such as fertility were crucially important and therefore had to be channelled. While for Catholics allowing unlimited fecundity was bending the body to the will of God, for Protestants it was bending the body to an imperfect, "worldly" nature that was fundamentally separate from God. It should be noted, however, that the Protestant discourses rarely set themselves up in direct opposition to Roman Catholic ideals.

In their quest to create an ideal married one-flesh body that was both mystical and ordered, Protestant denominations benefited greatly from their acceptance of the use of birth control by married couples to limit their children. Anglican and United Church couples were told to embrace methods of contraception in order to create families that fit within their financial means; this would separate their bodies from the disordered and uncontrolled Catholic bodies. Again, this was often framed in the context of the inability of people to obey natural law in the face of a fallen world; poverty and the burdens of humanity on an overpopulated globe were important considerations in how the one-flesh body could be used. According to the resolutions of the 1958 Lambeth Conference:

> The Conference believes that the responsibility for deciding upon the number and frequency of children has been laid by God upon the consciences of parents everywhere: that this planning, in such ways as are mutually acceptable to husband and wife in Christian conscience, is a right and important factor in Christian family life and should be the result of positive choice before God. Such responsible parenthood, built on obedience to all the duties of marriage, requires a wise stewardship of the resources and abilities of the family as well as a thoughtful consideration of the varying population needs and problems of society and the claims of future generations.[101]

Thus, the proper use of contraceptives was not just accepted but recommended by the Protestant denominations. Contraceptive use was thought to free a couple from the overbearing fear of unwanted pregnancy so that they could more fully engage in the spiritual benefits of the one-flesh body. Though the dominant historical metanarrative of birth control has been framed as woman's emancipation, the Protestant denominations' focus on the couple and disapproval of contraceptive use outside of marriage serves to disrupt this metanarrative. The use of limitation devices such as the Pill was seen in Protestant discourse as emancipating the male as well and, indeed, the family as a whole. As United Church authority Evelyn Millis Duvall noted in the article "What's Right with Today's Families," the future was bright because women had more choice and equality in marriage as well as sexual freedom within that institution. They continued:

> Modern man may not be master of all he surveys, but he is able to cope with more of his life's problems than his forebears did. He and his wife can now plan the number of children they will have and how they will space them to take into account educational plans, vocational preparation, and their more easily estimated family finances. At times a family man may be bogged down, but he is not so often overwhelmed as is the man whose children come faster than he can care for them.[102]

The Protestant denominations also echoed the medical community's parameters for the proper use of contraceptive methods. They explained that contraceptives were dangerous if used by a non-married couple; both the husband and the wife had to agree to limit their family and the method of such limitation must be mutually aesthetically acceptable; and finally, that while contraceptive use was to be encouraged, other birth control methods such as sterilization and abortion, except as part of a life-saving medical procedure, were morally wrong.[103] Further, the Protestant denominations agreed that it was abnormal – indeed pathological – to use contraception to avoid having children entirely or to limit the family to one child. To forestall or postpone children for selfish motives such as economic gain – rather than economic stability – was just as much a violation of the ordered body as uncontrolled reproduction was.

> It may be said, however, that responsible parenthood implies a watchful guard against selfishness and covetousness, and an equally thoughtful awareness of the world into which our children are to be born. Couples who postpone having children until certain financial goals are reached, or certain possessions gained, need to be vigilant lest they are putting their own comfort level ahead of their duty. Similarly those who carelessly and improvidently bring children into the world trusting in an unknown future or generous society to care for them, need to make a rigorous examination of their lack of concern for their children and for the society of which they are a part.[104]

The Protestant churches were walking the fine line between, and influenced by, competing ideals of capitalism and socialism. No right-thinking capitalist would produce children that would eventually become dependent on the state. At the same time, unrestrained consumption – "keeping up with the Jones" – was also deviant, as it placed too much emphasis on material goods rather than spirituality and the development of the family as the core unit of society. At the same time we can also see Protestant white middle-class values at work. Unrestrained fecundity, the inability or lack of intelligence to use tools such as contraception, was viewed as a characteristic of the poor and the non-white.[105] To maintain a properly ordered body, contraception was to be used to space children for their optimal development and to limit overactive fecundity to a reasonable level; procreation was still an important function though it no longer was a factor in every sexual union. As *The Hallowing of the Union* was careful to note, concluding the section describing different methods of birth control, "But no matter how the parents may plan for the spacing of births, the fact remains that the normal result of the expression of love between a man and woman in Christian marriage is the gift of children."[106]

The Protestant churches appropriated scientific authority in other ways than encouraging the use of birth control – science could bring order to the religious body in multiple ways. This engagement was often as simple as appropriating the emerging language of psychoanalysis. Both the United and Anglican churches made free use of terms such as "ego," "neurotic," and "Momism," as well as concepts such as the psychological inheritance of disturbed personalities and the disciplining of homosexual feelings to heterosexual norms.[107] These tactics gave religious doctrine additional authority by attaching the veneer of scientific "fact," even when the pronouncements were not made by scientists or when the case histories being described did not follow proper scientific method. For example, reference to statistics, often collected without even the most basic methodological rigour embraced by institutional social sciences, gave many lay publications the appearance of scientific authenticity and "objective" authority.[108]

Whenever possible, religious pronouncements were augmented by the voices of medical or scientific experts who believed in, and more importantly deferred their own authority to, the pronouncements of the Christian faith. Both the United and Anglican churches were able to make use of the authority of Dr. Marion Hilliard who, in addition to being a recognized expert on the female body, was also a devout churchwoman. Raised in the United Church, she later converted to Anglicanism, and she often served on ecumenical committees and other pan-Protestant education efforts.[109]

Hilliard's involvement is but another layer of the ambivalence that both Protestant denominations showed towards changing women's roles. A single working woman herself and closeted lesbian, Hilliard spoke out about the dangers of overbearing mothers and the need for children to have good masculine and feminine examples to aid them both in identifying their own gender roles and in choosing a mate. She subscribed to and promoted the connection of gender to biological sex, arguing, for example, that "woman is equipped with a reproductive system which, even if she never uses it, dominates her fiber."[110] At the same time, Hilliard, like Betty Friedan, felt it was healthy for women to have interests – including work – outside of the home. Her presence in the churches' discourse about gender roles was similar to the role she played in the *Canadian Medical Association Journal*. Her position created an interesting discursive space where the dominant ideal body was both supported and subverted, not only due to her sometimes unorthodox pronouncements on gender but also by her lived experience, the latter of which was well known (except her own sexuality) because of her celebrity and her popular publications, including her columns in *Chatelaine*.[111] In a sense,

Hilliard herself embodied the very tensions that both the United and Anglican churches were attempting to reconcile; while she supported the tenets of the one-flesh body, she herself was anathema to it.

While Protestant authorities assured their parishioners that they had every right to enjoy all the benefits that science and modern living allowed, the Protestant churches were not willing to subjugate their authority to that of the lay medical/scientific world. Though they did not go to the extreme of insisting that parishioners find physicians who shared their faith, it was clear that the medical episteme of the body was not to replace or subvert the religious episteme, only support it. To take the spiritual element out of the one-flesh doctrine was to reduce any sexual encounter to the simple mating of animals. As the committee members of the 1958 Lambeth Conference put it:

> First of all, the family is rooted in the elemental processes of life itself. Human reproduction – human parenthood – is vastly more complicated than the reproduction of plants or the simpler animals. Mankind has rightly come to see depths and possibilities in the process, and in the relationships which it establishes, which are, at best, only faintly suggested (if indeed they exist at all) in the lower orders of life.[112]

Science could help order the one-flesh body by providing contraception to limit fecundity or by helping to alleviate illness more generally, but it could not give sexual interaction its true, higher purpose.

In the postwar church the married body was first and foremost a sexual body. Though the concept of "one flesh" taken from the Gospel of Mark could be subject to multiple interpretations, the dominant Christian churches of Canada adopted it to serve the evolving role of married sex in their ministries and in the postwar world. This was because the married body was, above all, sexual. Though leaders of each faith decried the oversexualization of society – labelling society "sex-saturated" – their discourses contributed to the overall importance of sex and the specific importance of sexual activity within marriage. Their authoritative voices joined those of the medical community in educating married couples that having frequent, mutually satisfying sexual relations within their heterosexual marriage, including orgasm, was normal; if couples were not achieving this standard, their bodies were not only medically and psychologically abnormal, but also spiritually lacking. Both Protestant and Roman Catholic authorities used the one-flesh body to discipline their parishioner's bodies in ways that complied with their ideals of marriage and their respective schemas for gender roles, even if the Protestant churches left these vaguely defined.

The one-flesh body also helped to define and negotiate each denomination's relationship to the powerful discourses on married sexuality emerging from the medical sciences. The Roman Catholic Church, unable to absorb the authority of a system too foreign to its own beliefs, created a chimera of medical discourses spanning from several different eras in order to counter the modern medical body politic that the Protestant churches were able to more fully utilize. However, it should be noted that religious discourses differed from the medical in one critical way. Unlike the institutional biomedical authorities, who during the 1950s and 1960s were at the apex of their dominance over alternative medical ideologies, the religious community during the baby boom era was essentially a free market with many different types and levels of religious involvement from which someone could choose.[113] As long as persons bowed to the authority of one of the acceptable faiths and lived within a framework of morality associated with the church, the denomination or individual church had only minor importance to many members of society. Throughout this period, if the "faithful" felt that their needs were not being met at a particular church or denomination, they could (and did) change their allegiances or practise other forms of resistance such as non-attendance or selective adherence to religious doctrine. Some Catholics, for example, disappointed at Pope Paul VI's condemnation of birth control, became Anglicans, rationalizing their choice with the belief that the difference between Catholicism and High Anglicanism was insignificant. Further, a spiritual diagnosis for living well carried less weight than a medical one. Priests and ministers had a harder time gaining full patient compliance to their spiritual prescriptions as, in postwar Canada, immediate illness was a much more efficacious motivator than the potential of discomfort in a world after death.

Religious leaders of each denomination also created ideals of what defined an ordered sexual/spiritual body. Parishioners chose to try to live up to these ideals with varying degrees of success, especially as postwar theology stated that true perfection could never be attained on earth. Faced with unavoidable failure, parishioners were told to do their best and beg forgiveness for their inevitable failings in what was an imperfect world. This diffusion of authority was compounded in the Anglican and United churches by their adoption of biblical criticism and focus on the Bible as metaphorical. Doing so encouraged even lay parishioners to interpret God's teachings and infused their schema with a moral relativity that necessarily weakened their ability to discipline the body. Indeed, this moral relativity would continue to shape the Protestant denominations for years to come. Within Canada both churches eventually extended their definitions of sexual normalcy to include previously deviant bodies such as homosexuals.[114] Canadian Protestant one-flesh bodies would not only cease to become necessarily heterosexual (though this would be, and continues to be, contested), but sexuality would no longer have the same vague mysticism and holiness it achieved during this period.

While the doctrines of the three main Christian denominations might have been plural, and for the Protestants often ambivalent and conflictual, they added their authoritative discourse to others such as the medical community's to further use the sexual body to police the boundaries of postwar normalcy. Further, all three denominations contributed to the ideal that the heterosexual married couple and the nuclear family were not only the primary unit of society but also, excepting those with a Catholic vocation, the most important and viable unit of society. Like the medical community, the three denominations argued that achieving normalcy in this fallen world was difficult and could only be achieved if parishioners accepted the beneficence of God and, more importantly, the authority of the church. They also made it clear that to not attempt normalcy – in this case not to strive for the perfection found in the one-flesh body – was to withdraw oneself from the community of the faithful and society at large. Whether or not one believed in the potential for everlasting life, adherence to a dominant Christian denomination was another way postwar women, couples, and families could demonstrate their acquiescence to societal standards of basic morality and, therefore, postwar heterosexual normalcy.

Chapter Four

Bringing Down Goliath: Oral Histories and the Engagement of Individual Bodies with the Ideal

In the aftermath of World War II medical and religious elites created multiple and shifting idealized discursive bodies to help negotiate and make sense of postwar sexual and gender norms and to aid in rebuilding postwar Canada and strengthening it to face potential Cold War challenges. What happened when these idealized non-corporeal entities inevitability collided with the physical bodies of those women who were supposed to emulate them? How did individual women who lived with these leviathan figures of femininity engage with, acquiesce to, or defy their embodied messages day to day and moment to moment? How did the corporeality of their bodies disrupt or support their non-corporal counterparts? This chapter interrogates these multiple and shifting relationships by engaging with the sexual history narratives of eighteen women who were married during the postwar period.[1] The experiences of these eighteen narrators are not meant to constitute a representative sample of Canadian women or to be broadly generalizable, though their narratives do demonstrate some commonalities of experience along axes of generation, class, and social background. Instead, the narrations presented here are deep ethnographies that demonstrate the nuances of how individual lives interacted with large-scale prescriptive discourses. Their individual sexual landscapes (which included orgasmic ability, intimacy, childbearing, sexual violence, loneliness, infidelity, and even illegal abortion) simultaneously defied and supported idealized postwar gender and sexual norms. On the one hand, the narrators gave postwar ideals authority via their constant performance of those ideals' general dominant characteristics, such as compulsory heterosexuality. On the other hand, and as demonstrated in this and the following chapter, the very individuality of their corporeal experiences challenged the authority of these dominant norms, creating a situation where medical and religious ideals were both confirmed and conflicted. Ideal embodied knowledge schemas by their very nature are static and generalized. It is only ever possible to follow the spirit of their prescriptive discourses; no real body is ever a perfect carbon copy of the ideal. Rather than engaging in outright defiance, however, the majority of these narrators carried out a series of day-to-day and moment-to-moment negotiations with dominant body politics created by postwar authoritative discourses. These negotiations were usually strategic attempts to shift dominant social scripts to fit their lives and experiences while simultaneously protecting their ability as white heterosexual married women to collect on "the dividends of normality."[2]

In this chapter I interrogate five main sites where such strategic negotiations occurred: (1) the importance of gender role divisions within marriage; (2) generational constructs of the significance of sexual purity versus sexual knowledge; (3) the importance of pregnancy and children as a physical display of psychosexual normality; (4) the need for the mother body to modify itself to benefit the health and wellbeing of the family; and (5) the importance of sex as both a barometer and guarantee of the overall success and happiness of a marriage. In each of these cases the majority of the narrators echoed at least some parts of these dominant discourses, demonstrating at least partial acceptance of their overall messages while also problematizing those same discourses with the nuances of their own situations. I also interrogate two cases where idealized authoritative bodies were silent or insufficient in their policing of a particular sexual theme in the narrators' lives. Though several of the narrators discussed issues of marital infidelity and two narrators recounted experiences of sexual assault and danger, the ideal bodies rarely interacted with such events, creating silences around them and further demonstrating the weaknesses of idealized bodies to define all facets of sexual life.

Oral history has undergone great changes since scholars collected testimonials as static artefacts or unmediated conduits to a past truth that could be mined for data. Instead, each narration is now viewed as a complex text in and of itself requiring careful attention to its internal discourse; one must unpack the different tensions within it and how the circumstances of the interview, the relation of the interviewer and the narrator, and the life histories and biases of both influence the final product. Oral history, particularly feminist oral history, has increasingly moved away from science models of participant research that focus on large, anonymized samples used to create "statistically significant data," and towards a life history approach that unpacks how memories are used to create subjectivity in both the past and the present.[3]

If we accept that each interview is a unique text created in the moment of interaction between the interviewer and the interviewed to be deconstructed in its own right, then the meaning-making process of the interview must be made as transparent as possible when reviewing the results. Ground-breaking sexuality historians Elizabeth Lapovsky and Madeline D. Davies term this process "showing the seams."[4] Accordingly, this chapter includes, when possible, interviewer comments and the wording of questions, as well as silences and gestures that give the oral interview a further textual richness and meaning. In addition to this increased transparency, extensive interviewer self-reflexivity has gradually become the norm, where the interviewer not only reflects on how their presence may have shifted and changed the narrator's account but also how the circumstances of the interview, recruitment, and geographical location might also have helped to create the overall meaning.[5]

One of the persistent problems faced by feminist oral historians is recruitment. As historian Penny Summerfield notes, "Even when adopting the technique of 'slow scholarship' that allows time for trust to build, it can be hard to persuade any woman, burdened as we are by cultural constructions that diminish our value, to participate in projects."[6] The evidence of this phenomenon can be clearly seen within my interview sample. In order to cast as wide a net as possible I sought participants in two ways. The first was a cold call method involving sending recruitment packages that included an introductory letter, advertising posters, and information pamphlets to seniors' social and housing organizations throughout the western provinces. The posters invited women who were married between the years of 1939 and 1966 and who were willing to discuss their marriage to contact me. This process achieved a total of seven participants. Snowballing amongst this group was ultimately unsuccessful in part because these women were not part of an easily identifiable community and so lacked the connections and/or a wider desire to mobilize other participants, and also because the intimate topic matter encouraged reticence and kept women from attempting to recruit their friends.

My second strategy was to leverage my own status as the granddaughter of a (deceased) war bride to enlist the help of the war bride associations of British Columbia, Alberta, Saskatchewan, and Manitoba, who ultimately furnished me with the mailing list of all their surviving members. This allowed me to directly mail calls for interviews to each potential participant, resulting in a much higher success rate. However, a more direct recruitment approach only partially explains why this strategy was more successful. Unlike the women in the first group, the war brides had a defined and established community that allowed for some degree of snowballing. More important, and here I return to Summerfield's observation, was that Canadian war brides, unlike many other women of their generation, were able to move beyond the initial stumbling block of assuming that their lives were historically unimportant. By virtue of their history as war brides – both contemporary news coverage and later commemorative work – they had historical capital, which, though their experiences as war brides remained a relatively small part of the overall project, gave them the confidence to reach out to me in the first place.

Such an unbalanced sample is more common than not in feminist oral history, bedevilled by the over-representation of the unique or often "activist" woman in any given sample and causing its own set of methodological challenges. As both Summerfield and Valerie J. Korinek observe, not only does this over-representation create disturbing silences around the lives of more "ordinary" women who persist in viewing their stories as not worthy of recording or who wish to be historically anonymous, it also creates a certain amount of scripting within the unique/activist group.[7] The very fact that the war brides in my sample were part of a community shaped their narratives, as they shared a lexicon about their experiences and in many cases reflected the set scripts highlighted within the large numbers of commemorative and celebratory works written about war bride lives.

As a group, white war brides were cast as meaning makers even before the end of hostilities; their stories symbolized a happy ending to the conflict and either consecrated the ties between allied nations or proclaimed the creation of new bonds with former enemy states.[8] Theirs was the Cinderella ending to a war-torn love story, and they and their children became potent portents of the postwar renewal.[9] Such narratives wear a groove in historical imagination, and several war bride narrators dutifully repeated their own personal variations on this set sequence of events at the beginning of the interview process. My status as the granddaughter of a war bride seemed to further the focus on uncomplicated, commemorative histories. To move beyond it I often had to reframe questions and be particularly alert to seemingly off-hand comments or silences that hinted at life circumstances that did not fit the triumphal chronicle and signalled deeper stories to be told.

The social relationship between the interviewer and the interviewee, and their perceptions of that relationship, cannot help but influence the resulting text. In particular, whether the interviewer is viewed as an "insider" or "outsider" of the narrator's community can expedite or inhibit the creation of trust between the two interlocutors. Though "married women" is not a community in the traditional sense of the word, it is interesting that every narrator took pains at some point in the interview to ascertain my own status as to marriage and children. In some cases, particularly during the in-person interviews, the narrators drew on visual cues such as my wedding ring to situate me. Other times, such as during interviews that occurred between the end of August and October when I was in the first trimester of my pregnancy, I had to tell the narrators of my condition as I was refusing all food due to extreme nausea and did not want to appear rude.[10] Yet even through the more anonymous medium of the telephone, narrators made the effort to ascertain my situation and usually did so within the first fifteen minutes of the interview. Whether we spoke over the phone or in person, once my position as an (assumed) insider to the community of white, heterosexual, cisgendered married women was established, the tone of the interview relaxed.[11] I became less a researcher from a distant university and more a junior member in a club over which they viewed themselves as the prevailing matriarchs. I attempted to answer any questions they had about my own life as fully and as honestly as possible and included these answers in the transcripts with a few exceptions.[12] More frequently, the narrators gave me unsolicited advice about all matters relating to marriage, including managing money and my husband, gender roles, raising children and, most poignantly, how to survive financially and emotionally should my husband predecease me – something that had already happened to many of them. This kind of self-identification with me as a young married woman did a great deal to break down the barriers that normally exist in such situations and created an interesting power shift within our interactions, as the narrators often placed me in the subordinate position of disciple learning from expert elders. The advice they gave me, which ranged from always having a sense of humour, having my own secret nest egg, and letting my husband think he was in charge, also proved incredibly illuminating.[13] Upon further analysis, such advice revealed much about how they characterized their marriages as a whole, what they felt was important in maintaining a marriage, and what they saw as their roles and responsibilities as married women.

The narratives presented here are just that – stories; they are the organization of life events into coherent structures. Further, given the ages of the narrators, they are chronicles that encompass almost an entire life, viewed from the position of nearing its completion, often well rehearsed through multiple tellings, and filtered through the meaning-making lens of nostalgia.[14] These narrative structures are useful in their own right, as they often reflect the influence of authoritative discourses such as those described in the previous chapters, as well as resistance to them. After all, social discourses give us the vocabularies that we then must use to make sense of our own lives. Robert Rutherdale's research on postwar fatherhood, which parallels my own in many ways, confirms this; he notes that many of his narrators drew on a "common culture" in creating their own personal narratives. As he writes, "From colorful colloquialisms to crisp metaphors, shared and seeming popular tropes often suggested how certain masculinities were deployed and inscribed in the culture."[15] Rutherdale observed that these social vocabularies are usually utilized twice – first in understanding the events as they happened and then in the recreation of those memories as coherent life narratives. However, in my oral histories there were also several instances when narrators presented life histories that were internally contradictory, contradicted other narrations, or clashed with available historical data. Such moments of conflict, though initially frustrating, are excellent signposts for fruitful deconstruction.

A prime example of this occurred in the contrast between two very different accounts of sexual assault and danger during World War II and the hazards that mobilization could pose to sexually vulnerable populations of women and children. Karen Rand (all names are pseudonyms) (war bride, m. 1945) described the situation in her birth country of England in the following way:

> We were never afraid during the war. That was another thing too if you were walking along the road and an air raid siren went off you'd have to find the nearest place to get in, sometimes it was a ditch! And if there was any troops on the road at the time well he'd jump in the ditch with you but he'd hold his arm over you. You might be fifteen years old or sixteen years old but you were never afraid. You never felt afraid during the war of being ... and I mean it was a blackout totally darkness. You'd meet all these servicemen and they say "hi babe" if they were Canadians or whatever. You knew you were never going to be molested in any way at all. You just felt safe with them. It was a different era.[16]

Fiona Shortt (m. 1952) a young child living in England during the same period, presented a directly contrasting narrative. When I asked for clarification on a prior comment she had made – that the war made her afraid of men – she told this story:

> And there was one park that had wooden swings. And my sister wanted me to go there with her and I said no it was too far away for me. I was ... I didn't want to go so far but I gave in. And we were swinging and we

were just going to leave the park and this solider came up to us. And offered us a bar of chocolate. If I'd go with him you know? And my sister said "Don't! Don't!" And I went [with him] and she ran off home. And so that was it.[17]

The context as well as the language of these quotations is crucial. Karen made her statement near the end of the interview as part of a larger discussion comparing her marriage to her children's – a question I would pose to get my narrators to discuss how they thought times had changed. She went on to say:

It was a different era than today. I think that the young children at the age of twelve they're become so ... they're more advanced in every way, shape, or form as we were at the age of twelve. And as I say by fifteen or sixteen they have a boyfriend and they're upset because the boyfriend looked at another girl and that causes a fight. I mean we never went through that even during the war.[18]

In conceiving of the present as highly sexualized and concomitantly remembering the recent past as much more innocent, Karen was engaging in memory making and a particular type of memory work that oral historians, including Kate Fisher, have identified as common in elderly narrators recalling their youth.[19] Karen also viewed the war as a time of sexual safety due to her own personal experiences, including meeting the man whom she would later marry. The reference to soldiers saying "hi babe" is crucial; they were the first words her future husband said to her. They met when she was sixteen and corresponded throughout the conflict, getting married three years later at the war's end. Her memory of relative sexual safety during wartime and her framing of soldiers as protectors rather than predators was therefore highly influenced by her nostalgic image of her deceased husband and the romance they shared. Fiona's story, in contrast, is stripped bare, only sketched in. She expended more words explaining to me that she and her sister went to the park specifically to use the wooden swings (as the metal swings at the nearer park had been removed during a wartime scrap metal drive) than she did explaining the actual molestation. Her story is also specific, about a single event, rather than a generalization about a longer period.

In some ways both narratives are "true" in that they hold a verified resonance with the narrators and that future decisions and choices were made on the basis of those truths; Fiona's account, however, is more historically accurate. Karen felt safe during the war with the particular soldiers that were stationed near her family farm. They would get water from her house and gather around the family piano when they had time off. In her mind and memory she discursively linked those soldiers with the fresh excitement of young love, conducted within the safety of her own home under the watchful eye of her benevolent parents. However, as Fiona's narrative demonstrates, sexual safety during wartime was not a guaranteed reality, a fact confirmed by another war bride narrator, Florence Anderson (war bride, m. 1945). Florence recounted that she and her husband first met on a double date, as she and a girlfriend always chose to go on dates with soldiers together because of an incident where some military men sexually "interfered" with girls at a local secondary school, getting several of them pregnant.[20] By examining the three discourses together, and in relation to their individual contexts, we gain more information not only about Karen's relationship with her husband – a deep affection that continued to colour her memorialization of all military men during the war – but also about the realities of the positive and negative effects that the mobilization of thousands of young men far away from the watchful eyes of friends, family, and community could have on women and children.

Fiona's and Karen's stories also demonstrate the need, when doing oral history, to take a person's entire life into consideration rather than limiting the analysis to events that occur only within the study's time period.[21] Karen's perspective at the time of the interview as an economically comfortable widow, surrounded by loving children and grandchildren, helped her to see the past through the window of contented nostalgia. In contrast, Fiona's sexual narrative often focused on her perception of herself as a victim; molested as a child, she also fought off a sexual assault in her fifties. Neither of these events happened within the postwar era of my study, but they affected her relationship with her husband as well as the way she remembered that relationship and her sexual life as a whole, and so they must be included.[22]

In the previous chapters both the medical and religious discourses advocated the importance of keeping gender roles separate and admonished women that men should be protected from having to engage in any particularly feminized housework, including childcare. Given the strength of this discourse, it is not surprising that many women I interviewed expressed a preference for traditional gender role designation and separation. Nor is it unexpected that this attitude was slightly more pronounced among the older narrators. However, this phenomenon cannot be reduced to a positivist feminist narrative where a growing awareness of women's rights spurred by wartime advances progressed straightforwardly to culminate in the explosion of the second-wave feminist movement. All my narrators expressed ambivalent and even self-contradictory views about ideal gender roles, demonstrating the liminal nature of the postwar years and echoing the ambiguous advice given by the Protestant churches rather than the clear-cut boundaries advocated by medical experts. Even those women who initially expressed the need for distinct masculine and feminine roles within marriages belied that ideal by their lived experiences.

Lois Adamson (war bride, m. 1945), for example, centred her whole interview on how well she fulfilled the traditional roles of housewife and mother.

> But I never felt like oh I want to work and have my own car and that. The minute the babies – well not the minute – *before* the babies were born, I was home. I never had to go out and work. My husband wanted it that way so that when they came home from school I was there and I was very happy. I didn't need a car of my own to go to work and have some stranger bring up my babies while I worked.[23]

She went on to discuss her successes as a mother, clearly drawing pride, self-worth, and self-identity from that role much in the same way other narrators did from their working lives. Edith Small (war bride, m. 1945) had a similar response when I asked her opinions of second-wave feminism, expressing concern that women had gone too far and lost as much as they had gained, including their powerful position as mothers.[24]

Margaret Brown (war bride, m. 1947) had a very different answer to my question about feminism. She said it was sad that some of the more attractive feminist leaders did not find themselves a nice young man. She noted light-heartedly, "And Greer was good looking! I was surprised at that. Friedan I could see why, but Greer I thought: 'you know gee whiz I think a man would find you a nice companion!' Did she ever marry anybody?" When I informed her that Friedan was married she responded, "He must have been quite a bloke! No I'm ... I really still think that men were made as God created them. I think they were probably meant to be the strong influence."[25]

Margaret presented her assessment of feminism as a joke, but the subtext to her words makes it clear she considered feminism a pastime reserved for "ugly," unmarriageable women. This kind of gendered judgment that feminists were embittered masculine (or lesbian) women unable to get a man, especially coming from other women, has been a millstone around the neck of feminists since the first-wave suffragettes were lampooned in political cartoons as "spinsters who have never been kissed."[26] Indeed, Margaret's casual, joking reference to such stereotypes denotes just how pervasive they were and the uphill battle that second-wave feminists would have in counteracting such insouciant, ephemeral sexism as well as more direct misogyny from both men and women.[27]

On the surface, and taken in isolation, the above comments by Lois, Edith, and Margaret seem to be nothing more than the expression of antiquated gender roles. Yet there was no sense that this strategy made them, and others who made similar statements, feel disempowered. For these narrators, adhering to traditional gender roles was an eminently practical solution that not only made for peaceful interactions within their marriages but also helped their husbands, for whom they felt a great deal of love and affection, feel important and secure in their own role within the family.

Security is an important concept here, as all three of these narrators were war brides. While the wartime experience encouraged some women to challenge gender norms, for others it heightened the call to domesticity and equation of traditional gender roles with peacetime regularity. Even for these women gender roles were more ambiguous than their statements make them appear. Margaret's husband, for instance, brought her a cup of tea in bed every morning of their marriage for over fifty years and voluntarily completed other domestic chores, such as cooking and baking bread. All three women were involved in the family finances, with Margaret even temporarily supporting the family when her husband went back to school. Even Lois, who never worked outside of the home and discussed at length the proper ways a man should treat a lady (such as opening her door and pulling out her chair), admitted that she handled all the family finances.[28] Further, Lois did not see her status as secondary to her husband despite not contributing financially to the family in the form of an income. This was particularly clear when she talked about owning a home and the difference between her socio-economic status and that of her parents. "I had everything I could think of because in England we had very little ... My mom and dad paid rent until the day they died and I owned my house at eighteen ... I did! I owned it and it was very nice."[29] Her sense of ownership over the home – it is *her* house; note that she mentions possession several times – is particularly important as she is claiming the value, both materially and ideologically, of her unwaged labour in the home. In this way Lois's statement simultaneously presages second-wave discussions of the value of unwaged domestic labour while her overall focus on her home and the possessions within in, and her role in creating it as a domestic haven, reflect the housewife consumer identity that became synonymous with the 1950s and was particularly attached to young war brides.[30]

The above narratives demonstrate that even when women accepted the division of labour along gender lines their mentalities did not always follow the same tracks. Edith, Margaret, and Lois, more so than any of the other women interviewed, were able to "toe the party line" about separate gender roles because their husbands were particularly loving and considerate, and appearing to accept those roles had placed them in very comfortable circumstances. These three women were amongst the most well situated at the time of the interview, both socially and financially, and reflected upon their lives with a great deal of contentment. Yet at the same time as they appeared to epitomize postwar gender role acquiescence and framed their marriages as unequal, in reality they wielded a great deal of power in their relationship with their husbands.

There were other strategies to change the gendered power dynamics within a marriage while still accepting a stricter separation of gender roles. One approach was to acknowledge that it was important for husbands to be "the boss" while simultaneously rationalizing this need as a particularly male weakness. Ruth Bell (war bride, 1943) and Alice Hall (war bride, 1945) reflected this mindset in their narrations. Both adhered to that strategy in response to questions about what advice they would give to young women getting married today. Alice Hall stated quite baldly:

> ALICE: I think you have to let the husband be the boss.
> HEATHER: And how come?
> ALICE: Because it makes them feel stronger.
> HEATHER: And so do you mean in terms of the money or ...?
> ALICE: Well just overall I mean you can tell them what you think, give your opinion, but they can override you if they ... (*trails off*)
> HEATHER: So they kind of have the last say?
> ALICE: Yeah.[31]

Ruth elaborated upon her position more than Alice did:

> You know men are much more fragile than women. That is my opinion. And they need to feel that they have a ... they need to feel supported. They need to be – even if they're not really running things they need to feel [that] they are. And I think sometimes that modern young women have got to the point where they have to have their ability to control known to everybody and that has caused in some instances a lack of control. Sometimes the most important thing is they're not overt.[32]

Ruth's last statement about the covert nature of managing one's husband is key. It indicates that Ruth and the other women who employed such strategies were aware that they were claiming some kind of power over their husband and that they had to mask that power by situating it "behind the throne." It is clear that for many of the narrators, especially in the earlier era, letting their husband *feel* like the boss when he was either not inclined to exploit that privilege or was being carefully managed from the sidelines allowed some women to fulfil highly structured postwar gender roles and maintain a certain amount of agency. This passive-aggressive stance was certainly the Roman Catholic Church in Canada's prescription for a happy marriage; however, both Alice and Ruth were raised in the Anglican Church. That this discourse is found outside the Catholic community suggests that rather than creating new norms, the Roman Catholic Church was drawing on already existing marital tropes. The latter is again supported by Robert Rutherford's works on baby boom fatherhood. His narrators, reflecting on their roles as fathers, asserted their patriarchal authority over their wives and children based often in the authority they felt sprang from their role as the family breadwinner. It was very important not only to "wear the pants" in the family dynamic but to be seen by society to be taking on the leadership role.[33] That they were being carefully managed from within the family doesn't seem to have occurred to them.

Other narrators made similar statements about modern women emasculating men when asked to evaluate their children's marriages, usually when critiquing their daughters-in-law.[34] The latter presents an interesting, though perhaps unsurprising, inconsistency, as the narrators were more likely to push for equality of gender relations when it came to their daughters and their daughters' husbands and be regressive regarding their son's relationships with women. However, the same also seems to have held true for some of the men in this transition era. For example, Fiona Shortt noted that while her husband had strict expectations that Fiona would fulfil a more traditional role, he was horrified at the idea that his daughter would face similar constraints.[35]

Other narrators dealt with gender role divisions by embracing the exhausting double day prescribed by doctors R. Castro de la Mata, G. Gringas, and E.D. Wittkower ("Impact of Sudden Severe Disablement of the Father upon the Family," discussed above) and within the pages of the *Christian Home*. These women carefully arranged their lives so they could "do it all" without asking their husbands to move too far out of their gender roles by, for example, helping out around the house or participating in childcare. Karen Rand wanted to contribute financially to the building of their house. Though she trained as a nurse during the war, there was no nursing work in the town in which they lived and moving was not a consideration because her husband had a successful job where they resided. Instead, Karen accepted an unskilled job as a mess-hall cook at the nearby lumber camp. In order to be home for her children she worked only night shifts, while her husband worked days. She described her often gruelling schedule quite cheerily, noting the sole bad part was that she only got to see her husband for two hours a day and on weekends.

> I went to work and I worked for two years on night shift because he was on day shift and I had the two children and they were in school and it was long shifts, it was ten-hour shifts ... So I made the dinner. We had two hours. Made the dinner for the children when they came in from school. I was sleeping. All day. So then I would get up when the children came home off the bus which was about three o'clock. And then they'd wake me up. Because I came home six o'clock in the morning, I got off and home by seven. In time to get the children up, get their breakfast. He was gone to work and I would get their breakfast and send them off to school and that was it.[36]

Despite the fact that they were both working, Karen arranged her schedule so that her husband had the minimum amount of childcare responsibilities and was never called on to engage in particularly female-designated tasks such as the preparation of meals. While this seems deeply unfair to modern, feminist sensibilities, Karen made it clear that it was worth the exhaustion for her to have a feeling of ownership and contribution to the building of their dream home. Ironically, just as the house was nearing completion, her husband was transferred and they sold the property without ever having lived in it; Karen once again had to bend herself to new circumstances created by her husband's breadwinner role, which she did (allegedly) without complaint.

Joyce Martin (m. 1961) had a similar strategy to prevent her husband taking on any feminine tasks, but she made it clear when she returned to work as a teacher that she expected her children, a son and daughter, to pick up the slack, both within the house and for the female-signified farm chores such as caring for the home garden.[37] Interestingly, while she deemed it improper for her husband to help out with domestic tasks, this gender division did not apply to her son. Though her son tended to do more chores outside on the farm and her daughter to do more housework indoors, Joyce felt it was important that her son take some responsibility for, and be capable in, the domestic sphere.

> And I can remember coming home from taking her [Joyce's daughter] to music lessons once when our son was about eleven and when we walked

in the door at nine o'clock at night he's in the living room watching television and the supper dishes are sitting on the table. I rounded the corner to the living room and I said, "[son's name], the supper dishes need to be done. Both [daughter's name] and I are going to watch TV." I said, "around here when there is work to be done we work at it until it's all done and then we all have time off."[38]

Joyce's ambivalence towards the separation of gender roles went beyond raising her son to follow different standards than did her husband. As a teacher she felt strongly that having a stay-at-home mother was crucial to a child's development, yet she also felt that mothers were providing a service to society by staying home and therefore that they should be adequately compensated for that work out of public funds. "And as a kindergarten teacher all my life I would like to see the government to pay parents and pay mothers enough ... pay one parent enough to stay home with their kids until they're at least six years old. I think it would really help out society in a lot of ways."[39]

For these women, again mostly of the older generation, this seemingly ambivalent attitude worked for them. Whether they chose to let their husband be the boss, let him only think he was the boss, or found other strategies to combine outside work and household duties, their ability to strategically manipulate dominant gender expectations allowed them some freedom without engaging in active conflict with their husbands. Other narrators who engaged in more direct challenges to the status quo were not so lucky.

Marjorie Taylor (war bride, m. 1946), though stating that she had always seen herself as a modern woman, did not immediately identify with the feminist movement. She became increasingly activist when her daughters and a close female friend persuaded her of feminism's relevance. However, when Marjorie began to challenge her subordinate status within her marriage, her husband reacted badly and accused her of sexual infidelity, attempting, perhaps unconsciously, to use sexual censure to police what he saw as her gender role deviance. Although they remained married, Marjorie recalls that they became increasingly distant. She convinced him to seek marital counselling through their minister at the United Church, who succeeded in reassuring Marjorie's husband that she was not cheating on him and giving them both better tools to work together. The minister, however, did not suggest that Marjorie's husband was in any way in the wrong.[40]

A similar situation occurred with Jessica Bateman (m. 1964), a trained nurse whose husband worked as an unskilled labourer. After nine years of marriage and two children, Jessica, who had returned to work when her children were "a bit older," felt unsatisfied with the marriage and wanted a divorce. Her husband was at that time underemployed and reportedly threatened that if she left he would sue her for alimony and take half her pension. This frightening prospect, combined with a deep religious commitment to marriage, kept Jessica in the marriage. They eventually reconciled, until Jessica started her own business in 1989. According to her, the business grew out of a delivery error. During the 1980s, Jessica's husband was diagnosed with celiac disease, which was difficult to manage at that time due to the scarcity of gluten-free food products outside of major centres. Jessica solved this problem by contacting a gluten-free distributor in the nearest large city. She claims that at some point the company mistakenly thought she was ordering goods to distribute in her area, rather than a small order for personal use, and sent her an entire container truckload of gluten-free products. She used the surplus to begin a home-based business selling gluten-free foods out of her basement.[41]

I was immediately suspicious of this account, though Jessica stuck to the narrative when I questioned her. She never answered why, if it was the company that had made the mistake, she did not simply refuse to accept the order, redirecting the question however it was framed. The subtext of her narrative suggests that setting up the business was always her intent – she had already created many contacts through her husband's celiac support group as well as through her nursing experience – and that she constructed the explanation of the mistake to forestall her husband, who would never have allowed her to set up a business in their home. This strategy, however, did not work. According to her, her husband was furious because the business took up much of Jessica's time and he felt she ignored her domestic responsibilities; he had an affair in retaliation. At the time of the interview in 2010 the couple, though still married, were almost completely estranged and living in separate rooms in their house.

Even when Jessica attempted to manage her husband by massaging the truth about her desire to start a home business, she presented their difference in education and earning potential as constantly eating away at him and poisoning their marriage. When she attempted to change that dynamic, already strained by her higher education and greater work success, he retaliated by threatening her future and attempting to reassert his masculine dominance by having an extended affair.[42]

The varied strategies and responses to the idealized separation of gender roles clearly demarks the baby boom era as one of change, but not, however, linear progression towards increased freedom and rights for women. Instead, it was a messy negotiation undertaken by each woman on an individual basis. What is clear from all the interviews is that the authoritative ideal of separate and rigid gender roles transferred to men and women and, whatever the arrangement engaged in by the couple, had to be dealt with.

This is particularly evident in the narrations of Mary Johnston (m. 1952) and Jean Simpson (m. 1963), both self-proclaimed feminists married to men whom they identified as "feminist men." Mary recalled how she was the envy of the neighbourhood because her husband, who had been a widower with young children when they married, was extremely involved with all the children, even changing diapers.[43] Jean Simpson recalled that her husband was a "feminist" in part because he had grown up in a household of women, including six sisters.[44] Both women related these facts to me with a clear sense that their situation was distinctive and that they needed to give reasons why their husbands were able to break the mould. By focusing on that difference and the uniqueness of their situation, they actually demonstrated how pervasive such ideals really were. Further, it should be noted that while Mary's and Jean's definitions of what made a feminist man – being more involved with the children and giving their wives a more equal say in the marriage – would not be considered particularly radical by feminist standards today, they saw their husband's actions as a major step forward. Given the mental and physical gymnastics required by some of the other narrators to shift those norms even slightly, Mary and Jean's shared responsibly with their spouses takes on greater significance.

Prescriptive discourses, such as those investigated in the preceding chapters, when they are given authority and repeated enough create societies where people police themselves and each other. We can see this process when it comes to the expression of sexuality within marriage and what types of sexual actions and personas were seen as possible or desirable for women. In Kate Fisher's study of marriage and sexuality, *Birth Control, Sex, and Marriage in Britain 1918–1960*, she noted that many of the women she interviewed maintained a deliberate ignorance regarding sexual matters before and during their marriages to better protect the image of innocence that was central to their sexual identity.[45] Like Fisher's informants, many of my narrators used tropes of innocence as a key element in their sexual sense of self. However, in contrast to Fisher's narrators, their episodes of deliberate unknowing were not centred around birth control.[46] Instead the ideal of innocence before marriage and within the union was an elastic concept that could be deployed in different ways.

Some of the innocence tropes were clearly cases of deliberate ignorance. Edith remembered having a talk about the wedding night with her mother a few days before the ceremony.

> And I don't know what I was saying or wasn't saying but she (*pause*) my mother was a very shy person (*pause*) but she said, "Edith" she said "if you'd like me to tell you I will." And I remember putting my hand up (*puts hand up, palm out*) I said "no don't do it, I've got a funny feeling it would spoil it." So she never did tell me.[47]

Others such as Margaret Brown and Ruth Bell were not given the opportunity for such an education; their sexual innocence was mandated in part by the silences from their mothers and other potential informants on that subject. Margaret described how she was suddenly confronted by her lack of understanding of her own body on the eve of her own wedding.

> It was awkward. I remember when I knew I was getting married and of course I went back to [the Women's Auxiliary Air Force: WAAF] camp and I remember sitting in the bath and getting out and drying myself and I thought, how is it all going to work? We never looked at ourselves. I knew there was something going to happen but I couldn't imagine how it would happen.[48]

Similarly, Ruth Bell remembered with the humour of hindsight how she, not knowing it was normal for some virgins to bleed after their first time having sex, ceased sexual relations with her husband after their wedding night, believing that she had gotten her period. As she put it: "Now can you imagine? Nowadays I can't imagine that there's grade school children that are that innocent. But I was. I was completely virgin and I had no experience. (*laughs*) I didn't know what to expect, to be truthful."[49]

Florence Anderson, also a war bride, characterized her innocence slightly differently, remarking that while she had heard some things about the mechanics of sex while stationed with other young women in the WAAF, it was the emotional impact that she was unprepared for.

> FLORENCE: I sort of had an idea. But, um, Mother had never said anything. And you sort of heard odd bits and pieces after I joined the WAAF. I was an only child and I had no siblings to ... but once I was in the WAAF, um, and training I was thrown all of a sudden ... I was thrown into this hut with all these girls in. Some were married some weren't. Some were like

> myself engaged and, ah, and you kinda heard stuff eh? But you didn't really at least I didn't, um, I didn't worry about it. I don't think I really totally knew or even had an idea of, um, the emotions – the feelings?
> HEATHER: Were the emotions very intense?
> FLORENCE: For me they were. And I believe so for him too. And our relationship was a very loving, caring ... he was most considerate. And I think [he was] a little apprehensive you know? As I was too.[50]

Others such as Karen Rand extended their claim to innocence by remaining deliberately ignorant of their husband's sexual past. When I asked Karen how much she knew about her husband's sexual history she dismissed the question.

> KAREN: No, no he had lots of girlfriends. I mean before when he was in the army, um, I don't know ... I think he did anyway. He was very young. I mean they all did I'm sure. I mean he would go on leave somewhere and I never really ... um. But he certainly wasn't a virgin. I know that.
> HEATHER: And you didn't ever ask him about that or his ...?
> KAREN: No I never asked him about that.
> HEATHER: You just didn't want to know or didn't think it mattered?
> KAREN: No I never thought about it. You know I mean I was married to him and he was my husband and so I never needed to ask him what he did before.[51]

Claiming an innocent identity in the past could also serve contemporary political motivations, as demonstrated by Verna King's (war bride, m. 1942) assertions to me that I set the story straight about war brides' sexuality. Verna who found my sexual questions extremely "cheeky," said that one of the only reasons she agreed to be interviewed was that she and other war brides had suffered verbal abuse upon their arrival in Canada. Specifically, people suggested that the war brides "caught" their husbands by being sexually promiscuous. Her memories are borne out by the secondary literature. Though war brides were more likely to be welcomed as symbols of the future hope for the postwar era, war brides, particularly those who were non-white or from former Axis countries, were sometimes painted as femme fatales preying on unworldly young soldiers. Some of this came from concerns over foreign women "poaching" from a supply of young men already decimated by wartime death and disability. As the fighting ceased and final casualty lists were calculated, it was clear that not all young women were going to be able to share in the social and economic dividends promised by postwar married domesticity, and these factors made some people denigrate these new Canadians.[52] In her interview with me Verna was able to use the trope of innocence to counteract these damaging narratives and to gain some power over them in the present by correcting what she saw as a gross injustice. She forcibly declared:

> I would like people to know that all the people that came here were not whores. Some people were accused of it – you know they were they were ill treated. Quite a few of the war brides were eh? ... I think that people should know that a lot of the women were not whores.[53]

The above recollections are in direct contrast to those of the younger cohort of my study group. While the older women all noted their mother's reticence or complete refusal to discuss sexual matters, for the younger women their mothers were usually their primary conduit of sexual information. Though she could not recall the exact circumstances where her mother sat down and told her about the "birds and the bees," Jean Simpson knew that her mother did talk to her about sex. Laughingly, she said, "I think probably knowing my mother she gave me a book from the library." Diane West's (m. 1957) mother, a nurse, not only explained the mechanics of sex and reproduction to her but also encouraged her to get a diaphragm to avoid an unwanted pregnancy.

> DIANE: I guess when I was dating we talked about sex. "Don't let the boys go too far" and all that. Particularly when I started dating men that were older and were out of school and by older men I mean twenties.
> HEATHER: But she didn't talk to you about anything like birth control or ...
> DIANE: Yeah, we did. We did talk about [it] at one point before I was married because I knew about the, um, that rubber thing you put inside you.
> HEATHER: Oh a diaphragm?
> DIANE: (*nodding*) Sometimes words escape me for a few minutes.[54]

It is possible that Jean's and Diane's mothers were anomalies, perhaps due to their higher education level. However, there is further evidence for change over time in transmission of sexual information from mother to daughter. First, many of the earlier brides, in retrospect, expressed dissatisfaction with their lack of preparedness for marital intercourse. Marjorie Taylor mentioned that her sexual life was okay but that it would have been better if she and her husband had had more information going into the marriage and spent less time having to learn everything on their own. In addition, all the earlier brides noted that when it came to their own children, especially their daughters, they wanted them to be better prepared. Marjorie was particularly adamant that, unlike her parents, she recognized sex was important and passed that information on to her children.[55] Sexual innocence, it seemed, had lost much of its appeal as a female sexual identity by the end of the 1960s.

Sexual knowledge also had a significant spatial component. That is, narrators from rural backgrounds, specifically those who grew up on farms, rejected the trope of innocence as unsustainable given their upbringing. Without exception and no matter their age cohort, rural women described having an understanding of the sexual process prior to the time of conscious memory – it was something they were aware of their entire lives and, perhaps more importantly, they were given vocabularies and knowledges to speak and think about it rather than the silences that could characterize more urban experiences. When I asked Joyce Martin how she first learned about sex, she replied simply, "Behind the barn."[56] She elaborated about how living with animals generally led to her asking questions and receiving information about breeding and sex more generally. Nancy Wilson (m. 1966), also from a farming background, echoed this statement, noting that she did not need a sexual education course at school: "I lived in one!"[57]

It is also likely that the trope of innocence amongst the older narrators was influenced by a feeling of nostalgia for a time that they perceived, through the lens of reminiscence, to have truly been more innocent. This imagined past of incorruptibility, and the role of their own naivete within that past, was created in part to offset what they viewed as a hypersexualized modern society. Significantly, Alice Hall, when discussing what she saw as rampant over-sexualization in the modern world, said, "I would really prefer that the young people didn't have so much sex thrown on them on TV and I'm sorry for the boys that have to watch these girls with hardly any clothes on. I don't think it's kind at all. No I really do feel strongly about that."[58] In focusing her sympathy with the boys in being exposed to the girls, rather than the girls who were exposed, Alice demonstrated that while tropes of innocence may have lost much of their social value, older sexual ideals were still in play, including the idea that women, deemed to have greater sexual restraint than males, had to continue to police sexual encounters.

For most of the women in this study the immediate postwar period was a time of change where at least the appearance of sexual awareness was no longer seen as taboo. Yet the simultaneous, negative reactions of many of the narrators to the hypersexualization of society may have masked this and other signs of their early sexual "feminism" and resulted in a general image of them, and the period, as sexually conservative. At the same time the generational shedding of certain iterations of the innocence trope suggests a greater continuity between the seemingly quiescent immediate postwar years and the sexual freedoms of the so-called sexual revolution. Simply being able to discuss their own sexuality, both more publicly and within the confines of their own minds, and being given a vocabulary to do so, would have been extremely powerful as demonstrated by Michel Foucault's concepts of sexual repression. Specifically referencing the strictures of the Victorian era, he notes:

> These are the characteristic features of repression, which serve to distinguish it from the prohibitions maintained by penal law: repression operated as a sentence to disappear but also as an injunction to silence, an affirmation of nonexistence, and, by implication, an admission that there was nothing to say about such things, nothing to see, and nothing to know.[59]

The act of lifting the "injunction of silence" or what might be better paraphrased as the "injunction to ignorance" upon which the innocence trope was founded allowed the younger women in my interview cohort to stretch the image of white, middle-class, married sexual respectability. In doing so they were working within the dominant sexual discourses presented by the medical and religious knowledge schemas, which, as chapters 2 and 3 demonstrate, promoted a rationally managed sexual body, including self-knowledge, so long as actual sex acts remained socially contained within heterosexual marriage. Such rational knowledge also fit with the postwar North American zeitgeist of scientific advancement and the use of scientific knowledges to create progress.[60]

A large part of our false remembrances of the postwar era as domestically quiescent is driven by the postwar world's seeming obsession with children. A world where babies permeated every aspect of Canadian society and culture and female identity was tied to maternity was certainly evident in the authoritative discourses. For the medical community pregnancy was the only way that women could reach full psychological maturity, and all three of Canada's main Christian denominations upheld the ideal that no marriage was complete without children. Given this societal normalization of children as essential to marriage, it is not surprising that all the women I interviewed had families that included children.

Motherhood featured prominently in many of the interviews. For several women, their abilities as mothers were a source of pride as they looked back on their lives, and for some having children was the most profound experience in their personal history and their life's central purpose. For example, I asked Lois Adamson if she felt lonely being so far away from her parents, who were in England. She replied by reframing the discussion around her role as a mother.

> LOIS: No. I mean sometimes I would feel lonely, but like I said I had the puppy and I had my little girl. And I was a good little mum! Oh, I used to walk her to the clinic and get her weighed all the time and you would laugh if you knew some of the things I did. I used to slide her diaper to the side, a newborn baby, and hold her over the toilet and the cold air of course would make her pee! I'd open up one side, slide it around and hold her little legs and sure enough she'd give a little shiver and pee. (*laughs*)
> HEATHER: (*laughs*) So she was potty-trained really early.
> LOIS: Oh she was!
> HEATHER: And how did you know to do that? Was that in like a book you read or …?
> LOIS: No nobody! You know, there's no babies in my family … I had no trouble with any of them.[61]

In this excerpt, Lois was adamant that her motherhood skills were neither learned from a book nor from prior familial experience. She maintained that she was an excellent mother by natural instinct alone. Karen Rand echoed this ideal, saying that she too was not lonely because she had her two children to raise. "And I was not homesick either. Mind you, I was too busy. I had two children right away. I used to love it."[62]

Both Lois and Karen created an image in their narratives of their families as islands of intimacy populated mainly by themselves and their children, along with their husbands who returned to the domestic centre at specific times. Their ideals fit the postwar stereotype of the home as domestic stronghold of the nuclear family. Lois repeated the phrase "my own world" when describing her life, noting that while she lived in a suburb with many other mothers who had children the same age, she chose not to mix with them very much. "Yeah there were young people out where we were but it was, ah … we didn't have a car to get around so, you know, we'd have to take the tram and all this so I never really got involved with anyone else. I was quite happy in my own little world."[63]

The dominant discourse also constructed children as necessary to a woman's happiness in her domestic role and the most common cure should she become bored with it, something that Alice Hall referenced in her interview.

HEATHER: And do you mind if I ask why there was such a large gap between [your children being born in] '48 and '61?
ALICE: Well I'll tell you having two babies in two years (*laughs*) I didn't want to know anything about diapers for a while and then when they got to be in their teens I guess, one was thirteen and one was fourteen, I got the empty nest syndrome and my husband said "well we better have another baby or you better get a job."
HEATHER: (*laughs*) And you chose the baby.
ALICE: (*laughs*) Yes.[64]

Alice's boredom is a classic example of the "housewife dissatisfaction" discussed by myriad experts, from the medical community to Betty Friedan. The choice as presented by her husband – to either go out and get a job or stay home and have another baby – is interesting, as it clearly demarks a spatial and temporal divide between working women and homemakers. That is, Alice's husband was asking her to choose between remaining temporally tied to childbearing, in essence continuing to define herself as a mother/potential mother and staying home, and the alternative of severing her connection with that biology. It seems that while more progressive views about women's work as represented in the elite discourse by Marion Hilliard existed and allowed Alice the possibility of finding a new form of self-identity and fulfilment through work, the distinct segregation of motherhood and work remained. If Alice had chosen the work option she would have entered a new life phase and would be allowed to enter the outside workforce, as though her children would still need parenting, they were past the socially accepted age where they needed her constant presence; a happier version of the severing of biology and concomitant social role of motherhood as presented in the menopausal treatment advertisements in chapter 2 (images 3 and 4). By having another baby Alice delayed that severance and remained geographically tied to the home rather than that outside world. This socially endorsed compartmentalization of women's lives would have made it difficult for women who wanted or were forced by circumstances to blend the two identities and become working mothers; the continued taboo made structural changes needed to support working mothers, such as affordable childcare, very unlikely.[65]

Alice chose to stay home longer and have another child. Her choice, and the choices of many of the other narrators, make it clear that while authoritative discourses had immense influence in how women perceived the postwar world, they were not slaves to a particular vision. They had choices, even if these were limited by social mores and standards, and there is no doubt that many of the women interviewed truly wanted children and saw their vocation as mothers as one of the primary sources of their identity. Further, no one can blame Alice for choosing to have another baby. Even if she was ambivalent about having a third child, and it does not seem that she was, finding a job from a very limited number of options available and likely at low pay would not be attractive. Remaining tied to biological motherhood "cured" Alice's housewife boredom in a way much more likely to pay social dividends.

Given these dividends, both in the past and in my narrators' oral reconstruction of their lives, the centrality of motherhood to their overall narratives is not particularly surprising. What is surprising is how ambivalent, even blasé, those same narrators could be about fertility loss, miscarriage, and even infant loss. Far from equating their situations with a loss of femininity or of womanhood as suggested by the medical discourse, the majority saw these issues as acceptable bumps along the reproductive road.

Several of the women interviewed had complications in conceiving. The most complex case was that of Joyce Martin, who was diagnosed with low fertility of unspecified cause and had to take medication in order to increase her chances of becoming pregnant. When I asked about her experience with infertility, however, it was the annoyance she felt at the logistics of her treatment that was most prominent in her mind.

> HEATHER: So tell me a little about what it was like to be treated for infertility at this time. Was it ... 'cause a lot of women today find it really traumatic.
> JOYCE: It was a pain because I had to use the thermometer. I had to keep a record *and* I had to collect my urine for twenty-four hours and take it back. We were living in [town's name removed] and I was doctoring in [city about four hour's drive away] because we had been living in [city about four hour's drive away] when I was trying to get pregnant at first and I just kept with the same doctor. I don't know it just seemed like it was forever.[66]

For Joyce the experience was basically a nuisance due to the long drive and the mechanics of fitting the treatment into her busy life on the farm. Edith Small was equally unconcerned when her first pregnancy turned out to be ectopic and burst, destroying one of her fallopian tubes and cutting her chances of conceiving in half.

> HEATHER: And what did you think about that when they told you that you'd lost a fallopian tube?
> EDITH: Well I was so glad to be out of this thing – I mean it was pretty painful and pretty serious. And I don't really go into tizzies about things

you know, not unless it's really necessary. They had told me that it might be difficult to get pregnant then you see 'cause they said usually it's your best side that goes but I wasn't in the habit of worrying about things ahead of time and look at it we had six pregnancies after that so ...[67]

Edith Small was equally quiescent in retelling her story of a miscarriage that she only brought up by way of explaining the large gap between two of her children.

> HEATHER: And tell me about the miscarriage. How far along were you?
> EDITH: Um I think it would be about the three-month mark. I was running down this set of steps with something or other to do with the lunch and I fell. And then I never really thought too much about it 'cause I didn't hurt myself badly you know. But I was conscious of the fact that I was [pregnant] when I fell, I remember thinking this is not good you know? But anyways I did go to the doctor's the next time he was in town and everything seemed to be fine. But then, then I lost it so ... (*trails off*)
> HEATHER: And how was, what was that like?
> EDITH: Uh well it sort of happened during the night. I remember the doctor, there was a nursing home in town at that time and the doctor came and picked me up at the house and took me to the nursing home. And I can remember seeing [husband's name]'s face at the living room window seeming so anxious. You know he wasn't a worrying kind of person at all but he looked very concerned then.
> HEATHER: So was there a lot of sadness and grief about losing this baby?
> EDITH: Well there was some but it wasn't, ah, but it didn't terribly throw us for a loop. That was very much I think the way we felt. Certainly didn't make us feel "we're never going to do this again" sort of thing you know.[68]

How do we reconcile these contradictory discourses from women who both venerated motherhood and yet were seemingly unconcerned over issues of fertility and even miscarriage? Edith Small, Joyce Martin, and the others who had trouble conceiving, despite their unconcern about infertility, were no less involved with their children or willing to be mothers than Lois Adamson, Karen Rand, or Alice Hall, who constructed their children as central. Part of their nonchalance, especially regarding infertility, can be ascribed to the distance between the time they gave their account and the time of the actual event. Time may not heal all wounds, but it does dull emotion and give a sense of perspective. More importantly, both Edith and Joyce went on to have children, meaning that they ultimately fulfilled their expected roles as mothers and displayed the crucial physical evidence of their postwar gender role and sexual normality. If during the period of infertility, or in Edith's case the time between when she lost her fallopian tube and the conception of her next child, these women felt the social pressure of what dominant medical and religious discourses portrayed as social and biological inadequacy, this was likely eclipsed by their overarching identity and experience as mothers. Women who could not conceive or bear any living children would presumably have constructed their experiences of infertility as more central to their life's narrative rather than placing it on the periphery. Motherhood, preferably biological motherhood, was crucially important to most postwar women's sense of self but, once achieved, the process was largely overshadowed.

The corollary to this ambivalence about infertility can be seen in the similar ambivalence towards fertility reduction and control. Though all the narrators I interviewed used some form of fertility prevention to delay their first pregnancies and to limit their overall number of children, their birth control usage was a far cry from the careful management of fertility – including the spacing of children for their optimal development – imagined within the medical and Protestant discourses. For the oldest narrators, who bore children before there was easy access to relatively simple and effective birth control measures such as the Pill, their nonchalance was partially due to the unreliable nature of the available birth control methods, especially the rhythm method.

Lois Adamson laughingly told me that she became pregnant with her only son because her daughter saw the marks her mother made on the calendar each month (denoting her fertile periods) and, when told they marked "special days," proceeded to mess up Lois's system by marking down her Brownie picnic with a similar symbol and throwing off Lois's count.[69] Lois was not very upset at the time largely because such methods were not expected to be infallible and the hope was not for full control but to avoid the debilitating and often dangerous serial pregnancies that had been their mother's lot.

Those born in the later period, such as Nancy Wilson (m. 1966), Jean Simpson and Diane West (m. 1957), who did have easy access to the Pill as well as condoms and diaphragms, reported using those methods to delay pregnancy only for a set period of time, usually at the beginning of the marriage, and then resuming their use after the desired number of children had been born. All of them reported the intermediate time – the time when they chose to be mothers – as a being somewhat of a fertility free-for-all. As Nancy Wilson put it: "We chose not to have one for the first year and then after that we had fun."[70]

Birth control and class issues have been historically intertwined. Innovations such as the Pill and IUD cost money and required somewhat regular access to a doctor and a degree of forethought that was, and continues to be, constructed as beyond the abilities of the working-class and/or non-white populations.[71] While all the women enjoyed the trappings of middle- or even upper-class life when I interviewed them[72] – trappings such as comfortable living circumstances including home ownership as well as the fact that most had children and/or grandchildren receiving post-secondary education – many were born into working-class families or families that hovered on the brink between working- and middle-class status. Yet Nancy, born to a poor farming family and never having finished high school, espoused the same unconcern about fertility control as Jean and Diane, both of whom had a middle-class upbringing and university degrees. It seems that in the immediate postwar era regular contraception use was characterized by medical and Protestant authorities as markers of class status but that women such as my narrators could, and did, retain older views about childbearing as one specific and largely uninterrupted period in a woman's life, albeit now one that they could effectively truncate on their terms.

As each individual child was not deliberately planned, unanticipated situations such as miscarriage or initial difficulty conceiving were not seen as major events in contrast to the ways they are currently constructed in the modern, middle-class, female, embodied ideals. Instead, the important thing was to have some children at some point, and most women chose to take them as they came. This is especially clear in Glenda Baker's (m. 1945) narrative of the 1948 birth of her twins, a boy and a girl. Glenda told me, quite matter-of-factly, that the boy had died four days after his birth due to kidney failure. When I asked her how this affected her, Glenda admitted she was sad but quickly dismissed that emotion, stating that she was simply happy to "bring one baby home."[73] Again, it may be that time and distance help to explain some of Glenda's composure in relating this story. However, I argue that, given the evidence of the other narrators, her equanimity also stems in part from the fact that her surviving daughter meant that she was still a mother, still able to connect to that lodestone in constructing her identity, which helped her cope with the loss of her son.

The difference between choosing each conception/pregnancy and choosing to be a mother is slight but crucially important. It explains why my narrators were blasé about fertility complications and miscarriage while at the same time being devastated by maternal mental illness such as postpartum depression. Maternal mental illness was described by those who admitted to suffering it as a very traumatic experience. Women with maternal mental illness felt unable to fulfil their goal of motherhood, and this made them feel, as Marjorie Taylor described, less than a woman.[74] For Marjorie the social role of mother was connected to her understanding of herself as a female much more so than was her biology. Even Fiona Shortt, who had a hormonal imbalance during pregnancy and was "fine" afterwards, framed her depression as a problem only because she could not take care of her children who were already born while she was experiencing symptoms.

> It was horrible. Because I would be standing baking or something and it was like a blanket coming down. I could feel it coming all the way down my body. And I would say if I run to the other side of the room it won't get me. That's how physical it was! And with my second child I was very, very depressed and I thought I'd have to kill myself and my daughter because I couldn't leave her for my husband to look after.

Fiona ties remembrances of her depression with the domestic task of baking, demonstrating the clear break in her mind between her functioning as normal, engaged in a household task and properly fulfilling her role as a mother, and the time during the depression. In the latter circumstance Fiona conceptualized herself as a failure as she was not only unable to take care of her eldest daughter but was a danger to her. It is important to note that Fiona's concern that she might kill her living daughter was not extended to her unborn child, demonstrating that she considered the relationship with the two entities as fundamentally different: to her daughter she was a mother, while she had not taken on that role in regard to the fetus.

Fiona's separation of her living daughter and her fetus into two distinct categories presages what would become a pillar of secular second-wave feminist ideas about the unborn and the pregnant body. It is significant, however, that this pregnancy happened prior to that time, in the late 1950s and when Fiona was still a practising Roman Catholic. Despite the Roman Catholic Church in Canada's attempt to gain parishioner compliance in giving control over their bodies to God and the church, none of my Catholic narrators seem to have taken this doctrine to heart. For example, all the Catholic narrators (Lois, Mary, and Fiona) and those with Catholic husbands (Margaret and Glenda) used some form of birth control, and only Lois limited herself solely to the (somewhat) sanctioned form of the rhythm method. As was noted in the previous chapter, there was a grey area for Catholics prior to the publication of *Humanae Vitae* in 1968 wherein the church's position on birth control was in some doubt, and it could be argued that these narrators were taking advantage of this lack of clarity. Mary Johnston problematizes this assumption. Mary and her husband were both devout Catholics, and they practised the rhythm method to limit and space out the children they had together. However, after they added five biological children to the three children from her husband's previous marriage, Mary's family doctor wanted to put her on the Pill as he worried that having additional children would put too much emotional strain on her husband, then in his fifties, as the breadwinner to an already large family. Mary agreed to do so without even discussing the issue with her husband and remained on the Pill for several years until she was safely within menopause.

In so doing, Mary contravened both the Catholic Church's ban on artificial birth control and the wider medical and religious discourses decreeing that a woman's fertility was the common property of herself *and* her husband. When I asked if she had ever confessed her contraceptive use to her priest, she replied in the negative: "I just didn't think it was any of their business."[75] With this statement, and though she mitigated her deviance somewhat by portraying the decision as crucial to her husband's health rather than her own, Mary's decision to end her fertile period by going on the Pill was an asserted claim over her own reproductive system both in the past and in her reconstruction of her life.

One of the strongest characteristics of the wife/mother body in the medical and religious discourses was that it was constructed as always willing to sublimate its needs to serve the needs of the family. Mothers were expected to modify their behaviour and their very bodies to emotionally and physically manage the household even if doing so was detrimental to their own health and mental well-being. To avoid doing so was to reject one's identity as a woman. There are elements of this ideal in the narratives of many of the women I interviewed and, indeed, Mary's framing her contraceptive use as protecting her husband's health rather than out of her own desire to stop having children fits this discursive pattern.

One of the most unflinching, unconflicted portrayals of personal sacrifice for the family occurred in Diane West's history. Diane found great joy and fulfilment in her employment as a teacher, and continued teaching after her first child, a daughter, was born and throughout the pregnancy of her second child. However, just two weeks after her son was born, her husband unexpectedly died. Diane undertook extra work, such as selling Tupperware, to make ends meet, and eventually she decided to leave teaching because of her inability, as a single parent, to deal with her son's constant ill health while working at a demanding job.

I discovered that teaching is not the answer for a single mom with a teenager and a sick baby 'cause [son's name] was born premature and he had real lung problems at first. You wouldn't know it now he's a big strapping man but at that time he was sick a lot. So I thought I'm going to go back to school and I'm going to take business administration and I'm going to work in human resources.[76]

Later in the interview when I asked Diane about what was most important in her life, she went back to her experience as a teacher.

> DIANE: Oh yeah. I loved teaching far more than I ever loved working in business. You're teaching and you're working to try and explain something to a child and you go six ways from Sunday and nothing seems to work and you aren't getting through and all of a sudden you see that light go on. And it makes your whole day worthwhile.
> HEATHER: Yeah. So was it really hard to give up then since you had to give it up?
> DIANE: I had to give it up because I just didn't have the energy for it.
> HEATHER: And was that another loss almost?
> DIANE: It was tough. It was another loss. Yeah I would say that.[77]

Diane went on to talk about how she had regained some of that lost experience through her involvement in her local Rotary Club's adopted school. However, it was clear that leaving the job she loved to go into the much less demanding business administration sector was a sacrifice she made for her family, specifically her son, in the wake of her husband's sudden death. It was a sacrifice made at the cost of her own happiness and sense of fulfilment in her work.

Diane's story, in which she makes a clear decision in congruence with the dominant ideals of the motherhood role, is somewhat of an anomaly. There were other narratives of sacrifice and modification, including sacrifices that were particularly embodied, but in those cases the narrative scripts were altered and, as in the case of Mary's contraceptive use, the dominant discourse surrounding that act was distorted and reframed to give it new meaning.

Embodied and emotional sacrifices also did not always live up to their authorative discourses. According to Fiona Shortt, her marriage was not healthy. Her husband emotionally abused her before suddenly divorcing her and leaving her in a difficult emotional and financial position at the time of her interview. When they were still together Fiona consistently modified herself and her situation throughout their marriage in an effort to please her husband and bring her family together. She agreed to leave her entire birth family and emigrate to Canada, internalized the blame for her husband's passive-aggressive bouts of silence, and agreed to stop having children when he said they had had enough.[78] Fiona even went back to work on the advice of her husband's doctor.

> FIONA: I can remember my ex-husband had high blood pressure in his thirties and so he was taken into hospital. [The hospital doctor] said to me "your husband will live a minimum of ten years and a maximum of twenty-five so get off your butt and go out to work and take some of the financial strain off of him!" I was in a state of shock. So I phoned my doctor and he said, "Well Fiona that could be true." He said, "Not only that he could die and you'll have all of them to look after." You know the children to look after.
> HEATHER: And that didn't happen though obviously.
> FIONA: No. I saved him. (*laughs bitterly*) I was told not to let him worry. If there were any problems with the school I dealt with it. I dealt with my children. I never, you know, took problems to him and I just did whatever I could. And then we moved to [city name] and I went out to work and my son said to me "please mum don't go out to work." I said to him "it's better that I be a working wife than a working widow." I never told [my husband] what the doctor said.

Fiona framed this sacrifice as stemming from a failure to live up to the assurance of family safety and harmony promised to her by the dominant discourses. According to both the medical and religious doctrines, her constant work to please her husband and protect her family should have carried them through these crises. Instead, she continued to struggle and blamed the miscarriage of her third child on overstretching herself and the stress of her husband's condition.

> About a year later I went into shock. I was just going to bed and I collapsed on the living room floor crying my eyes out. And I knew it was shock. [My husband] said, "What's the matter? What's the matter?" And I didn't tell him. And that's when I had a miscarriage. I became pregnant and I was terrified of having another child. I mean we'd always planned on having another child before. But I was thinking, with high blood pressure and another mouth to feed and after what the doctor'd told me. I was absolutely terrified. And I think that's why I lost the child. I'm convinced that's why I lost the child. I've heard it said that babies know when they're not wanted.[79]

Margaret Brown's narrative of having an illegal abortion provides an interesting counterpoint to Fiona's marriage story. In both the medical and religious discourses, obtaining an abortion was the ultimate act of selfishness on the part of a woman; it signalled her emotional and spiritual alienation from the family and her innate maternal urges. Instead, Margaret framed her abortion as a supreme sacrifice that she made for her family. Far from being a singular or selfish act, it was one she undertook with her husband as a married couple. As she tells it, her husband, who originally had trained as a television antennae installer, had to quit his job because of a bad back injury. He returned to school to train as a teacher, and Margaret went back to work temporarily as a bookkeeper in a real estate office to make ends meet.

> And anyway suddenly I found out I was pregnant. And we I cried a lot. I cried and I said, "You know what this'll be the end of the dream. You'll have to stop what you are doing ... I don't know what you're gonna do." It spoiled everything. And of course him being Catholic, he was pretty upset. I said, "I want ... I'll have to get an abortion." I knew that's what I had to do. And then I thought well that's easy [husband's name] who gives them? Who do I know that does that?[80]

A short time later Margaret found out the name of a doctor who would perform illegal abortions from a male colleague at work. She went to a secret office with her husband and had the procedure. She described the aftereffects: "It was worse than having a baby. Oh God! 'Cause then you lose it. That was when I lost it and oh we did cry. We both cried. I wish I had never done it. But I had no choice! It was either that or I don't know what he would have done for a living. He had no other skills."[81] Margaret further explained that both she and her husband would have liked to have another child had the circumstances been different. She vehemently rejected the idea that her choice was a shameful one, instead saying, "I feel regretful though. I'm sorry I had to do it."[82] According to the prescriptive body discourses, such an event should have shattered the relationship between Margaret and her Catholic husband; instead, the abortion was both a shared decision and a shared pain that brought them much closer together, and at the time of the interview they were still married and continued to care deeply for one another.

These discrete events aside, there was a general sense from most of the women, particularly those who were married in the earlier years of the study period, that they would have to bend more than their husbands and to be the emotional managers of the family to make the marriage work.[83] Glenda Baker talked about the difficulty in returning to see her family in England, as she always had to travel there with her children by herself. Her husband, whom she explained had had a "bad war," refused to return to a place so fraught with painful memories.[84] Other war brides, such as Lois Adamson, Verna King, and Alice Hall spoke of repressing the loneliness of being so far away from their parents and other relatives and refocusing their energy, most often towards their children, when life got really difficult to bear.[85]

Florence Anderson and Karen Rand dealt with the more serious issue of their husband's drinking problems, which they viewed as coping mechanisms to deal with the men's war experiences. Karen notes that she finally learned to drive properly when she could no longer rely on her husband to be sober enough to drive them home.[86] Florence almost left her husband, even packing her bags and going to the Greyhound bus station, while her husband was out drinking and her boys were asleep. However, Florence said she realized that her husband's drinking was not his fault and so she returned home without him ever knowing she had left. She noted that though she had seen some of the devastation of the war while working in the WAAF, it did not compare to the horrors her husband had witnessed.

> It's hard to say this because I saw a lot myself at the [WAAF] station where I was. I saw these people coming in off the planes just scraps of humanity, badly wounded, liberated from the camps, just skeletons. I saw that. But my husband saw worse. And was actually living in it. Like I was in England. I was safe. You know those men they came home to Canada or wherever they were and they weren't given the help. They weren't given the understanding. Their refuge – a lot of them – was to go to the different clubs you know Army, Navy, Legion, different veterans' clubs where they could commiserate and be with their buddies. Well that I guess instead of really helping them it just continued it you see?[87]

War brides such as Florence may have had an easier time in shouldering this emotional management burden because it could be, and was, framed as a continuation of the home front spirit in which they engaged during the conflict. That is, these women already had a socially sanctioned script that told them how to be their family's emotional managers and portrayed that role as serving a much greater cause beyond their individual unions.[88]

In contrast, later narrators did not have such a clear-cut discursive strategy to conceptualize inequalities. Either they expected that they and their husbands would both have to undertake some modifications to ensure marital accord, as Mary Johnston, Joyce Martin, and Nancy Wilson did, or they found themselves at a loss to explain why they alone had to bend themselves to suit the family, signalling the immediate postwar years as a liminal period in gender relations. Jessica Bateman (m. 1964), for example, could never articulate why she endured the inequalities within her marriage even as she protested them, and there were times that this inability caused her to become uncomfortable and even hostile during the course of the interview.

In previous chapters the ideal that marital accord was manifested within, and reliably predicted by, sexual frequency and mutual enjoyment was the most coherent and consistently presented ideal. Medical and religious authorities continuously reinforced the sexualization of marriage; each time that they wrote about it, debated the issue, or sought to repress certain expressions of it, they increased its prestige in the social consciousness.

Some interviewees, when asked about the role sexual intercourse played within their marriages, echoed these dominant discourses by giving it a central importance to their overall union and lives. Those who constructed their married lives within the narrative framework of grand love story – the meeting of two soulmates – were especially likely to do so. Karen Rand, though widowed relatively young, remained steadfast against the possibility of marrying again, stating, "I'm a one-man woman." She had a nostalgic and even roguish smile on her face as she recalled her sexual relationship with her husband. "We had excellent sex. We did. We had a very good marriage, very compatible marriage and, um, oh sex was always there. He was (*chuckles and pauses*) *very* virile. Yeah he always liked his sex." Karen then confirmed that she liked their sexual contact as much as he did.[89] Nancy Wilson, also widowed, likewise described her marriage as fated, even divinely constructed. She noted that sexuality was a key part of their connection to each other throughout their lifetimes. "It's just a wave of energy. That just is ... I don't even know how the words ... it's so intense it blows your mind, you don't even know what your mind's doing. It's just so intense!"[90] Ironically, Nancy, who followed New Age teachings, was a self-professed "indigo child" (a special person with a unique destiny), and rejected mainstream religion, most closely echoed the Anglican and United churches' sexual mysticism when describing her experiences.

When I asked Edith Small if sex remained an important part of her relationship throughout her marriage, she replied:

> It was pretty well steady right throughout the marriage really. One of my most beautiful memories is the night before he went into hospital before he died. We knew it was serious but had no idea in our heads that this would be the last time we would be in a bed together, and that was the last

time that we had [sex]. But, um, and it was very poignant because even though we didn't realize this was the end we must have realized it was pretty bad.[91]

For these three women, their sexual relationships met the tests of both the dominant medical and religious discourses: sex was frequent, satisfying for both parties, usually included female orgasm, and was part of their larger feeling of contentment within their prescribed postwar social and biological roles. They all firmly denied ever having sex solely to fulfil their husband's needs, indicating that in addition to emotional compatibility these couples were also highly sexually well suited. Further, all three affirmed that sexuality was a lasting feature of their marriage in which they engaged throughout their lives, including in times of ill health or in the face of encroaching old age.

These women demonstrate the transmission of at least the main themes of the dominant discourses discussed in the previous two chapters. However, they rarely provided a clearly defined line of transmission between themselves and those discourses where they claimed, for example, to have taken a lesson directly from a religious or medical authority and then credited that lesson as contributing to the success of their marriage and the sexual component within it. Instead, they expressed a sense of "rightness" regarding their marriage, and this romanticism was in direct contrast to the logical, even dispassionate search for compatibility as demonstrated in the medical and religious discourses. These women used a romantic frame to narrate their acceptance of postwar sexual norms, weaving their sexual lives with their husbands into a great story of romance and "fated" connection. By framing their sexual congruence in this way, these women both fulfilled and subverted, if only slightly, the dominant prescriptive discourses in telling the stories of their own lives.

Much more deviant were the many women who, when asked about their married sexuality, were noncommittal, almost indifferent, about their experiences. When I asked Marjorie Taylor to characterize her married sex life she merely said it was "not wildly exciting," even after she learned to orgasm during penetrative sex. When I pressed her for further details she noted that she never really initiated sex, though she usually went along with it when her husband initiated. She concluded that, as a whole, their sex life was "fine." Marjorie then directed the conversation to other aspects of marriage such as her children, her tone making it clear to me that in her assessment of her marriage's overall success, sex was a minor variable at best.[92] These themes were repeated in other interviews. Verna King's only comment when I inquired as to the quality of her sexual relationship with her husband was that "it was regular."[93] Other women made it clear that sex within marriage was more important to their husbands than to themselves. They either noted, as Fiona Shortt did, that they would attempt to avoid sexual contact or fake an orgasm to end the encounter as quickly as possible, or that, like Marjorie, they went along with it if their husband initiated the contact but more out of affection for him than a personal sexual desire.[94]

For these narrators married sexuality was something that was either never a priority or only one during the early "honeymoon" phase of their marriages. In this, they rejected the dominant discourses that made sexuality the primary arbitrator of marital compatibility and longevity, destabilizing the triangular interconnections of coitus, heterosexual norms, and female gender roles that the medical and religious elites relied on to police married sex and postwar families. It is true that some of them, such as Fiona Shortt, ended up seeing their marriages end via divorce; however, the majority remained married and expressed their overall contentment with their unions because their criteria for judging their relationships were different from those of dominant postwar sexual ideals. For many of these narrators, particularly the oldest brides, it was their husband's ability to fulfil other, non-sexual aspects of the male gender role that meant their marriage was a success. Of these, the most commonly mentioned were that their husbands were consistent providers and hard workers and that their husbands were good fathers to their children; the latter criterion was largely satisfied if they were better fathers than men of the previous generation.

In focusing on their husbands' successes as a breadwinner and parent, these narrators demonstrate both the strengths and weaknesses of the authoritative ideals. That is, a male's ability to be both a good provider and father were key features of the dominant gender discourses, and unlike the sexual schema, which was undergoing recodification during this time, the gender ideal of the male as good provider had a much longer and uninterrupted history as a barometer marital success.[95] Thus, while their husbands may not have awakened in them a long-burning connubial passion – something seen as abnormal and problematic by many postwar discourses on heterosexual marriage – by foregrounding their husband's gender role compliance and at the same time exhibiting the outward signs of gender normalcy and sexual compatibility, these women displayed perfect congruence with postwar ideal embodied schemas, at least in the public eye.[96] In a sense these women took the triangle of sex, heterosexuality, and gender roles and distorted it so that gender roles became the arbitrator of sexual satisfaction rather than sexual satisfaction demonstrating proper adherence to gender roles.

Both the medical and religious discourses, in their assumption of scientific authority, used numbers and statistics whenever possible to demonstrate scientific accuracy as well as to project the image of scientific detachment. The discourses thus, in creating the contours of normality, mapped humanity along the bell curve with behaviours on either extreme end constructed as abnormal. When it came to questions of sexual frequency, my narrators demonstrated almost complete adherence to this specific understanding of "normal." In nearly every interview when I asked the narrator about the frequency of their sexual congress with their husbands, they unhesitatingly replied with some variation of "average." In doing so they were, in fact, claiming their sexual normality, as "average" took on a very different meaning during the immediate postwar era. Canadian historian Mary Louise Adams notes, in her examination of teenage sexuality and the family, that "average" or "typical" increasingly became linked with the idealized visions of normality and general sameness associated with middle-class Canadian suburban life rather than a statistical or aggregate norm. In fact the suburb itself, including the idealized Forest Hill suburb of Toronto, which was described as having "infinite variety, yet eternal sameness," became a metaphor for this new definition of average as reflective of white middle-class family norms.[97] Jenny Ellison in her examination of fat activism notes that a similar slippage between "normal" and "average" occurred in her interviews with women in the 1990s, suggesting that that the duality of these terms had considerable staying power.[98] Therefore "average," which would be taken as almost an insult by many today, was an aspirational goal in both postwar Canada and the United States, one that was simultaneously created as normal and typical and at the same time promoted as unobtainable to multiple "undesirable groups" such as persons of colour, Indigenous Canadians, and the working class.[99]

However, while being seen as average increasingly meant being seen as adhering to such class- and race-based social norms, "average" also remained ill defined and took a great deal of power from its ephemerality. When I would press my narrators to define what they understood as an average amount of sexual activity, there usually occurred a break in the interview as they struggled to find their way out of this paradox. Most of my narrators wanted to assert their sexual normality because normality was crucial in the postwar world and to their remembrances of that time, but medical, religious, and other authoritative discourses rarely defined "average" with an actual number. And at this point in the interview, as they attempted to find a way out of this dilemma, many of the narrators shifted the way they related to me. Though, as I noted earlier, the narrators tended to see me more as a junior member of a club, in need of instruction and guidance, in this moment they placed me back into the role of the distant educated expert. Viewing me as the closest approximation to an authority on sexual frequency at hand, almost all the narrators tried to elicit from me a quantified "average" with which to identify; they required a number before they could claim normality in this particular situation. Such was the power of the concept of "average" – as long as you were "average" you could claim normality. However, by not putting actual numbers to the concept of "average," dominant discourses protected its exclusivity and prevented outsiders from attempting to claim its benefits.

Only in one case, in an interview with Jean Simpson, did I actually provide an actual number. Her response is important not because she and her husband as an couple did not conform to the North American numerical average of sexual contact, but because of her desire to change her answer once she inadvertently found herself in the "abnormal" category.

> HEATHER: Yeah. So after the children were born did the sexuality remain the same?
> JEAN: Yeah I don't know. Well that's not true I'm thinking probably average. You know.
> HEATHER: What would you consider average?
> JEAN: What would we consider average? I don't know would it be somewhere between two and four times a week?
> HEATHER: That's actually above average.
> JEAN: Is it? Yeah. You see I think that's another myth that one has this idea that if you're happily married you're sort of having sex all the time yeah but nobody tells you what is an average amount. Well you know that is interesting ... so maybe I am closer to two than four I don't know. I was going to say two to three and then I thought four covers the whole thing.[100]

Upon hearing that her marriage was more sexually active than the average North American marriage – something that many people would not see as problematic or even view as worth boasting about – Jean backtracked to drastically reduce her number.[101] Further, it is obvious that Jean, highly educated with a master's degree in social work, was at least partially aware that her desire to be average was something imposed upon her by outside authoritative forces. She made the attempt both here and at other points of her interview to examine her sexual life as an outside academic observer might. Yet despite her discussion of the "myth" of average sexuality, she still ended the dialogue by trying to change her answer to place herself and her marriage within the bounds of "average" and thereby assert her and her husband's conventionality.

This desire to at least appear normal to the public, in this case represented by me as interviewer, also manifested itself when narrators became difficult, or even hostile, during the interview process. The clearest instance occurred in my interview with Jessica Bateman, who had evasive and even aggressive responses to many of my questions despite being briefed as to the interview's content as part of the process of informed consent. I wondered for a long time after the session why she had chosen to contact me for an interview at all. It was only in reviewing the transcripts later that it became clear to me that Jessica was deeply conflicted about her sexual normalcy and the role of sex within her marriage. Having been brought up a strict Lutheran, Jessica admitted that she was taught that "sex was dirty"; this view was reinforced by her mother, whose own sexual history, which included being molested by her uncle and being forced to marry Jessica's father, was complex and often tragic.[102] Jessica stated that she enjoyed having sex with her husband at the beginning of the marriage and rated it "a nine out of ten."[103] Later, her desire to return to full-time work as a nurse and subsequently open her own business strained the gender dynamic between her and her husband and caused them to become estranged, though they remained married and lived together. Near the end of the interview Jessica's sexual conflict became truly illuminated. When I asked her if she had ever wanted to break up with her husband or have an affair after he had engaged in one during their estrangement, she answered forcefully in the negative. She said that she would never have an affair, not out of loyalty to her husband (as she said she had very little left), or due to of lack of opportunity, but because she was not interested. She explained she was currently taking high blood pressure medication that had the side effect of drastically lowering her libido and described the medication as "a bit of blessing," while at the same time admitting her reaction meant that "something was wrong with [her]."[104] Jessica then related how her upbringing, combined with her experience as a community nurse, where she once witnessed a threesome during a nursing home visit, as well as what she perceived to be the sexually casual attitude of young people, caused her to view sex as a profoundly degrading act. She ended her story with the statement, "Who needs it?"[105]

Jessica's original hostility during the interview process was part of her struggle with a desire to tell a story that she felt was true and important but incongruent with authoritative norms. The only positive sexual experience she could draw on was the early sexual encounters with her husband. After their estrangement, which Jessica blamed on her husband's continued enforcement of patriarchal gender relations, she noted that those early sexual experiences became tainted with overtones of submission and degradation; the was further fueled by her own upbringing within a religious dogma that had not yet moved to celebrate married sex rather than portraying it as a necessary evil. Perhaps due to her training as a nurse, she also knew her sexual tastes were defined as aberrant; as noted above, she stated that "something was wrong with [her]." Characterizing her blood pressure medication as a blessing had less to do with its lowering her already diminished libido and more with its giving her a reason to normalize her existing lack of desire.

Jean's reframing of her answer, Jessica's difficulty in expressing her "abnormality," and the desire of all the narrators to be seen as "average" demonstrate that, despite individual nuances in how they conceptualized aspects of dominant discourses, the overall message that normality was desirable and important was clearly internalized. This tyranny of the average was present even in cases when the narrators had no actual number on which to focus.[106]

The bodies of the narrators, as white, heterosexual, cisgendered, and largely middle-class women, were rarely in direct defiance of dominant postwar norms. Their inherent social capital meant they could work within the boundaries of "normal" to create small individual changes rather than being forced into direct opposition to ideals. However, there were two cases where narrators found themselves in a state of subversion, not because they defied the norms directly or indirectly, but because their experiences were almost completely unaddressed by, and so outside the control of, the dominant schemas. Returning to Foucault's characteristics of repression and the creation of silences or non-acknowledgment, we can see that while some silences such as those inherent in the sexual innocence trope began to able to be communicated during the postwar era, other sexual and gendered aspects of heterosexual marriage remained subject to "affirmation[s] of non-existence."[107]

Though not completely absent, marital infidelity remained one of those silences within the dominant discourses. In the Catholic doctrine there was near complete silence, as marriage was viewed as insoluble and the couple would be expected to work things out with the guidance of their priest, who would be trained to deal with such issues deemed beyond lay capabilities. Though infidelity had a more obvious presence in the Protestant religious documents, it was never the focus of the intense study or debate to which other aspects of marriage were subject. People looking for guidance in the face of a partner's unfaithfulness were likely to be given some brief Christian homilies about forgiveness before the article, paper, or pamphlet moved on to another topic. In the medical discourse, infidelity, when it did appear, was even more problematic; whether the affair was her own or her husband's, it was pathological for the female in the marriage. She was at fault either because she had betrayed her natural feminine reticence to become a sexual aggressor or she had failed to fulfil the requirement of the mother body to manage the family so as to prevent such a catastrophe.

These silences meant that there was little in the way of a script created either within dominant discourses or resulting social mores that was offered to women who discovered their husbands had cheated and who then had to somehow make that betrayal fit within the narrative of their marriages and their own sexuality in those unions. Some of the narrators, such as Jessica Bateman, felt they had no choice but to ignore the indiscretion and move forward holding the marriage together the best they could, especially if they deemed the affair to be primarily physical or if they had no proof than an indiscretion had occurred.[108] Indeed, several of the narrators went out their way to make sure their suspicions that their husbands were unfaithful were never confirmed, which I see as a protective measure given their lack of alternatives. More difficult were cases such as Diane West's, whose first husband had an affair that she deemed both sexual and emotional and that she had no choice but to acknowledge. Diane's sister, who came to her house to clean while Diane worked, caught her husband and the woman in the act.

> DIANE: My sister told me. I was teaching you see and so I was working full time and so she used to do my housecleaning for me. And one day she came in and caught them.
> HEATHER: Oh my goodness.
> DIANE: So she told me what had happened and so I confronted him and I was angry. Oh I was angry!
> HEATHER: And did it take a long time to forgive him?
> DIANE: Yeah it took probably a while ... quite a while I would think. It took a while to trust him more than ... Forgive I could do. Trust was harder.

Diane was the only narrator who sought out an authority – her female United Church minister – to obtain marital counselling in response to infidelity. The interview continued:

HEATHER: And what kind of advice, like what kind of stance did she take?
DIANE: More of a, you have to learn to forgive and you have to learn to forget. And once you've forgiven you have to learn to forget or sort of put it out of your mind.
HEATHER: And what did she say to him?
DIANE: That he had to be faithful. She was quite blunt about it. But as I said we were working at such odd times we weren't connecting at that point. He was on ... he wasn't at sea at that time he was on land. He was on land based and so I don't know. It was tough. It was a really hard time.
HEATHER: And did you ever talk about that with him later?
DIANE: I don't ... I think once we got past it we didn't no we never talked about it again. It was over.[109]

All of the analysis in this passage comes from Diane, who attempted to understand what had happened from her husband's perspective and deconstruct any contributing factors. In contrast, her minister focused on creating further silences by merely stopping the infidelity and getting Diane to move past it in order to encapsulate the episode outside the larger story of Diane's marriage and marriages in general. However, one must wonder what other advice other than to forgive and forget Diane's minister could give to her. Religious and other authoritative ideals were built on the foundation that married sex was a positive barometer of marital happiness; sexual infidelity in marriage signalled that the union was fundamentally broken – abnormal. At the same time, though increasingly accepting of divorce as a last resort, many dominant discourses were invested in keeping marriages together. These two priorities conflicted with each other and essentially paralysed the authoritative sexual schemas in regard to this issue, making forgiveness, accepting blame, or careful ignorance some of the only options available to women; this was one more way ideal bodies, when confronted with the reality of real fleshy bodies in actual marriages, were weakened by that interaction.

The second, much more glaring silence was the almost complete absence of sexual danger within dominant married sexual discourses. When impossible to deny fully, according to Foucault, undesirable aspects of the sexual landscape are pushed to the margins of society. Sexual danger, unthinkable for the respectable white married woman, was seen as the fate of "bad" or damaged women who engaged in risky behaviours such as sex work, while the nuclear family was constructed as a place of safety. Sexual misconduct within marriage such as marital rape was deemed, by its absence, an impossibility. Yet, as feminism has striven to point out throughout the latter twentieth and into the twenty-first centuries, any woman can be subject to sexual danger. The fallacies of these silences were exposed by two of my narrators: Fiona Shortt and Edith Small.

As I noted at the beginning of this chapter, Fiona framed her sexual life as being bookended by two violations. The first occurred when she was molested as a young child, the second during the 1980s when she was in her fifties and after her husband had left her, when a strange man grabbed her and attempted to force her into the home she shared with her son, who was away working at the time. She started by describing how, as she was getting off the bus, a gust of wind blew her coat aside.

> FIONA: Showing my leg and I thought my God I'm inviting rape. And I walked down the lane. And I was putting my key in the lock to open the back door there was just three little steps up. And this arm came up between my legs. Like this. And the other one around my waist. And I had my hand up and the head was under here (*gesturing under her arm*). And the shoulders. And I pulled the key out right away. And I started pummelling like this (*mimes hitting him with both her fists*). "Let go! Let go! Let go!" I thought you stupid twit. (*laughs*)
>
> HEATHER: And did he just run off?
>
> FIONA: Nope. He stood up and I was there I was backed against the door you see. Couldn't do anything 'cause he was there. And he was telling me all the "nice" (*said sarcastically*) things he was going to do to me. And I couldn't scream, I couldn't call for help I couldn't do anything because I'd (*sharp intake of air*) you know. Atrophied or whatever, I couldn't do a thing. So I … I … I stood there. Just stood there. I couldn't do anything. Anyway, I began to get my voice back because I (*emits high-pitched sound*) – this little squeak coming out! And he started backing off. And then the home at the bottom of the road was being renovated and the carpenters had come back to work and they were hammering. And I was getting my voice back so I think he began to understand that I might really be yelling soon. So he started backing off … backing off. And I went to put the key in the lock and he jumped so I pulled it out again. And by this time I'm yelling a bit more. So he backs off more and I get the key in the lock and open it and jump in and then slam the door! And I sit down and I think should I call the police or shouldn't I? 'Cause I didn't get raped. And then I thought don't be so stupid he might go after someone else. And I called the police. It took them about half an hour to come.[110]

Initially Fiona said she felt fine, but later she began to experience symptoms of anxiety and fear. Luckily, the police had left her a handbook with resources for assault survivors, including the sexual assault hotline. Fiona used these services and credits the hotline in particular in helping her deal with the attack.

I was shocked by Fiona's narrative, both when she first recounted it to me and later when I transcribed it. I was surprised by how often she laughed in the retelling of what was a horrific and traumatic event in her life. It was only when I interviewed Edith Small that I began to formulate a hypothesis as to why these two women framed their experiences as they did.

Edith Small seemed even less concerned than Fiona when she narrated the story of her attack, which occurred while she was working at a greenhouse as part of the Women's Land Army during the war. She did not even frame the attack as a significant event, only mentioning it in passing as part of her larger explanation of why her first boss was highly influential in her life. The exchange, though lengthy, is worth including in its entirety as it demonstrates how often Edith veered away from the topic, which I argue indicates her discomfort at its inclusion in her life's sexual narrative.

> EDITH: Yes, well I, he [her first boss] became a great friend really. And I think the foreman of the place was of call-up age but he'd got an exemption because of his job. Um, I couldn't stand the man. He once jumped me in a ... in a shed. They'd borrowed a horse from somebody to do some work at one point, and I was the only one there that knew anything about horses and so I used to have to get up early in the morning and this animal was shedded not too far from where I was living. It was sort of on my way to the nursery. And so I used to, um, to go to this barn and look after the horse and take him to the nursery if we were using him. (*long interjection talking about wartime food shortages*) And so we borrowed this horse. I think that was the time that we harvested the potatoes. And of course I felt like somebody; 'cause here was me driving on the main road through from London with a horse and cart (*laughs*) when everyone else was on four wheels. And stopping this horse at the traffic lights (*laughs*), now I can remember I just felt like somebody up there. Everybody looking to see this woman. But um ... (*trails off*)
> HEATHER: So you said he jumped you. Do you mean he sexually assaulted you?
> EDITH: Um, he really ... he came in the shed and I didn't know he was there. And he had nothing to do there. 'Cause it was quite a distance from the ... from the premises where we worked and just a place that we had rented for the short time we had this horse. Um, anyway I was harnessing up the horse and all of a sudden somebody grabbed me from

behind and put their arms around my neck and pulled themselves right tight to me. And I turned around and it was him and (*laughs*) oh dear I gave him an elbow in the face for one thing.

HEATHER: And so nothing happened you didn't ...

EDITH: No. Nothing happened. But that's what he came there for so ...

HEATHER: So when you gave him the elbow in the face did he just sort of give up?

EDITH: Well he went very red. He was mad! He went red in the face. But I mean ... I'd never ... I couldn't ... I didn't like the man anyways so I certainly never encouraged him. But ... and he had a wife and family! But I'd gathered that this wasn't the first time that he'd ... done this sort of thing so ... He was good at his job but I don't think anybody liked him as a person. You know he was I think they only kept him there because he was a very good foreman and he knew as much about growing things under glass as the owner did.

HEATHER: And you didn't report him to your boss or anything?

EDITH: I told the boss's son who was the one that most of us talked to. And who I kept in touch with until after he died and after that with his wife because they were very good to me, um, especially around the time I got married. My mom was pretty upset about this whole thing, my marriage – she was heartbroken and so I think that his wife kinda stepped in and helped me find stuff 'cause during the war you had to travel miles to find stuff for the wedding, and I borrowed her veil I remember. Because we couldn't get one.

HEATHER: So what did the son say?

EDITH: Hmm?

HEATHER: What did the boss's son say about this guy attacking you?

EDITH: Oh, he was furious and, um, he told me he spoke to him and had a good talk with him and he said [to the man], ah, "If it weren't for your wife and children," he said, "you would be gone." And of course it was very difficult to get anybody in his place because they were all away in the war. And he said, "If there's even a hint of this again," he said, "you will be gone." So I guess he worked there until he retired but, um ...[111]

She then switched to another subject entirely.

Initially Edith was not planning to discuss the details of the assault at all, excising it from her sexual life narrative in the same way Diane was encouraged to expunge her husband's infidelity. Only when I prompted her did she expand the story, and even then she veered off on several tangents, including discussions of war shortages and the work of the Women's Land Army to combat them. Her tone, which remained even throughout the story as if these tangents had the same emotional impact on her as the assault, was also confusing to me. However, upon later analysis of her and Fiona's story together, I concluded that their seemingly inexplicable reactions to their assaults using humour and indifference were coping mechanisms, especially given the historical time period – long before #MeToo and other sexual assault awareness campaigns – in which the assaults had taken place. I was surprised that Edith continued to work at a place where a man who had assaulted her was permitted to stay; Edith suggested that the man had attacked other girls, indicating this was habitual behavior for her attacker rather than a singular event. However, in addition to her living in a culture prior to second-wave feminism that often overlooked sexual assault, it was wartime and the British national motto was "Keep calm and carry on." Edith also emphasized that it was an excellent, enjoyable job. Nor is it surprising that the boss's son, though sympathetic, did not dismiss the man, citing both his need for skilled employees during the war and the man's family. Indeed, the son's discussion with the man, in which he reminded him of his role as a breadwinner and provider, was congruent with the medical opinions of the time prescribing marriage and the nuclear family as a cure-all for many sexual deviances. Edith had few options and little real power at a time when war propaganda urged women to make sacrifices and when sexual assault was the unspoken consequence of a social system that painted men as natural sexual aggressors. Indifference, with the notable exception of her assertion that *she* had nothing to be ashamed of, avowing her innocence and his guilt, was one of the only ways she could cope and minimize the long-term impact that the event had on her.

Similarly, Fiona used humour, calling the man a "stupid twit" in her discourse to take back some power, even if only rhetorical, from her attacker. Fiona was more open about the dramatic nature of her experience both because it occurred later, in the 1980s when feminists were beginning to have some, though limited, successes in reframing violated women as innocent and also due to her own personality. Perhaps because she was able to access better counselling resources, Fiona seems to have more fully processed the event and was better able to subsume it into her sexual history in a way that Edith could not.

Contemporary and historical studies of the prevalence of rape and sexual assault suggest that out of the eighteen women I interviewed, statistically, more than two would have had such experiences. According to legal historian Constance Backhouse, experts agree that few women in Canada who experience sexual assault disclose their experiences to even close confidants and even fewer – only 6 per cent of all cases – talk to the authorities about the incident(s).[112] In her book *Carnal*

Crimes: Sexual Assault Law in Canada, 1900–1975, Backhouse recounts an interview with Velma Demerson, who at sixteen was raped by a twenty-seven-year-old chemist she was on a date with in the 1930s. Velma's testimony demonstrates the fears that women had in coming forward, demonstrating that many familiar themes such as blaming the victim were present in both the prewar and postwar eras. As Velma notes:

> I didn't tell anybody about what had happened. I didn't even tell my best friend. Why not? If I'd gone to the police, I would have been disgraced ... It would have been my fault, of course, because I went out in the car. When you think about it, thousands and thousands of us got raped this way, and never told anybody.[113]

Despite the statistical likelihood that some of the other interviewees had experienced some form of sexual assault and the fact that I asked each narrator about any negative sexual experiences, Fiona and Edith were the only narrators to reference sexual danger in their life stories. It is possible that the other sixteen women were lucky enough to avoid these situations, especially given their social advantages. However, it is also probable that some of them experienced sexual assaults but chose to keep them private. Fiona's story, though still undeniably frightening and traumatic, was particularly unusual as her attacker was a complete stranger; most sexual assaults occur closer to home, either in the workplace amongst acquaintances, as Edith's did, or in the victim's immediate circle of close friends and family. To admit that such an attack happened closer to home, especially in cases of incest, would be extremely difficult to share with a comparative stranger. Further, as Karen Dubinsky demonstrates in her study of sexual conflict, patriarchy, and assault in Ontario's industrial age, shame kept almost all the women in her study quiet about their assault, as the very fact that they were assaulted immediately put their own morality into question. As Dubinsky argues, "Good women were not associated with such sordid matters as forced sex." This automatic shaming and blaming of the victim only increased if the case "fell beyond the tightly drawn boundaries of victimhood."[114] Women raped or assaulted by strangers were more likely to be believed despite the fact that many more women were sexually assaulted or exploited by those known them.[115] As Dubinsky demonstrates, any woman engaged in heterosexual courtship behaviour outside the patriarchal bounds of propriety, such as meeting a man without a chaperone, was immediately labelled a "bad girl."

Very few women had the sexual and social capital to be viewed as pure enough to be believed over men (unless the man was non-white or of a lower class), and even those who were believed, took their cases to court, and won were subject to lingering doubts and questions within the wider society.[116] Neither Fiona nor Edith was involved in what would have been characterized as "risky" or "immoral" behaviour such as being out late, visiting bars or unsavory parts of town, or keeping company with men, which would have been used against them both in the legal courts and in the court of public opinion. They were also protected by their whiteness. As authors including Jean Barman, Robin Jarvis Brownlie, and Backhouse have demonstrated, racialized bodies, particularly Indigenous bodies, have historically been viewed as both inherently sexual and sexually available, particularly to white men, and therefore often faced a second victimization in seeking justice or redress.[117] Despite her socially prescribed racial advantage, Fiona still referenced a "blame the victim" mentality when she mentioned "inviting rape" when her coat blew open, thus demonstrating that discourse's permeating power. The other reason that Fiona and Edith might have been more willing to tell their stories is that their attackers were unsuccessful; they fought off the men and prevented a rape from actually occurring. Other women, attacked during a time when the victim of rape was culturally conditioned to feel shame, might have abided by the injunction to be silent about a more complete violation.

The eighteen women profiled in this chapter, both as a unified whole and, in some cases, separated from their bodies reaped enormous benefits from and yet simultaneously defied dominant postwar discourses such as those described in chapters 2 and 3. Their whiteness, class status, and heterosexual marriages signalled their normality to the postwar world and, as Karen Dubinksy observes, "To the normal go considerable spoils."[118] Safe in their outward appearance of normality, these women could make micro-changes to the dominant discourses usually without engaging in direct conflict. Or, to borrow a metaphor from cultural historian Susan M. Carini, the narrators' corporeal experiences served as "Coney Island" funhouse mirrors; sometimes they reflected only minor distortions and other times disfigured the image so greatly as to obscure the original picture.[119]

In many cases distortion occurred within the narrators' own consciousness as they creatively misunderstood, replaced, or reorganized dominant discourses to fit their own embodied life circumstances. Both Alice Hall and Ruth Bell distanced themselves from the feminist movement, denying its relevance to their lives and lived experiences and noting, in Alice's words, that "those feminist women were a bit crazy."[120] Yet both Alice and Ruth sought to redress what they saw as an untenable power imbalance within their marriages by reframing their acquiescence to stringent gender role separations as necessary due their husbands' particularly masculine weakness and demonstrating at least an awareness that the natural gender role separation was anything but natural. This subtle shift in the social script had a wide-reaching if individualized impact, changing the meaning of a particular event. Other times change was created by playing competing narratives against each other. Margaret Brown's refusal to feel shamed by her abortion narrative, rewriting that event as a sacrifice rather than as the epitome of selfishness, demonstrates this principle. Though Margaret utilized the "mother as martyr" dominant ideal to disempower and disregard another, more unpalatable, dominant embodied discourse that painted "women like her" as selfish and mentally disturbed, she still used her body to challenge the status quo.

In many ways it was the narrators' very corporeality that most exposed the inherent weaknesses of the dominant ideals that they were supposed to emulate – that is, the inability of those ideal bodies to encapsulate the individuality of their corporeal reality. Fiona Shortt's narrative demonstrates how an individual body could serve as a historical actor in destabilizing the efficacy of the ideal body. According to the hegemonic discourse, Fiona's actions in modifying her maternal body to preserve the health of her husband should have been rewarded by greater familial health and happiness overall. Instead of reflecting this image of domestic bliss, however, Fiona's body portrayed the distorted and broken image of her miscarriage and, later, her eventual separation and divorce.

It is unsurprising that the more generalized messages of normality enjoyed the strongest reproduction in the bodies of the informants: the broader the message, the greater chance it could be internalized by more people. All eighteen narrators clearly understood the importance of sexual normality to postwar society, and they looked for ways to demonstrate their normality to me as their lives' chronicler. This is demonstrated in the ubiquitous response of "average" to questions about sexual frequency and the fractures that occurred in the interview when I pushed narrators to specify the parameters of "average" and therefore define their own concept of the category of "normal." In their looking to me to give them a distinct number against which to define their life experience, we can observe the importance of outside expert evaluation in postwar sexual identity. Most of my narrators had internalized the ideal that elite outsiders could evaluate their bodies and embodied actions as being correct, and in the absence of any other seeming authority, they turned to the closest approximation of one – me – for that validation. They wanted me to tell them that they were doing it properly.

These moments of fracture or difficulty in the interview act as signposts to fissures inevitably occurring when narrator bodies, or embodied experience, could not be fitted into dominant discourses. We can see this within the stutters, silences, and seemingly inappropriate emotional responses in the face of marital infidelity or sexual assault. Such sexual situations were placed outside the boundaries of "normal," despite the fact that they occurred in otherwise "normal" lives and caused the narrators to struggle to articulate them as part of their overall sexual life stories. In promoting these silences, the dominant discourses also demonstrated their limited usefulness. Over the long term, those dominant ideals that could not adapt would become increasingly irrelevant. As the 1960s progressed, more self-proclaimed activist women and bodies, particularly those of colour, lesbian women, and women workers, were forced to directly challenge the status quo, but dominant ideals were also weakened from within, demonstrating Foucault's argument that every hegemony contains within itself the seeds of its own resistance and destruction.[121]

Chapter Five

Conclusion: Making Good (Sex)

In the aftermath of World War II Canada seemed to stand on the precipice of moral disaster. Two sustained international conflicts bookending an economic catastrophe caused massive shifts in the social organization of female and male gender roles, the role of the family, and the place of marriage in broader society. The Cold War atmosphere added new urgency to postwar rebuilding while at the same time its nature as a "cold" war meant that social experts finally had the breathing room and general social stability to attempt to redress the issues they saw stemming from the upheavals of the first half of the twentieth century. Ironically, and despite the current nostalgia-fueled image of the immediate postwar era as a sexually uncomplicated time, experts in the medical and religious fields attempted to create dominant discourses to recover social equilibrium and reinstate an idealized postwar status quo of gender role separation and family unity. Sex was a matter of national importance and for Western civilization as a whole. These experts sought to (re)create structures of sexual knowledges around ideal bodies to make sense of this seeming chaos and by policing bodies, especially female ones, to steer society into a new era of growth, stability, and moral certitude.

The question became, then, how does one steer something one cannot actually see? Unlike homosexuality, which was often policed through direct surveillance, denying LGBTQ2S+ folx the right to sexual privacy, one of the "dividends of normality" in the postwar era was the lack of direct scrutiny over the sexual bodies of white, middle-class, heterosexual, cisgendered marrieds. Instead, authoritative discourses and the elites who created them relied on a combination of self-regulation and indirect bodily governance.

Self-regulation is a classic example of Foucault's concept of disciplinary power, whereby citizen compliance is gained not through direct oppression but via the complex process of internalization of standards and norms that promote embodied usefulness.[1] This phenomenon can be clearly observed in the previous chapter in my narrators' desire to be seen, and represented, as sexually normal. The ubiquitous answer of "average" to questions about sexual frequency and the concomitant meaninglessness of that word, as none of my narrators could define an "average" amount of married sex, demonstrate both the pervasiveness of the overall message – be normal, and average equals normal – and the impossibility of ensuring complete compliance.

The second method, regulation through indirect governance, was more complex. Sex, sexuality, and gender roles were not distinct entities in the postwar era. In both the medical and religious discourses they came together to create a triad whereby each category drew strength from, and more importantly could be policed through, the others. Though doctors, psychiatrists, religious leaders, and moral pundits could not be in the bedrooms of the nation critiquing the frequency and sexual technique of each married couple, they could and did make assumptions about "the bedroom" based on observable factors such as gender role adherence.

In the medical discourse gender role adherence served both a diagnostic and curative function. Gender role deviance, such as a young woman wanting to continue working while her children were still very young, could cause biological symptoms such as painful periods or excessive nausea during pregnancy. Conversely, gender role adherence, the faithful and rigorous practising of gender norms, could bring reproductive organs back into a state of health. This linking of the mind, body, and social norms empowered Canadian medical men not only to treat the fleshy body but also to medicalize normal processes such as pregnancy and menopause and to prescribe social norms as part of their treatment. The fact that the mother body was permeable and communal, with the potential to be made ill by the deviations of other members of the family and vice versa, only served to further increase that medical territory and helped to solidify medical control over female sex, sexuality, and gender roles. This same kind of embodied gender role surveillance, with the important exception of homosexual men, was not applied to male bodies.

The three dominant churches did not have medicine's power to compel "patient compliance" amongst the population; postwar Canadians could and did treat religion as an open marketplace. However, the Roman Catholic, Anglican, and United churches also created and promoted the symbiotic relationship of sex, sexuality, and gender roles within their doctrines. The passive Roman Catholic woman, led sexually by her more dominant husband, was also supposed to be submissive to him socially. Her biological pull to motherhood was likewise echoed in her supposed distaste for non-procreative sex, and the church, by denigrating artificial contraception, placed itself in the role of protector of mothers, whose theology kept them from being degraded by their husbands' lust. The Protestant churches, despite their superficial advocacy of increased equality in marriage, reflected their gender role ambivalence in the ephemeral quality of their sexual theology, and "good sex" for married couples became a Band-Aid solution that belied the Protestant difficulty and hesitation in adapting to shifting moral landscapes.

On the surface, the medical and religious discourses drew strength from each other. After all, they were working towards the same general goal of promoting monogamous, heterosexual, married sex and the creation of contemporaneous ideal female bodies. However, women could and did use the nuances of each body politic against the others to make choices regarding their sexual embodiment. Mary Johnston, a devout Catholic who taught Sunday school and had five biological children with her equally devout husband, used her doctor's medical authority to override the doctrines of her priest when she decided to start taking the Pill after her fifth child was born. She justified her decision by invoking her doctor's medical concern that her fifty-year-old husband's health would be severely compromised by the need to support another child. However, with three stepchildren and five of her own, it is likely that Mary was also content to stop having children. Her use, perhaps largely unconscious, of one dominant sexual discourse (the medical ideal that birth control was positive for married couples and that the mother body should modify itself as necessary to ensure the health of the family) to counteract a personally less palatable one (the anglophone Roman Catholic focus on preserving the potential for conception in all sexual acts) demonstrates that divergent discourses could be read in conflict.

Similarly, internal contradictions and fissures within discourses could be manipulated to create new narratives that better reflected women's actual corporeal experiences. Margaret Brown's reframing of her abortion narrative as an embodied sacrifice for her family, similar to Mary's above, helped to protect her from social norms ready to paint such an action as selfish, immoral, and anti-maternal. In her recontextualization of the event Margaret engaged in what cultural scholars term "alternative readings," where the normative and dominant message of a text is subtly subverted. Alternative or oppositional readings are private forms of activism – the changes they create are often held solely within the person engaged in that reading.[2]

Other forms of activism happened in the privacy of narrators' own minds. Ruth Bell and Alice Hall both fulfilled the stereotypical housewife roles and observed strict gender divisions within their marriages but simultaneously denied that such divisions were natural. Instead, they represented their adherence to gender roles as evidence of their strength and their husbands' weakness; their acts were only necessary to protect inherently fragile male egos. Emotional management of the family, especially husbands, was a recurring theme within many of the interviews. Indeed, sixty years later it is still common for mothers to invoke their maternal sacrifice – their role in "holding it all together" – as a source of power and identity rather than as a legitimate social complaint against the patriarchal organization of society. The idea that "if mother does not do it then nobody will" can be, though not unproblematically, negotiated into "nobody but mother *can* do it." This complex dance along a spectrum spanning from subordinated victim to maternal four-star general successfully organizing the household and the lives within it demonstrates that power cannot be limited to the oversimplified binary of those who have it oppressing those who do not. Though dominant embodied discourses only allowed women, including those interviewed, a very narrow range of legitimate identities in which to engage, it also empowered those who were willing and able to fulfil those roles.

Bodies could also give "alterative or oppositional readings" to dominant discourses by acting in ways contrary to the accepted ideal and opposed to the needs and desires of the consciousnesses inhabiting them. According to both the medical and religious dogmas, Fiona Shortt's constant modification of herself both behaviourally and bodily should have resulted in long-term family harmony. That was to be the the "carrot" to help her bear the constant emotional and physical adjustments required by her husband and the society that empowered him. Yet this did not happen: her husband still left her and the emotional strain of carrying the weight of the family alone caused her, in her mind, to miscarry. Her damaged body became a testimony to the betrayal of the dominant ideal.

Bodies were not the only outside force working against the hegemony of dominant discourses. The geographical spaces that those bodies occupied also affected the sexual identities of some of the narrators as well as mitigating the power of some aspects of medical and religious body politics. Though rurality is often given a similar nostalgic framing as the postwar era, with both regarded as bastions of family stability and conservative values, rural living was more likely to destabilize than enhance postwar sexual authority.[3] In the first place, the trope of sexual innocence simply could not be sustained by those who lived with the constant evidence of sexual activity that livestock provided. Narrators who grew up in those circumstances established sexual knowledges and vocabularies long before marriage and were usually much more matter of fact and open in discussing sexuality with me.

Moreover, in rural spaces a general lack of services and a corresponding attitude of "make do" disrupted both medical and religious claims to authority. Several of the war brides interviewed who had grown up attending their local parish church in their particular sect found denominational fealty impossible in the Canadian rural west; the general lack of denominational diversity made barriers between sects extremely fluid. Florence Anderson, raised in the Anglican Church, attended Lutheran services whenever the itinerant minister came to preach in their small Prairie town because the only other religious option was the Ukrainian Orthodox Church. Though the Lutheran services required a fairly large theological adjustment, the alternative was yet more daunting, as the services were conducted in Ukrainian.[4] Living in an isolated logging town, Karen Rand had to content herself with attending occasional Anglican services with a friend in the nearest large centre, and only when that friend had access to a car.[5] Denominational scarcity resulted in many women being exposed to several different religious knowledge structures over their lifetimes, weakening the hold of a single sect on their own corporeal experience. Others chose to practise their faith privately rather than attending alternative services, effectively removing them from contact with their faith's hierarchy and limiting direct religious control over their embodied experiences.

The dominant medical discourse was almost completely urban in its make-up. Medical training, as well as major medical investigative studies, were (and remain) necessarily housed in major institutions, which are only feasible in large cities. The institutional biomedical model is also more generally based on an idealized urban setting where a physician, in treating a patient, has access to a variety of diagnostic tools and apparatuses, specialist consultations, and support as necessary from medical structures such as pharmacies, paramedics, and hospitals. In the absence of such structures, the idealized postwar relationship between the doctor and the patient changed, creating a different power exchange not based on the appearance of detached infallibility.

When Verna King's son became seriously ill with bronchial pneumonia while they were living in an isolated Prairie town, the local doctor, the town's sole car owner, drove the boy and Verna to the nearest hospital during a blizzard. An accident along the way damaged the driver-side door, which would no longer close. The doctor drove the rest of the way with one arm out the window holding that door shut. Such a comical image was in direct contrast to the dignified doctor persona that the *CMAJ* attempted to convey.[6] Joyce Martin's doctor diagnosed her, and her family, largely over the phone because it was expensive and difficult for them to get into town to meet with him in person. She would describe the symptoms to him and he would either send a prescription by mail or tell her how to treat the illness with what she had on hand, including, in one case, veterinary medicine they had for their livestock.[7] These kinds of personal interactions disrupted the dominant authoritative role of the emotionally detached medical man who inspired patient compliance via his wielding of a dominant knowledge structure, and replaced it with a deeper, more individual, sense of trust that came from physician and patient working together. Verna and Joyce both felt that they were partners working with the doctor to ensure their families' health. As Joyce put it, "Things like that just meant a lot to us because we had no money and a trip to the doctor for no reason was unheard of. And we just had such a good working relationship."[8] Joyce's use of the phrase "working relationship" is particularly illuminating: it denotes a collegial rather than authoritarian rapport.

Whether urban, suburban, or rural, the narrators profiled in this book commanded a great deal of social capital that they used to enact resistances and to create spaces within the dominant discourses rather than challenging them outright. Even when they did directly contradict authoritative body politics, however, they were able to leverage their normality to minimize any potential negative consequences. We can see this performed by the significant number of the women I interviewed, particularly amongst the older cohort, who denied sex as a crucial factor in marriage or barometer for the success of their unions. Sex, for them, just was not that important. In making this claim they outright rejected not only the core doctrines of the medical and religious female body politics but also the many other authorities from government agencies to popular culture who promoted the same ideal that good sex was one of the most (if not the most) crucial criteria in maintaining and evaluating heterosexual marriage.

Instead these women looked to older, more established indicators of their overall marital success. Most substituted gender role adherence for sexual frequency and quality, praising their husbands for being reliable, consistent providers rather than accomplished lovers. In doing so, these narrators again demonstrated the power that they had to stretch the boundaries of "normal," and at the same time demonstrated the fundamental weakness in the postwar attempt to use public displays of gender to police private sexuality. That is, using gender roles to signal sexual

Conclusion: Making Good (Sex) 143

compliance only worked if society as a whole agreed that sex, sexuality, and gender were all part of the same unit; clearly not everyone did.

How do we reconcile the multiple paradoxes that characterize the sexual landscape of the postwar era? How can we comprehend the irony of a seemingly sexually quiescent and norm-conforming generation of women that yet would raise the women who swelled the ranks of the second wave of feminism and the sexual revolution, and in some cases joined those ranks themselves? Years before the first publication of *Our Bodies, Ourselves*, before the first performance of *The Vagina Monologues*, before *Cosmopolitan* and *Sex and the City* made the word "vagina" part of public vocabulary, how did women understand and relate to their sexual organs? What did postwar wives and mothers, reduced by popular reimagining to a straw avatar cheerfully vacuuming in her heels, actually think about sex and their own sexual embodiment?

The answer, as this book demonstrates, is necessarily complex. It begins with abandoning the myth that the immediate postwar era was a bucolic, desexualized oasis in history, epitomized by the pop culture image of twin beds in the master suite chastely separated by a nightstand. Further, we must understand that bodies, in order to create change, need not be in direct contravention of the dominant ideal. The majority of the time, in the majority of ways, the bodies of the narrators profiled in this book conformed to the general prescriptions of authoritative ideals. Indeed, they benefitted from their veneer of normality. Yet it was from this position of power that their bodies, in their inescapably individuality, could realize change. Some of these changes were the result of conscious choices to rework the boundaries of the sexual frameworks that constrained them. Others were artefacts of the day-to-day, minute-to-minute negotiations required to make individual lives fit generalized ideals. Indeed, it is this simultaneous paradoxical mix of moments of progressive consciousness with the wholesale rejection of feminism expressed by many narrators – the blending of radical and conservative viewpoints – that makes the evaluation of the embodied political standpoints of postwar women so difficult. Protected by their white heterosexual bodies, these women were still like fractured or distorted "Coney Island" mirrors, yieldinging imperfect reflections of the ideal bodies they were meant to emulate.[9] Instead of producing a never-ending series of perfect copies as two intact, parallel mirrors would do, real "fleshy" bodies rebounded their own distortions back onto the ideal body, creating imperfections within that ideal by demonstrating its unreality.

Such challenges and changes were often private and always privileged, but still helped to shape the contours of the concept of "good sex" that maintains an enormous presence in present-day Canada. Recently democratized to include relationships beyond heterosexual marriage, it is ubiquitous: one only has to tune into the latest celebrity psychologist television show or browse the covers of the many lifestyle magazines at the grocery store checkout aisle to be inundated with the message that good sex is important to adult relationships (and myriad tips to achieve this crucial benchmark.) What Canadians do not seem to recognize is that good sex does not just stem from the free lovers or the explosive sexual revolutions of the late 1960s and the 1970s. Its history is equally rooted in the conservative need for embodied citizen control and social rebuilding that characterized the immediate postwar years.

Appendix: Interview Data

Note: all names are pseudonyms.

Interview participants were recruited via a series of advertisements and targeted information campaigns focused on western retirement social and housing organizations in order to attract participants of the right age. Additionally, in cooperation with the provincial war bride associations of British Columbia, Alberta, Saskatchewan, and Manitoba, information packages were sent to their member mailing lists. Interested women who viewed the call for participants then contacted me to arrange for interviews in person or via telephone. The targeted mailing of the war bride member lists resulted in a majority of interview participants coming from that group. What follows is limited contextual data about each narrator and the relevant topics of this work. These data remain necessarily limited due to the research ethics protocols under which the original research was done, which require that no details be given about any of the narrators that would allow them or any third party (particularly their family members) to be identified. Each interview was loosely structured and participant led, meaning that details vary greatly between each narrator.

Lois Adamson

Date and circumstances of interview: Via the telephone, 19 March 2010.

Date and circumstances of marriage: Married in 1945 at the age eighteen as a war bride in England. Widowed and remarried at time of interview.

Children and pregnancies: Four children. No mention of other pregnancies.

Religious circumstances: Raised as a Catholic but was married in the Anglican Church because the Catholic priest refused to marry them in the church without her fiancé going through the required Catholic training. They could not do this because he was about to be deployed. After the war ended they had their marriage blessed by a Canadian Catholic priest. Adamson remained active in the Catholic Church throughout her life. Her husband did not convert.

Additional medical knowledges: None.

Living environment: Suburbs outside a large Prairie city.

Florence Anderson

Date and circumstances of interview: Interviewed in her home, 20 September 2010.

Date and circumstances of marriage: Married in 1945 at unknown age as a war bride in England. Widowed at time of interview.

Children and pregnancies: Three children. No mention of other pregnancies.

Religious circumstances: Raised and married in the Anglican Church. Husband was Lutheran. She and husband converted to the United Church upon settling in Canada because it was the closest available church to their birth faiths. Other nearby churches were Ukrainian Orthodox. They both remained active in the church throughout their lives.

Additional medical knowledges: None.

Living environment: Took over her husband's father's farm in the rural Prairies.

Glenda Baker

Date and circumstances of interview: Interviewed in her home, 20 September 2010.

Date and circumstances of marriage: Married in 1945 at age nineteen as a war bride in England. At time of interview her she had remarried after her first husband's death and had been widowed for a second time.

Children and pregnancies: Three children, including a set of fraternal twins, one of whom died soon after birth.

Religious circumstances: Raised and married in the Anglican Church. Husband was a Roman Catholic, but she did not want to convert or have the pared-down ceremony required if both participants were not converted.

Additional medical knowledges: None.

Living environment: Small rural towns and smaller cities in the Prairies.

Jessica Bateman

Date and circumstances of interview: Interviewed in her home, 19 July 2010.

Date and circumstances of marriage: Married in 1964 at age twenty-two. At time of interview she was still married to her first husband but almost completely estranged from him and the two occupied separate bedrooms. Neither she nor her husband were considering divorce due to their religious beliefs.

Children and pregnancies: Three children. No mention of other pregnancies.

Religious circumstances: Raised and married in the Lutheran Church. She and her husband received premarital counselling in that church. She remained active in her faith.

Additional medical knowledges: Trained as a nurse, so had increased exposure to and knowledge of medical discourses.

Living environment: Initially, small rural areas of the Prairies, and then moved to a larger city.

Ruth Bell

Date and circumstances of interview: Interviewed in her home, 21 September 2010.

Date and circumstances of marriage: Married in 1943 at age seventeen in England as a war bride. Widowed at time of interview.

Children and pregnancies: Four biological children and one foster daughter.

Religious circumstances: Married in the Anglican church. Attended the United Church, as it was the only church near her home, but never officially converted. Her children were baptised in the United Church.

Additional medical knowledges: None.

Living environment: Both rural areas and small towns in the Prairies.

Margaret Brown

Date and circumstances of interview: Interviewed in her home, 27 June 2010.

Date and circumstances of marriage: Married at 1947 at age nineteen as a war bride in England; still living together at time of interview.

Children and pregnancies: Four children and one illegal abortion.

Religious circumstances: Raised in the Anglican Church. Husband raised as a Catholic. They had to be married in the Anglican Church because wartime circumstances did not allow time for the process of being married in the Catholic Church. All of the children were raised Catholic. Brown attended the Catholic Church with her husband throughout their lives, but she never converted and does not take communion. They have both bought burial plots in the Catholic cemetery. Brown refused to convert officially, as she felt she had given up enough to marry her husband and to emigrate to Canada.

Additional medical knowledges: Had increased interaction with the medical and psychiatric community because she developed agoraphobia when her children were young.

Living environment: First in the rural Prairies, then returned to live in England for several years before living in large cities in Ontario and British Columbia.

Evelyn Carter

Date and circumstances of interview: Interviewed in her home, 20 September 2010.

Date and circumstances of marriage: Married in 1945 at an unknown age as a war bride in England. Widowed at time of interview.

Children and pregnancies: Three children from three normal pregnancies.

Religious circumstances: Married in the Presbyterian Church. Husband was raised in the United Church.

Additional medical knowledges: None.

Living environment: Rural areas in the Prairies.

Alice Hall

Date and circumstances of interview: Interviewed in her home, 28 June 2010.

Date and circumstances of marriage: Married in 1945 at age twenty-four as a war bride in England. Still married and living with her husband at time of interview.

Children and pregnancies: Three children. No mention of other pregnancies.

Religious circumstances: Raised in the Anglican Church. Husband was raised in the United Church. They started attending the Anglican Church after the war, and the first two children were baptised in the Anglican Church. They later converted to the United Church, where their last child was baptised.

Additional medical knowledges: None

Living environment: Suburb of a large Prairie city.

Mary Johnston

Date and circumstances of interview: Interviewed in her home, 19 April 2010.

Date and circumstances of marriage: Married in 1952 at an unknown age, to a widower with three young children. Widowed at time of interview.

Children and pregnancies: Step-mother to three children from her husband's previous marriage. She and her husband had five more children, for a total of eight.

Religious circumstances: Devout Roman Catholic who had taught in a Catholic school. Her husband was also a Roman Catholic, and they were married in the Roman Catholic Church. Oddly, she does not recall having premarital counselling in the church.

Additional medical knowledges: None.

Living environment: Lived just outside, and later within, a large city in the Prairies.

Verna King

Date and circumstances of interview: Interviewed in her home, 20 September 2010.

Date and circumstances of marriage: Married at age twenty as a war bride in 1942 in Scotland. Widowed at time of interview.

Children and pregnancies: Had three children. No mention of other pregnancies.

Religious circumstances: Raised and married in the Presbyterian Church. Her husband was United Church but rarely attended. She attended the United Church in Canada because there was no Presbyterian Church nearby her home. She noted that the church was not really a large part of her adult life.

Additional medical knowledges: None.

Living environment: Several small rural areas and one large city in the Prairies.

Joyce Martin

Date and circumstances of interview: Interviewed via telephone, 4 October 2010.

Date and circumstances of marriage: Married at age twenty-one in 1961 in a double wedding with her sister to save money. At time of interview she and her husband were still married and living together.

Children and pregnancies: Had two children after being successfully treated for infertility.

Religious circumstances: Raised and married in the United Church. Her husband was a Prairie Mennonite but did not attend services. She remained involved in the United Church and taught Sunday school but left the church when they started allowing openly gay ministers to preach. (*Note*: The United Church started discussing the question of gay ministers in the 1980s, and the first openly gay minister was ordained in 1992.)

Additional medical knowledges: Had extended relationships with doctors due to being treated for infertility and so had increased exposure to medical discourses.

Living environment: Small towns in the rural Prairies.

Karen Rand

Date and circumstances of interview: Interviewed in her home, 7 July 2010.

Date and circumstances of marriage: Married in 1945 at age nineteen as a war bride in England. Widowed at time of interview.

Children and pregnancies: Three children. No mention of other pregnancies.

Religious circumstances: Raised and married in the Anglican Church. Husband's family were prominent Methodists, but he had converted to the United Church. They were given pre-marriage counselling by the army padre. She cannot remember what denomination the padre represented. She converted to the United Church upon arriving in Canada. All of the children were baptised in the United Church. Gradually started only attending church on special occasions due to lack of churches in some of the areas they lived in.

Additional medical knowledges: Trained as a nurse during the war so had some extra exposure to and understanding of medical discourses.

Living environment: Rural areas and a larger city in British Columbia.

Fiona Shortt

Date and circumstances of interview: Interviewed in her home, 5 July 2010.

Date and circumstances of marriage: Married at age twenty in England in 1952. (She was not a war bride.) At time of interview she had been divorced after thirty-six years of marriage. Her husband had remarried but she had not.

Children and pregnancies: Three children with four pregnancies and one miscarriage. Attempted to adopt an older child early on in the marriage, but it was not a good fit and the child was returned to public care after one week. Had severe anxiety and depression while pregnant.

Religious circumstances: Raised a Catholic. Her husband was not a Catholic but underwent the teaching process so they could be married with a limited ceremony in the Catholic Church, though he did not convert. She remained active in the church until her oldest child was old enough to go to Sunday School. She then decided that the Catholic Church was harmful and left, though she remained a non-practising Christian.

Additional medical knowledges: None.

Living environment: Married in England and emigrated to Canada early in the marriage. Within Canada she lived in medium and large cities in Ontario and British Columbia.

Jean Simpson

Date and circumstances of interview: Interviewed in her home, 5 July 2010.

Date and circumstances of marriage: Married at age twenty-four in 1963 by a Unitarian minister. The only couple to be married outside a church, as they were married in her sister's backyard. At time of interview she and her husband were still married and living together.

Children and pregnancies: Two children and one pregnancy that ended in a miscarriage.

Religious circumstances: She and her husband received some premarital counselling by the Unitarian minister who officiated their wedding. She came from an ethnically Jewish background; her husband was raised in the United Church. Neither she nor her husband were particularly involved in any religion throughout their adult lives.

Additional medical knowledges: Trained as a social worker and husband was a family doctor, so she had increased exposure to and understanding of medical and social science discourses. She and her husband went to a psychiatrist for marital counselling when their children were young.

Living environment: Large and medium cities in Ontario and British Columbia.

Edith Small

Date and circumstances of interview: Interviewed in her home, 19 September 2010.

Date and circumstances of marriage: Married in 1945 at age twenty-one as a war bride in England. Widowed at time of interview.

Children and pregnancies: Five children and seven pregnancies, including one miscarriage and one ectopic pregnancy that burst one of her fallopian tubes.

Religious circumstances: She and her husband were both raised as Anglicans and were married in the Anglican Church. They continued to be very involved in the church throughout their married lives. Small was ordained after she was widowed later in life.

Additional medical knowledges: Except about the ectopic pregnancy, none.

Living environment: Small towns in the Prairies.

Marjorie Taylor

Date and circumstances of interview: Interviewed via telephone, 17 October 2010.

Date and circumstances of marriage: Married in 1946 at age twenty-one as a war bride. Widowed at time of interview. She and her husband had been estranged for much of their marriage, though she had reconciled with him near the end of his life.

Children and pregnancies: Two children. She suffered badly from postpartum depression after each birth.

Religious circumstances: She and her husband both attended the Anglican Church as part of their role in the navy. She was in the Women's Royal Naval Service (WRNS). They were married in the Congregational Church, though it is unclear why they chose that denomination and whether either of them had been raised in it. Once in Canada she and her husband converted to the United Church. They received marital counselling through their church in the middle of their marriage to address her husband's issues with jealousy. Just prior to the interview she had converted to Unitarianism.

Additional medical knowledges: None.

Living environment: Suburbs of large cities in Quebec, Ontario, and British Columbia.

Diane West

Date and circumstances of interview: Interviewed in her home, 19 July 2010.

Date and circumstances of marriage: Married in 1957 in the United Church at age twenty-one. She and her husband had premarital counselling in that church. Her first husband died almost immediately after the birth of their second child. She was then engaged to another man but broke it off. She remarried in the 1980s and was living with her second husband at time of interview.

Children and pregnancies: Two children. Husband died a few weeks after the second child was born.

Religious circumstances: Raised Anglican but moved to the United Church because she had a disagreement with the Anglican Church Sunday School teacher as a child. As a young girl she was also involved in the Canadian Girls in Training, which was affiliated with the United Church. After her second marriage she returned to the Anglican Church, as she felt it had a more robust liturgy.

Additional medical knowledges: Her mother was a nurse and so she had some extra exposure to medical knowledges and discourses regarding puberty and sex.

Living environment: Large and medium cities in British Columbia and in the Prairies.

Nancy Wilson

Date and circumstances of interview: Interviewed in her home, 19 April 2010.

Date and circumstances of marriage: Married at age nineteen in 1966 in an unknown location. Widowed at time of interview.

Children and pregnancies: Three pregnancies, one of which she miscarried. Her fertility was limited in part by natural infertility that was not treated.

Religious circumstances: Throughout her life she believed in New Age spiritualism, including spirit guides, auras, and astrology. She believed she was an "indigo child," meaning that she had special abilities, including a heightened empathy and clairaudience, that allowed her to hear messages from the spirit world. Her belief system also led her to believe she and her husband were destined to meet each other. She distrusted many doctors and followed New Age healing, including naturopathy, herbal remedies, and acupuncture.

Any special medical interactions: She had an interest in herbalism and naturopathy and was self-educated in this by reading books and consulting practitioners. She and her husband had a brief interaction with a psychiatrist to address marriage problems but Wilson disliked it and so they stopped going.

Living environment: Grew up in the rural Prairies and then lived in large and medium cities and small towns throughout British Columbia and in the Prairies.

Notes

1. Breaking Free from the "Nostalgia Trap": History and the Paradox of Female Sexuality in the Postwar World

1 The Boston Women's Health Collective, *Our Bodies, Ourselves: A Book by and for Women* (New York: Simon and Schuster, 1973).
2 For Australia see for example Lisa Featherstone, "'The One Single Primary Cause': Divorce, the Family, and Heterosexual Pleasure in Postwar Australia," *Journal of Australian Studies* 37, no. 3 (2013): 349–63; John Murphy, *Imagining the Fifties: Private Sentiment and Political Culture in Menzies' Australia* (Kensington: UNSW Press, 2000). For Britain see for example Marcus Collins, *Modern Love: An Intimate History of Men and Women in the Twentieth Century* (London: Atlantic, 2003); Claire Langhamer, "The Meanings of Home in Postwar Britain," *Journal of Contemporary History* 40, no. 2 (2005): 341–62. For France see for example Kelly Ricciardi Colvin, "'A Well-Made-Up Woman': Aesthetics and Conformity in Postwar France," *French Historical Studies* 38, no. 4 (2015): 691–718; Sarah Fishman, *From Vichy to the Sexual Revolution: Gender and Family Life in Postwar France* (Oxford: Oxford University Press, 2017).
3 Stephanie Coontz, *The Way We Never Were: American Families and the Nostalgia Trap* (New York: Basic Books, 1992). There are myriad examples of concern about social and moral decay that will be explored throughout this work. Significantly, postwar Canada was compared to the last days of the Roman Empire. Historical works of that time often repeated the dominant narrative that it was a fundamental breakdown in society and morality that caused the Roman Empire to collapse. See Reverend Canon W.H. Davidson, *The Nature of Marriage* (Montreal: R.A. Regnault, 1946), 3; United Church Archives of Canada (hereafter "UCAC"), Accn. 77051C, f. 177-2, pamphlet, David A. MacLennan, "Family Life," n.d.

4 For a discussion of the different ways that discourse can become hegemonic common-sense truths, see for example Trevor Purvis and Alan Hunt, "Discourse, Ideology, Discourse, Ideology, Discourse, Ideology ...," *British Journal of Sociology* 44, no. 3 (1993): 473–99.
5 Privacy was, of course, a dividend of middle-class heterosexuality. Many authors have demonstrated how gay men sought out semi-private spaces such as public toilets and bath houses for sexual encounters, which facilities were subject to surveillance and raids by law enforcement. See for example Gary Kinsman and Patrizia Gentile, *The Canadian War on Queers: National Security as Sexual Regulation* (Vancouver, UBC Press, 2010); Valerie J. Korinek, *Prairie Fairies: A History of Queer Communities and People in Western Canada, 1930–1985* (Toronto: University of Toronto Press, 2018); Steven Maynard, "Through a Hole in the Lavatory Wall: Homosexual Subcultures, Police Surveillance, and the Dialectics of Discovery, Toronto, 1890–1930," *Journal of the History of Sexuality* 5, no. 2 (1994): 207–42.
6 Karen Dubinsky, *The Second Greatest Disappointment: Honeymooning and Tourism at Niagara Falls* (Toronto: Between the Lines, 1999), 228.
7 Gerard Bouchard, "La sexualité comme practique et rapport social chez les couples paysans du Saguenay (1860–1930)," *Revue d'histoire de l'Amerique française* 53, no. 2 (2000): 183–217.
8 Sandra Bartky, *Femininity and Domination: Studies in the Phenomenology of Oppression.* (New York: Routledge, 1990), 74–5.
9 Michel Foucault extensively examines the process of creating silences and the policing of bodies. For his work on silences created to police the sexual body see *The History of Sexuality: An Introduction, Volume I*, trans. Robert Hurley (New York: Vintage Books, 1990). On how bodies are policed through the institutional biomedical model see *The Birth of the Clinic: An Archeology of Medical Perception*, trans. A.M. Sheridan (London: Routledge, 1989). On how people are taught to police their own embodiment see *Discipline & Punish: The Birth of the Prison*, trans. Alan Sheridan (New York: Vintage Books, 1995). This book is theoretically informed by these works and by Foucault's essays collected in *Power/Knowledge: Selected Interviews and Other Writings, 1972–1977*, ed. Colin Gordon, trans. Colin Gordon et al. (New York: Pantheon Books, 1980); and in *Abnormal: Lectures at the Collège de France, 1974–1975*, ed. Valerio Marchetti and Antonella Salmoni, trans. Graham Burchell (New York: Picador 1999).
10 Foucault, *History of Sexuality*, 17–35.
11 Joanne Meyerwitz, ed., *Not June Cleaver: Women and Gender in Postwar American, 1945–1960* (Philadelphia: Temple University Press, 1994); Valerie J. Korinek, *Roughing It in the Suburbs: Reading* Chatelaine *Magazine in the Fifties and Sixties* (Toronto: University of Toronto Press, 2000); Jennifer A. Stephen, "Balancing Equality for the Post-War Woman:

Demobilising Canada's Women Workers after World War Two," *Atlantis* 31, no. 1 (2007): 125–35; Veronica Strong-Boag, "Home Dreams: Women and the Suburban Experiment in Canada, 1945–60," *Canadian Historical Review* 72, no. 4 (1991): 471–504.

12 Marlene Epp and Franca Iacovetta, eds., *Sisters or Strangers?: Immigrant, Ethnic, and Racialized Women in Canadian History*, 2nd ed. (Toronto: University of Toronto Press, 2016); Franca Iacovetta, *Gatekeepers: Reshaping Immigrant Lives in Cold War Canada* (Toronto: Between the Lines, 2006); Joan Sangster, "Incarcerating 'Bad Girls': The Regulation of Sexuality through the Female Refuges Act in Ontario, 1920–1945," *Journal of the History of Sexuality* 7, no. 2 (1996): 239–75; Sangster, *Regulating Girls and Women: Sexuality, Family, and the Law in Ontario, 1920–1960* (Oxford: Oxford University Press, 2001).

13 Doug Owram, *Born at the Right Time: A History of the Baby Boom Generation* (Toronto: University of Toronto Press, 1996), 82.

14 Mary Louise Adams, *The Trouble with Normal: Postwar Youth and the Making of Heterosexuality* (Toronto: University of Toronto Press, 1997); Mona Gleason, *Normalizing the Ideal: Psychology, Schooling, and the Family in Postwar Canada* (Toronto: University Press, 1999). See also Magda Fahrni and Robert Rutherdale, eds., *Creating Postwar Canada: Community, Diversity, and Dissent, 1945–75* (Vancouver: UBC Press, 2008).

15 For histories of sexual activism see Brett Beemyn, ed., *Creating a Place for Ourselves: Lesbian, Gay, and Bisexual Community Histories* (New York: Routledge 1997); John D'Emilio and Estelle B. Freedman, *Intimate Matters: A History of Sexuality in America* (New York: Harper & Row, 1988); Elise Chenier, "Rethinking Class in Lesbian Bar Culture: Living 'The Gay Life' in Toronto, 1955–1965," *Left History* 9, no. 2 (2004): 85–118; Cameron Duder, *Awfully Devoted Women: Lesbian Lives in Canada, 1900–65* (Vancouver: UBC Press, 2010); Jonathan Ned Katz, *The Invention of Heterosexuality* (Chicago: University of Chicago Press, 1995); Katz, *Love Stories: Sex between Men before Homosexuality* (Chicago: Chicago University Press, 2001); Gary Kinsman, *The Regulation of Desire: Sexuality in Canada* (Montreal: Black Rose Books, 1987); Gary Kinsman and Patrizia Gentile, *The Canadian War on Queers*; Korinek, *Prairie Fairies*; Tom Warner, *Never Going Back: A History of Queer Activism in Canada* (Toronto: University of Toronto Press, 2002); Martha Vicinus, *Intimate Friends: Women Who Loved Women, 1778–1928* (Chicago: Chicago University Press, 2004).

16 Patrizia Gentile and Jane Nicholas, eds., *Contesting Bodies and Nation in Canadian History* (Toronto: University of Toronto Press, 2013); Jane Nicholas, *The Modern Girl: Feminine Modernities, the Body, and Commodities in the 1920s* (Toronto: University of Toronto Press, 2015); Nicholas, *Canadian*

Carnival Freaks and the Extraordinary Body, 1900–1970s (Toronto: University of Toronto Press, 2018).

17 Embodied history is an emerging discipline and has been most consistently used by early modern historians, though others have begun to make inroads. See Edward Berhrend-Martinez, "Manhood and the Neutered Body in the Early Modern Spain," *Journal of Social History* 38, no. 4 (2005): 1073–93; Joanna Bourke, *Dismembering the Male: Men's Bodies, Britain and the Great War* (Chicago: University of Chicago, 1996); Joanna Bourke, *The Story of Pain: From Prayer to Painkillers* (Oxford: Oxford University Press, 2014); Barbara Duden, "History Beneath the Skin," *Michigan Quarterly Review* 30, no. 1 (1991): 174–90; Gentile and Nicholas, *Contesting Bodies and Nation*; Nicholas, *The Modern Girl*.

18 I have taken this term from Joanna Bourke's article "Sexual Violence, Marital Guidance, and Victorian Bodies: An Aesthesiology," *Victorian Studies* 50, no. 3 (2008): 419–36.

19 Duden, "History Beneath the Skin, 174–75.

20 See for example Bourke, *Dismembering the Male*; Joanna Bourke, *Fear: A Cultural History* (Emeryville, CA: Shoemaker Hoard, 2006); Lisa Helps, "Body, Power, Desire: Mapping Canadian Body History," *Journal of Canadian Studies/Revue d'études canadiennes* 41, no. 1 (2007): 126–50; Elaine Scarry, *The Body in the Pain: the Making and Unmaking of the World* (Oxford University Press, 1985); Joy Parr, "Notes for a More Sensuous History of Twentieth-Century Canada: The Timely, the Tacit, and the Material Body," *Canadian Historical Review* 82, no. 4 (2001): 719–45.

21 Carolyn J. Dean, *The Frail Social Body: Pornography, Homosexuality and Other Fantasies in Interwar France* (Berkley: University of California Press, 2000); Duden, "History Beneath the Skin"; Moira Gatens, *Imaginary Bodies: Ethics, Power, and Corporeality* (New York: Routledge, 1996).

22 For further information on the importance to sex and sexuality to the Canadian nation see Heather Stanley, "Primal Urge/National Force: Sex, Sexuality, and National History," in *Reading Canadian Women's and Gender History* ed. Nancy Janovicek and Carmen Nielson (Toronto: University of Toronto Press, 2019), 225–77.

23 Gatens, *Imaginary Bodies*, 21–7.

24 See for example Tina Block, *The Secular Northwest: Religion and Irreligion in Everyday Postwar Life* (Vancouver: UBC Press, 2016), 56–8; Brian Clark and Stuart Macdonald, *Leaving Christianity: Changing Allegiances in Canada since 1945* (Montreal & Kingston: McGill-Queen's University Press, 2017), 67–70, 141–9, 164.

25 This is one of the main arguments in Nancy Christie and Michael Gauvreau, *A Full-Orbed Christianity: The Protestant Churches and Social Welfare*

in Canada, 1900–1940 (Montreal & Kingston: McGill-Queen's University Press, 1996).

26 The question of whether "the fifties" presented a gendered break between the advances made by women in World War II and the second-wave feminist movement is largely ancillary to the main argument of this book. However, I do see the "wave" metaphor as overly simplistic and often the result of focusing primarily on white, cisgendered, middle-class, heterosexual women's definition of activism. Using such a limited definition of activism, many of the women interviewed for this book saw themselves as apolitical or directly defined themselves against "women's libbers" of the second-wave feminist movement in Canada. Yet, as chapters 4 and 5 demonstrate, these women were also engaged in disrupting the gendered status quo. This work therefore aligns with other scholarship seeking to broaden concepts of activism and resistance and sees lines of continuity in the search for gender equality between World War II and the Cold War era. In the Canadian context, Joan Sangster has written extensively about these lines of continuity. See for example Sangster, "Radical Ruptures: Feminism, Labor and the Left in the Long Sixties in Canada," *American Review of Canadian Studies* 40, no. 1 (2010), 1–21; "Creating Popular Histories: Reinterpreting 'Second Wave Canadian Feminism,'" *Dialectical Anthropology* 39 (2015): 381–404; and, with Linda Kealey, "Introduction," in *Beyond the Vote: Canadian Women and Politics*, ed. Linda Keeley and Joan Sangster (Toronto: University of Toronto Press, 1989), 3–15. See also Sandra Burt, Lorraine Code, and Lindsay Dorney, eds., *Changing Patterns: Women in Canada* (Toronto: McClelland & Stewart, 1988; Dorothy Sue Cobble, *The Other Women's Movement: Workplace Justice and Social Rights in America* (Princeton: Princeton University Press, 2004); Micheline Dumont, "The Origins of the Women's Movement in Quebec," trans. Carol Cochrane, in *Challenging Times: The Women's Movements in Canada and the United States*, ed. Constance Backhouse and David H. Flaherty (Montreal & Kingston: McGill-Queen's University Press, 1992), 72–89; Nancy Hewitt, *No Permanent Waves: Recasting Histories of U.S. Feminism* (New Brunswick: Rutgers University Press, 2004); Jill McCalla Vickers, "Feminist Approaches to Women in Politics," in *Beyond the Vote: Canadian Women and Politics*, ed. Linda Kealey and Joan Sangster (Toronto: University of Toronto Press, 1989), 16–36.

2. Embodying Family Values: The *Canadian Medical Association Journal* and the Creation of the "Mother Body"

1 R.A.H. Kinch, "Sexual Difficulties after 50: The Gynecologist's View," *Canadian Medical Association Journal* (hereafter *CMAJ*), 29 January 1966, 211.

2 Wendy Mitchinson, *The Nature of Their Bodies: Women and Their Doctors in Victoria Canada* (Toronto: University of Toronto Press, 1991); Mitchinson, *Bodily Failure: Medical Views of Women, 1900–1950* (Toronto: University of Toronto Press, 2013).
3 Cheryl Krasnick Warsh, *Prescribed Norms: Women and Health in Canada and the United States since 1800* (Toronto: University of Toronto Press, 2010).
4 Cynthia R. Comacchio, *Nations Are Built of Babies: Saving Ontario's Mothers and Children, 1900–1940* (Montreal & Kingston: McGill-Queen's University Press, 1993); Denyse Baillargeon, *Babies for the Nation: The Medicalization of Motherhood in Quebec, 1910–1970*, trans. Donald W. Wilson (Waterloo: Wilfred Laurier University Press, 2009). Additionally, Katheryn McPherson and Helen Lenskyj examine similar interactions among the concepts of femininity, motherhood, the body, and sexuality in the professions of nursing and women's sports, respectively. McPherson, *Bedside Matters: The Transformation of Canadian Nursing, 1900–1990* (Toronto: University of Toronto Press, 2003); Lenskyj, *Out of Bounds: Women, Sport and Sexuality* (Toronto: Women's Press, 1986).
5 With the exception of Wendy Mitchinson's valuable insights in *Fighting Fat: Canada 1920–1980* (Toronto: University of Toronto Press, 2018), 270–3, there are very few studies examining the history of the *Canadian Medical Association Journal*. The majority are written by medical men writing as amateur historians and in which the *CMAJ* is mentioned only briefly. See John Sutton Bennett, *History of the Canadian Medical Association, 1954–1994* (Ottawa: CMA, 1996); H.E. MacDermot, *History of the Canadian Medical Association, 1888–1983* (Toronto: Murray Printing, n.d.).
6 Unfortunately, the data do not seem to include how many of those printed journals went to paid subscribers, making it suggestive rather than conclusive. Circulation and printing figures beyond 1958 appear to be missing, though it is recorded within the meeting minutes that circulation continued to increase throughout the period under review. Library and Archives Canada (hereafter *LAC*), Mfm M-4787 "Minutes of the Meeting of the CMA Executive Council, 1946–1962."
7 Mitchinson, *Fighting Fat*, 272.
8 Foucault discusses this method of silencing in *The History of Sexuality: An Introduction, Volume 1*, trans. Robert Hurley (New York: Vintage Books), 17–18.
9 Medical and scientific theories that ranked bodies according to intersecting categories of race and gender reach back to antiquity. See for example Adele Perry, *On the Edge of Empire: Gender, Race and the Making of British Columbia, 1849–1871* (Toronto: University of Toronto Press, 2001); Londa Schiebinger, *Nature's Body: Gender in the Making of Modern Science* (New Brunswick: Rutgers University Press, 2013); Nancy Stepan, *The Idea*

of Race in Science: Great Britain, 1800–1960 (London: Macmillan, 1982); Stepan, "Race, Gender, Science and Citizenship," *Gender & History* 10, no. 1 (1998): 26–52; Ann Laura Stoler, *Carnal Knowledge and Imperial Power: Race and the Intimate in the Colonial World* (Berkley: University of California Press, 2002); Melissa N. Stein, *Measuring Manhood: Race and the Science of Masculinity, 1803–1934* (Minneapolis: University of Minnesota Press, 2015); Andrew Wells, "Confusion Embodied: Epistemologies of Sex and Race in *Memoirs of a Woman of Pleasure* (1748–49) and the *Histoire naturelle* (1749–1804), in *Bodies, Sex and Desire from the Renaissance to the Present*, ed. Kate Fisher and Sarah Toulalan (London: Palgrave Macmillan, 2011); Marli F. Weiner with Mazie Hough, *Sex, Sickness, and Slavery: Defining Illness in the Antebellum South* (Urbana: University of Illinois Press, 2012).

10 See for example Dorothy Roberts, *Killing the Black Body: Race, Reproduction and the Meaning of Liberty* (New York: Vintage Books, 1998); Schiebinger, *Nature's Body*; Susan L. Smith, *Sick and Tired of Being Sick and Tired: Black Women's Health Activism in America, 1890–1950* (Philadelphia: University of Pennsylvania Press, 1995).

11 El Chenier comes to a similar conclusion about the ways psychiatry took over from eugenics-based therapies for "sexual deviances" such as homosexuality. See Elise Chenier, *Strangers in Our Midst: Sexual Deviancy in Postwar Ontario* (Toronto: University of Toronto Press, 2008), 22–3, 122–3.

12 For works on the general history of psychology and the place of psychoanalysis within it, see Thomas E. Brown, "Dr. Ernest Jones, Psychoanalysis and the Canadian Medical Profession, 1908–1913," in *Medicine in Canadian Society: Historical Perspectives*, ed. S.E.D. Shortt (Montreal: McGill-University Press, 1981), 315–60; John C. Burnham, *After Freud Left: A Century of Psychoanalysis in America* (Chicago: University of Chicago Press, 2012); Anne Digby and Jonathan Andrews, *Sex, Seclusion, Class, and Custody: Perspectives on Gender and Class in the History of British and Irish Psychiatry* (New York: Rodopi, 2005); Nathan G. Hale Jr., *The Rise and Crisis of Psychoanalysis in the United States: Freud and the Americans 1917–1985* (Oxford: Oxford University Press, 1995); J.D. Keehn, *Master Builders of Modern Psychology: From Freud to Skinner* (New York: New York University Press, 1996); Mark S. Micale, *Traumatic Pasts: History, Psychiatry and Trauma in the Modern Age* (Cambridge: Cambridge University Press, 2001).

13 H.O. Foucar, "Emotions and Human Relations," *CMAJ*, September 1947, 282.

14 Ibid.

15 N. Viner, "Treatment in Mental Disease: Especially the Psychoneuroses," *CMAJ*, August 1946, 102.

16 M. Tyndel, "The Role of the General Practitioner in Psychiatry," *CMAJ*, 6 February 1960, 324.

17 C.B. Farrar, "Psychotherapy in Medical Practice," *CMAJ*, December 1947, 519.
18 Ibid., 101–2.
19 Martin Roth, "The Phenomenology of Depressive States," *Canadian Psychiatric Association Journal* (hereafter *CPAJ*) *Special Supplement*, 19–21 March 1959, 533.
20 Robert O. Jones, "Discussion" *CPAJ Special Supplement*, 19–21 March 1959, 533. Throughout the *CPAJ* there are many examples of this kind of limiting language, as the majority of contributors noted that their research was in most cases not broadly generalizable and that the human mind's complexity made oversimplifying the research studying it (as was commonly done within the *CMAJ*) dangerous. Some examples of such language include D.G. McKerracher, "President's Foreword," *CPAJ*, January 1956, 1; H.E. Lehmann, "Psychiatric Concepts of Depression? Nomenclature and Classification," *CPAJ Special Supplement*, 19–21 March 1959, 51; R.A. Cleghorn and G.C. Curtis, "Psychosomatic Accompaniments of Latent and Manifest Depressive Affect," *CPAJ Special Supplement*, 19–21 March 1959, 513; Villars Lunn, "Discussion," *CPAJ Special Supplement*, 19–21 March 1959, 522; Ian Gregory, "Factors Influencing First Admission Rates to Canadian Mental Hospitals 1: Analysis of Trends, 1932–1953," *CPAJ*, July 1956, 115; Nicholas Destounis, "Complication of Pregnancy – A Psychosomatic Approach," *CPAJ*, 6 December 1962, 279–90; Donald R. Gunn, "Psychiatric Recognition of Anxiety and Depression," *CPAJ Special Supplement*, 1962, S1–S2; Wendell Muncie, "Depression or Depressions?" *CPAJ*, August 1963, 217.
21 This increase in psychoanalytical content was also due in part to patient and societal pressure from outside the medical profession. According to Chenier, advocates of psychoanalysis aggressively "sold" the idea of mental health to the public, which greatly increased its influence during this time. Chenier, *Strangers in Our Midst*, 31.
22 The most noted example of this thesis is found in Barbara Ehrenreich and Deidre English, *Complaints and Disorders; The Sexual Politics of Sickness* (Old Westbury, NY: Feminist Press, 1973). See also Barbara Ehrenreich and Deirdre English, *For Her Own Good: 150 Years of the Experts' Advice to Women* (Garden City, NY: Anchor Books, 1979); Mitchinson, *The Nature of Their Bodies*; Warsh, *Prescribed Norms*.
23 Michel Foucault, *The Birth of the Clinic: An Archeology of Medical Perception*, trans. A.M. Sheridan (London: Routledge, 1989), 34.
24 This need to be trusted by the public manifested itself in several articles on both the issue of socialized medicine and the need for a public relations campaign. Notably, many of these articles were published in both French and English – something that rarely occurred with other articles.

See "National Health Service Prospects in Great Britain," *CMAJ*, February 1946, 171; H. Holye Campbell, "Total Rehabilitation and Organized Medicine," *CMAJ*, June 1950, 600–2; "Panic and Public Relations," *CMAJ*, April 1952, 386–9; Ian MacNeill, "Is the Profession Misunderstood?" *CMAJ*, January 1952, 79–82; A.D. Kelly "Why Bother with Public Relations?" *CMAJ*, May 1952, 493–6; Robert R. Robinson, "Public Relations: Prescription for M.D.'s," *CMAJ*, December 1953, 648–9; L.W. Holmes, "Public Relations Forum: Enter the Patient," *CMAJ*, 1 December 1955, 908–9; M.B. Etziony, "Letter to the Editor: Repetitio ad nauseam," *CMAJ*, 15 December 1955, 992; L.W. Holmes, "Public Relations Forum: The Doctor and Community Relations," *CMAJ*, 15 January 1956, 158–9; L.W. Holmes, "Public Relations Forum: The Doctor and the Press," *CMAJ*, 1 February 1956, 224–8; L.W. Holmes, "Public Relations Forum: Medicine on the Air," *CMAJ*, 1 April 1956, 571; L.W. Holmes, "Public Relations Forum: The Doctor Speaks," *CMAJ*, 1 March 1956, 396–7; L.W. Holmes, "Public Relations Forum: Doctors on Camera," *CMAJ*, 15 April 1956, 652–4; L.W. Holmes, "Public Relations Forum: Public Attitudes towards Doctors," *CMAJ*, 1 January 1957, 46–7; L.W. Holmes, "Public Relations Forum: Preventative PR," *CMAJ*, 1 February 1957, 229–30; Francis T. Hodges, "Public Relations Forum: Medicine's Seven Deadly Sins," *CMAJ*, 15 April 1957, 660–2; Harry Baker, "Doctor-Patient Relationship or Doctor-Public Relationship," *CMAJ*, 15 January 1958, 128–31; J.B. Benson, "Letter to the Editor: Public Relations," *CMAJ*, 15 March 1958, 450–1; "Doctors on Television," *CMAJ*, 1 June 1958, 866; "What Patients Think of Doctors," *CMAJ*, 27 August 1960, 440–2; F.W. Hanley and F. Grunberg, "Reflections on Doctor-Patient Relationship," *CMAJ*, 2 June 1962, 1022–4; "News & Views on the Economics of Medicine: Recommendations of the Royal Commission on Health Services," *CMAJ*, 1 August 1964, n.p.

25 "The Doctor and His Wife," *CMAJ*, 8 January 1966, 93. Unsurprisingly, the doctor by default is defined as male in a heterosexual relationship.

26 The image of the sexually quiescent Victorian woman had been eroding consistently since the turn of the century, undergoing successive shocks such as was posed by "the flapper" in the 1920s. However, given the sociopolitical upheavals of the first half of the twentieth century, it seems that the post–World War II era was one of the first times that social experts were able to turn their full attention to women's sexuality. See Jane Nicholas, *The Modern Girl: Feminine Modernities, the Body, and Commodities in the 1920s* (Toronto: University of Toronto Press, 2015). For discussions of the changing nature of sexual womanhood prior to World War II see Beth L. Bailey, *From the Front Porch to the Back Seat: Courtship in Twentieth-Century America* (Baltimore: Johns Hopkins University Press, 1988); John D'Emilio and Estelle B. Freedman, *Intimate Matters: A History of Sexuality*

in American (New York: Harper & Row, 1988); Susan K. Freeman, *Sex Goes to School: Girls and Sex Education before the 1960s* (Urbana: University of Illinois Press, 2008); Kate Fisher, *Birth Control, Sex, and Marriage in Britain 1918–1960* (Oxford: Oxford University Press, 2006); Angus McLaren, *Twentieth-Century Sexuality: A History* (Oxford: Blackwell, 1999); Kathy Peiss, *Cheap Amusements: Working Women and Leisure in Turn-of-the-Century New York* (Philadelphia: Temple University Press, 1986); Joan Sangster, *Regulating Girls and Woman: Sexuality, Family and the Law, 1920–1960* (Oxford: Oxford University Press, 2001); Veronica Strong-Boag, *The New Day Recalled: Lives of Girls and Women in English Canada, 1919–1939* (Toronto: Copp Clack Pitman., 1988); Marianna Valverde, *The Age of Light, Soap and Water* (Toronto: McClelland & Stewart, 1991).

27 Endometriosis, discovered in 1860, occurs when cells from the lining of the uterus are found outside the uterus, which can cause pain and infertility. The physical nature of the disorder was understood in the period under review.

28 M. Bruser, "The Common Occurrence of Endometriosis in Young Women," *CMAJ*, 1 February 1955, 191.

29 Veronica Strong-Boag notes that psychological ideals of family and motherhood made it beyond the purely medical discourse and were featured in popular-culture magazines such as *Chatelaine*. See Veronica Strong-Boag, "Home Dreams: Women and the Suburban Experiment in Canada: 1945–1960," *Canadian Historical Review* 72, no. 4 (1991): 482.

30 In Freudian psychoanalysis displacement is an unconscious defence mechanism where a person shifts negative feelings from one target to a different target (person or object) to avoid distress or anxiety. In many cases the original target is either too powerful to be challenged or confrontation would be too painful.

31 Of course this was nothing new: women's reproductive systems had been medically constructed as sites of danger since Galen and Hippocrates. It was simply a new way to frame this relationship. For other histories of the construction of the reproductive system as a site of danger see Thomas Laqueur, *Making Sex: Body and Gender from the Greeks to Freud* (Cambridge, MA: Harvard University Press, 1990); Schiebinger, *Nature's Body*; Mitchinson, *The Nature of Their Bodies*.

32 J.N Fortin, E.D. Wittkower, and F. Kalz, "A Psychosomatic Approach to the Pre-menstrual Tension Syndrome: A Preliminary Report," *CMAJ*, 15 December 1958, 978.

33 Ibid., 980.

34 Ibid. Of course blaming mothers is not new, nor is it confined to gendered bodies. For example, Wendy Mitchinson notes in her work *Fighting Fat* that obesity of children, teens, and even husbands was often blamed on

mothers. Furthermore, instead of focusing on mothers as feeders, doctors and psychologists blamed mothers for making their family members obese because they were assumed to be deficient in showing proper and healthy affection and love for those family members and food was made into a substitute for that lack of love. Mitchinson, *Fighting Fat*, 191–3. Michitson's conclusions are echoed in Deborah McPhail's work on the embodied family. See McPhail, "What to Do with the 'Tubby Hubby'? 'Obesity,' the Crisis of Masculinity and the Nuclear Family in Early Cold War Canada," *Antipode* 41, no. 5 (2009): 1021–50.

35 Daniel Cappon, "Some Psychodynamic Aspects of Pregnancy," *CMAJ*, February 1954, 148.
36 Ibid., 149.
37 Gordon W. Preuter, "Trifluoperazine in Nausea and Vomiting Pregnancy," *CMAJ*, 1 July 1959, 22. Though the image of the extramarital sexual mother as damaged and socially disruptive was clearly dominant, occasionally contrasting viewpoints were published, creating pockets of resistance. For example, in a short 1951 article Dr. H.J. Skully noted, "A young, healthy, unmarried women comes in for a check up. It hardly needs elaborating as to what this patient is anxious to know. Her emotional state is such that she needs sympathy and encouragement at this time." Skully "The Patient's Viewpoint," *CMAJ*, July 1951, 64.
38 M. Straker, "Psychological Factors during Pregnancy and Childbirth," *CMAJ*, May 1954, 512.
39 Mitchinson, *Fighting Fat*, 274.
40 It should be noted that neither Bonamine nor Mornidine were thalidomide drugs.
41 Donald C. McEwen, "Ovarian Failure and the Menopause," *CMAJ*, 1 May 1965, 962.
42 Ibid., 967–8.
43 For further information on Hilliard's column in *Chatelaine*, see Valerie J. Korinek, *Roughing It in the Suburbs: Reading* Chatelaine *Magazine in the Fifties and Sixties* (Toronto: University of Toronto Press, 2000), 272, 295–300, 306, 337, 370.
44 Hilliard, "The Diagnosis and Treatment of the Menopause," *CMAJ*, 1 January 1957, 1.
45 In the period under review there were a total of seven cases reported in the *CMAJ*. See David D. Kulcsar, "Intersexuality (with Report of a Case)," *CMAJ*, August 1948, 144–8; J.E.C. Stollmeyer and J.P.A. Latour, "Pseudo Hermaphroditism," *CMAJ*, November 1950, 494; L.T. Barclay, "Artificial Vagina," *CMAJ*, January 1954, 67; J.C. Pattee, D.M. Wyse, and R. Palmer Howard, "Female Psuedohermaphroditism Treated with Oral Cortisone," *CMAJ*, October 1954, 358; Murray L. Barr, "The Sex Chromatin and Its

Bearing on Errors of Sex Development," *CMAJ*, 15 March 1956, 419–22; D.A. Hillman, "Fetal Masculinization with Maternal Progesterone Therapy," *CMAJ*, 1 February 1959, 200–1; M. Kosowski, "Letter to the Editor: Congenital Absence of Vagina," *CMAJ*, 2 January 1960, 43; J.B. Costello and E.J. Badre, "Construction of an Artificial Vagina," *CMAJ*, 17 September 1966, 631–2. It is estimated that intersexual cases occur at most in 2 per cent of live births. During the postwar period intersexed or hermaphroditic infants were most often made into biological and social females, as it was deemed cruel to assign a male gender to such persons because they would be forever effeminized by having a very small penis. For further information see Elizabeth Reis, *Bodies in Doubt: An American History of Intersex* (Baltimore: Johns Hopkins University Press, 2009).

46 Barr, "The Sex Chromatin," 421–2.
47 Ibid., 419.
48 A vaginal passage was required for the patient to be able to physically engage in heterosexual intercourse.
49 Barclay, "Artificial Vagina," 68.
50 Of course the ultimate biological marker of femininity was a functioning uterus, but this was beyond the ability of medical science to provide. For further information on the feminization of nursing in Canada, see Katheryn McPherson, *Bedside Matters*.
51 Canada's birth control and abortion historiography remains sparse. Existing important works include Dianne Dodd, "Women's Involvement in the Canadian Birth Control Movement of the 1930s: The Hamilton Clinic," in *Delivering Motherhood: Maternal Ideologies and Practices in the 19th and 20th Centuries*, ed. Katherine Arnup, Andrée Lévesque, and Ruth Roach Pierson (London: Routledge, 1990), 150–72; Erik Dyck, "Sterilization and Birth Control in the Shadow of Eugenics: Married, Middle-Class Women in Alberta, 1930–1960s," *Canadian Bulletin of Medical History/Bulletin canadien d'histoire de la medicine* 31, no. 1 (2004): 165–87; Erika Dyck and Maureen Lux, *Challenging Choices: Canada's Population Control in the 1970s* (Montreal & Kingston: McGill-Queen's University Press, 2020); Angus McLaren and Arlene Tigar McLaren, *The Bedroom and the State* (Toronto: McClelland & Stewart, 1986); Mitchinson, *The Nature of Their Bodies*, 125–51; Christabelle Sethna and Gayle Davis, eds., *Abortion across Borders: Transnational Travel and Access to Abortion Services* (Baltimore: Johns Hopkins University Press, 2019); Christabelle Sethna, "The Evolution of the *Birth Control Handbook*: From Student Peer-Education Manual to Feminist Self-Empowerment Text, 1968–1975," *Canadian Bulletin of Medical History/Bulletin canadien d'histoire de la medicine* 23, no. 1 (2006): 89–118; Sethna, "The University of Toronto Health Service, Oral Contraception, and Student Demand for Birth

Control," *Historical Studies in Education* 17, no. 2 (2005): 265–92; Shannon Stettner, ed., *Without Apology: Writings on Abortion in Canada* (Edmonton: Athabasca University Press, 2016). Wendy Mitchinson's discussion of birth control in the first half of the twentieth century also notes that birth control proponents advocated its use for the spacing of children and to prevent having so many children that families could not provide proper care for them – especially in the wake of the Great Depression. She also notes that some people saw it as preventing the great sin of abortion, which I did not find echoed in the later literature presented here. Mitchinson, *Body Failure*, 161–2.

52 "Oral Contraceptives," *CMAJ*, 10 August 1963, 270.
53 J.H. Dickinson and G.G. Smith, "A New and Practical Oral Contraceptive Agent: Norethindrone and Mestranol," *CMAJ*, 10 August 1963, 242.
54 L. Carlyle Lyon, "A Menstrual Chart," *CMAJ*, August 1948, 172.
55 LAC, "Minutes of the Meeting of the CMA Executive Council," Mflm 7491.This was the same attitude the Canadian medical community espoused in regard to abortion: both were acceptable so long as they were under the ultimate control of medical doctors.
56 "The Legal Aspects of Sterilization," *CMAJ*, May 1948, 512–13.
57 C.A. Douglas Ringrose, "The Emotional Responses of Married Women Receiving Oral Contraceptives," *CMAJ*, 5 June 1965, 1207.
58 Fred L. Johnson, F.R. Doerffer, and J.E.A. Tyson, "Clinical Experience with Margulies Intrauterine Contraceptive Device," *CMAJ*, 2 July 1966, 15.
59 Sethna, "The University of Toronto Health Service"; Sethna, "The Evolution of the *Birth Control Handbook*."
60 "Birth Control," *CMAJ*, November 1947, 489; G.P.R. Tallin, "The Legal Implications of the Non-Therapeutic Practices of Doctors," *CMAJ*, 4 August, 1962, 207–13; "Medical News in Brief: The Physician and Family Planning," *CMAJ*, 24 September 1966, 689.
61 The first "test tube baby" born as a result of in vitro fertilization was Louise Brown, who was born in England 25 July 1978.
62 This was a precursor to the current treatment of intrauterine insemination, or IUI.
63 There were no cases put forward in the *CMAJ* of women desiring AID (donor) in order to have a child on their own (or as part of a lesbian couple). Whether this absence is due to the social constructions of the day making planned single motherhood an unthinkable option for women, or *CMAJ* contributors simply refused to countenance such a practice, or a combination of the two, is unknown.
64 Tallin, "Legal Implications of Non-Therapeutic Practices," 208.
65 "The Law and Artificial Insemination," *CMAJ*, 15 May 1956, 832.

66 S.S.B. Gilder, "The London Letter: Conception after Adoption," *CMAJ*, 5 June 1965, 1209.
67 W.W. Watters and J. Sousa-Poza, "Psychiatric Aspects of Artificial Insemination (Donor)," *CMAJ*, 16 July 1966, 106–13.
68 See also "Editorial and Comments: The Law and Artificial Insemination," *CMAJ*, 15 May, 1956, 832–3; "News in Brief: Donor Insemination to Be Punishable in Germany," *CMAJ*, 15 April 1956, 80; William A.R. Thomson, "The London Letter: Artificial Insemination," *CMAJ*, 3 September 1960, 553–4; G.P.R. Tallin, "Legal Implications of Non-Therapeutic Practices," *CMAJ*, 4 August 1962, 207–13.
69 C. Crawford Lindsay and C.V. Ward, "Potassium Permanganate as an Abortifacient," *CMAJ*, November 1954, 465–7; J.J. Lederman, "The Doctor, Abortion, and the Law: A Medicolegal Dilemma," *CMAJ*, 4 August 1962, 216; Tallin, "Legal Implications of Non-Therapeutic Practices," 207–15; Walter Simpson, "Letter to the Editor: The Doctor, Abortion, and the Law," 13 October 1962, 821–2; C.P. Harrison, "Letter to the Editor: The Issue of Legalized Abortion," *CMAJ*, 9 February 1963, 329–30; S.G. Stern, "Letter to the Editor: The Issue of Legalized Abortion," *CMAJ*, 27 April 1963, 899; "The London Letter: Abortion," *CMAJ*, 23 September 1963, 679; D.F. Osborne, "Attempted Abortion with Retention of an Intrauterine Foreign Body," *CMAJ*, 15 February 1964, 494–5; P.M. Grant, "Letter to the Editor: On the Futility of Legalizing Abortion," *CMAJ*, 22 October 1966, 879; Peter M. Grant, "Letter to the Editor: On the Futility of Legalizing Abortion," 24 September 1966, 688.
70 Harrison, "The Issue of Legalized Abortion," 329.
71 D.E. Zarfas, "Psychiatric Indications of the Termination of Pregnancy," *CMAJ*, 15 August 1958, 230–6.
72 Though a woman's status as an immigrant was mentioned in only a small percentage of the overall cases where a woman was pathologized as overly masculine, the fact that ethnicity was included at all suggests that patients who did not present as having a clear Anglo-Saxon background were more likely to be, and were more heavily, pathologized in the immediate postwar years. E.S. Heath and D.G. McKerracher, "Short Communication: Impressions of a Common Psychiatric Entity," *CMAJ*, 1 June 1958, 896; Zarfas, "Psychiatric Indications," 232; Advertisement, *CMAJ*, 1 June 1955, 877; A. Russell and M. Sambhi, "Intrafamilial Aggressive Patterns: A Pilot Study to Develop a Classification of Family Relationships," *CMAJ*, 26 May 1962, 977–80; "Editorials and Annotations: Venereal Disease and Young People," *CMAJ*, 23 May 1964, 1230.
73 Cartoon, *CMAJ*, 15 July 1958, p. 35.
74 "The Legal Aspects of Sterilization (Part II)," *CMAJ*, July 1948, 80.
75 "Legal Aspects of Sterilization," 512.

76 Erika Dyck, *Facing Eugenics: Reproduction, Sterilization, and the Politics of Choice* (Toronto: University of Toronto Press, 2013). See also Amy Sampson, "Eugenics in the Community: Alberta's Sexual Sterilization Act, 1928–1972," *Canadian Bulletin of Medical History/Bulletin canadien d'histoire de la medicine* 31, no. 1 (2014): 143–63.
77 Dyck, *Facing Eugenics*.
78 Ibid, 169.
79 See also Molly Ladd-Taylor, *Fixing the Poor: Eugenic Sterilization and Child Welfare in the Twentieth Century* (Baltimore: Johns Hopkins University Press, 2020); Jane Harris-Zsovan, *Eugenics and the Firewall: Canada's Nasty Little Secret* (Winnipeg: J.G. Shilingford, 2010); Wendy Kline, *Building a Better Race: Gender, Sexuality, and Eugenics from the Turn of the Century to the Baby Boom* (Berkeley: University of California Press, 2001); Mark A. Largent, *Breeding Contempt: The History of Coerced Sterilization and the Politics of Choice* (New Brunswick: Rutgers University Press, 2008); Angus McLaren, *Our Own Master Race: Eugenics in Canada, 1885–1945* (Toronto: McClelland & Stewart, 1990).
80 R. Castro de la Mata, G. Gringras, and E.D. Wittkower, "Impact of Sudden, Severe Disablement of the Father Upon the Family," *CMAJ*, 14 May 1960, 1015.
81 Ibid., 1016.
82 Ibid.
83 Ibid.
84 Ibid.
85 F.E. McNair, "Psychosis: Occurring Postpartum: Analysis of 34 Cases," *CMAJ*, December 1952, 638.
86 Ibid., 639.
87 Robert Rutherdale, "'I'm a Lousy Father': Alcoholic Fathers in Postwar Canada and the Myths of Masculine Crises," in *Making Men, Making History: Canadian Masculinities across Time and Place*, ed. Peter Gossage and Robert Rutherdale (Vancouver: UBC Press, 2018), 410–11, 414.
88 It was not considered that doctors' wives might have greater access to and thus a greater ability to abuse legal drugs than those in the control group or that their husbands would be more likely to seek biomedically based solutions to marital discord. "The Doctor and His Wife," 93.
89 It should also be noted that the article does not suggest intimacy was impossible for doctors – that they would become impotent – but instead that they were too busy and distant to romance their wives to get them to the point where they would willingly engage in marital intimacy.
90 S.R. Laycock "Homosexuality – A Mental Hygiene Problem," *CMAJ*, September 1950, 245–50; B. Kanee and C.L. Hunt, "Homosexuality as a Source of Venereal Disease," *CMAJ*, August 1951, 138–40; Marvin

Wellman, "Overt Homosexuality with Spontaneous Remission," *CMAJ*, 15 August 1956, 273–9. For a deconstruction of the social theme of the homosexual man as engaged in "risky" behaviour, see Susan Sontag, *AIDS and Its Metaphors* (London: Penguin, 1989).
91 Laycock, "Homosexuality," 246. It is somewhat unclear what Laycock means by the term "impotent." He could mean that he believed very effeminate homosexual men were unable to sustain an erection at all in either homosexual or hetereosexual relations. However, it is likely that Laycock uses "impotent" to refer to cases of heterosexual relations because he viewed homosexual sex as invalid, and so did not consider homosexual sex as actual sex.
92 Wellman, "Overt Homosexuality," 273–4.
93 Ibid., 276, emphasis added.
94 In all the issues of the *CMAJ* in the period under review I was only able to find one dissenting voice in the narrative of homosexual as dangerous sexual deviant. The article, published in 1962 and entitled "The Other Side: Living with Homosexuality," was written in the first person by a self-identified, though anonymous, non-medical homosexual man; it describes the issues facing a homosexual man and calls for sympathy. Anonymous, "Living with Homosexuality," *CMAJ*, 12 May 1962, 875–7.
95 Ian K. Bond and Harry C. Hutchinson, "Application of Reciprocal Inhibition Therapy to Exhibitionism," *CMAJ*, 2 July 1960, 24.
96 El Chenier also refers to this particular case in *Strangers in Our Midst*, were she notes that psychologists such as Bond and Hutchison had a very ambiguous view of wives of offenders such as the one profiled here. Though mothers were often portrayed as the cause of such sexual deviance, wives were often blamed for cases of recidivism. Indeed, according to Chenier, in this case such a relapse did occur. Chenier, *Strangers in Our Midst*, 133–5.
97 The most famous example of this remains Boston Women's Health Book Collective, *Our Bodies, Ourselves: A Book by and for Women* (New York: Simon and Schuster, 1979).
98 Chenier, *Strangers in Our Midst*, 32.

3. Sex, Marriage, and the "One-Flesh" Body: Married Sexuality in the Anglican, United, and Roman Catholic Denominations

1 Angus McLaren, *Impotence: A Cultural History* (Chicago: University of Chicago Press, 2007), 35–7; Judith C. Mueller, "Fallen Men: Representations of Male Impotence in Britain," *Studies in Eighteenth Century Culture* 28 (1999): 92–3.
2 I am confining myself to the three most prevalent Christian denominations within Canada during this time. Thus, "religion" or

"denomination" should be seen to refer in these pages to the Anglican, United, or Roman Catholic Church unless otherwise specified.

3 See for example Tina Block, *The Secular Northwest: Religion and Irreligion in Everyday Postwar Life* (Vancouver: UBC Press, 2016); Nancy Christie and Michael Gauvreau, *A Full-Orbed Christianity: The Protestant Churches and Social Welfare in Canada, 1900–1940* (Montreal & Kingston: McGill-Queen's University Press, 1996); Ramsay Cook, *The Regenerators: Social Criticism in Late Victorian English Canada*, 2nd ed. (Toronto: University of Toronto Press, 2016); and David B. Marshall, *Secularizing the Faith: Canadian Protestant Clergy and the Crisis of Belief, 1950–1940* (Toronto: University of Toronto Press, 1992).

4 See for example Michael Gauvereau, *The Catholic Origins of Quebec's Quiet Revolution, 1931–1970* (Montreal & Kingston: McGill-Queen's University Press, 2005); Paul-Andre Linteau et. al, *Histoire du Québec contemporain: Le Québec depuis 1930* (Montreal: Boréal Express, 1989); Brian Young, *A Short History of Quebec*, 2nd ed. (Toronto: Copp Clark, 1993).

5 Gilles Routhier, "Governance of the Catholic Church in Quebec: An Expression of the Distinct Society?" in *The Churches and Social Order in Nineteenth- and Twentieth-Century Canada*, ed. Michael Gauvreau and Ollivier Hubert (Montreal & Kingston: McGill-Queen's University Press, 2006), 292–314.

6 Dominion Bureau of Statistics, *Ninth Census of Canada 1951* (Ottawa: Dominion Bureau of Statistics, 1953), table 1; Dominion Bureau of Statistics, *1961 Census of Canada* (Ottawa: Dominion Bureau of Statistics, 1962), table 42.

7 Brian Clarke and Stuart Macdonald, *Leaving Christianity: Changing Allegiances in Canada since 1945* (Montreal & Kingston: McGill-Queen's University Press, 2017), 164–5. Clarke and Macdonald note that in the immediate postwar era all censuses were taken by individual census takers who interviewed the head of the household, and that this personal interaction likely contributed to the smaller numbers of people willing to say that they or their family members had no religious affiliations.

8 These legal requirements had a long history in Canada, particularly in policing the intermarriages of Indigenous women and white men as well as religious minorities such as the polygamous Mormon sects. Laws governing who could marry a couple and under what circumstances a couple could legitimately marry were part of a larger nation-building project. They served to make church marriages an enduring norm. For these histories see Constance Backhouse, *Petticoats and Prejudice: Women and the Law in Nineteenth Century Canada* (Toronto: Osgoode Society, 1991), and Sarah Carter, *The Importance of Being Monogamous: Marriage and Nation*

Building in Western Canada to 1915 (Edmonton: University of Alberta Press, 2008).

9 Monsignor J.D. Conway, "Enlightenment for Confused Spouses," *Prairie Messenger*, 16 January 1958, 4, reprinted from the "Question Box" in *Catholic Messenger*.

10 Neil Semple, *The Lord's Dominion: The History of Canadian Methodism* (Montreal & Kingston: McGill-Queen's University Press, 1996), 342; Marshall, *Secularizing the Faith*, 136.

11 Mary-Ann Shantz notes a similar use of psychological concepts in Anglican advice to parents about raising children in her examination of Anglican churches in Calgary. Shantz, "Centring the Suburb, Focusing on the Family: Calgary's Anglican and Alliance Churches, 1945–1969," *Social History/Histoire sociale* 42, no. 84 (2009): 430, 433.

12 Reverend Canon W.H. Davidson, *The Nature of Marriage* (Montreal: R.A. Regnault, 1946), 3; United Church Archives of Canada (hereafter UCAC), Accn. 77051C, f. 177–2, pamphlet, David A. MacLennan, "Family Life." N.d.

13 Francis A. Marrocco D. D., Auxiliary Bishop of Toronto, "A Diocesan Family Life Programe," in *The Christian Family Apostolate*, Report of the Seventh Annual Session of the Catholic Social Life Conference, 9–10 October 1959, Sudbury, ON, 94.

14 See *This Is a Great Sacrament* (Ottawa: Le Droit, 196?), 349–51; *Toward a Christian Understanding of Sex, Love and Marriage* (National General Council of the United Church of Canada, 1960), 14; *The Hallowing of the Union* (Toronto: Diocesan Marriage Services, 196?), 6.

15 Doug Owram, *Born at the Right Time: A History of the Baby Boom Generation* (Toronto: University of Toronto Press, 1996), 28–9.

16 Elsie Robinson, "Frank Talk about Realism in Marriage," *Prairie Messenger*, 18 May 1950, 3.

17 "Movies and Marriage," *Prairie Messenger*, 17 January 1946, 8.

18 UCAC, Accn. 83.051 f. 177–5, Folder Plans for the *Christian Home*.

19 Unlike the Anglican and United churches, which have central organizational arms within Canada, the Roman Catholic Church retains a more central power structure. Thus, there is the Roman Catholic Church *in* Canada rather that the Roman Catholic Church *of* Canada.

20 ACC, C.S. 75–100, box 12, folder 3, Marriage Counselling Committee 1950–1962, letter from Miss Nora Lea (informational secretary) to Reverend R.S. Mowry, 7 December 1962.

21 *This Is a Great Sacrament*, 155, emphasis in original.

22 Ibid., 337.

23 Ibid., 332.

24 "Fulfillment for the Lonely Heart in a Single Woman," *Prairie Messenger*, 7 October 1954, 3, reprinted from *The Catholic Herald*; "The Unmarried

Woman – Spiritual Motherhood," *The Prairie Messenger*, 17 January 1946, 3; Dr. Doris Boyle, "Homemaking Most Difficult Work," *Prairie Messenger*, 12 June 1958, 1.

25 This is only one of the ways that Gauvreau's representation of Catholic Action's Service de Préperation au Mariage (SPM) differed from the evidence in *This Is a Great Sacrament*. According to Gauvreau, the SPM actively promoted the rhythm method as acceptable birth control, allowed for women to orgasm separate from any penetrative sexual act (i.e., not in the act of procreation), and had more current psychological concepts and language. This suggests that western anglophone Catholic authorities were actually more conservative in their doctrinal interpretations. However, more detailed comparisons of Catholic marriage preparation materials, both within Canada and internationally, are needed before a definitive reason for these differences can be vouchsafed. Gauvreau, *Catholic Origins*, 175–246.
26 Ibid.
27 Ibid., 364.
28 "The Family in Canada," Statement of the Canadian Hierarchy, in *The Christian Family Apostolate*, 51–2.
29 William A. Dyson, "Husband-Wife Relationships" *Social Thought* 61, no. 2 (1960), 8.
30 Attempting to give motherhood a professional veneer and status was a common postwar containment tactic outside of religion.
31 "The Family in Canada." Statement of the Canadian Hierarchy. In *The Christian Family Apostolate*, 51.
32 His Grace the Most Reverend J. Gerald Berry D.D., Archbishop of Halifax, "The Christian Family Apostolate," in *The Christian Family Apostolate*, 64–7.
33 *This Is a Great Sacrament*, 109–10.
34 Ibid., 126.
35 Ibid., 112.
36 Ibid., 104.
37 See Wendy Mitchinson, *The Nature of Their Bodies: Women and Their Doctors in Victorian Canada* (Toronto: University of Toronto Press, 1991); Londa Schiebinger, *Nature's Body: Gender in the Making of Modern Science* (New Brunswick: Rutgers University Press, 2013).
38 *This Is a Great Sacrament*, 102–4. For information on the four humours, humoural theory, and its connection to Catholicism and gender roles, see Caroline Walker Bynum, *Holy Feast and Holy Fast: The Religious Significance of Food to Medieval Women* (Berkeley: University of California Press, 1987).
39 "Catholic Doctors Answer Questions on Medical Ethics," *Prairie Messenger*, 10 July 1958, 1; Msgr. John C. Knott, "Everyman's Family – Doctor's

Advise Priests to 'Mind Your Own Business,'" *Prairie Messenger*, 5 January 1966, 8, 10; Most Reverend Alexander Carter, "Report of the Family Life Survey of Sault Ste. Marie," in *The Christian Family Apostolate*, 83–93; *Catholic Family Life Survey – City of Saskatoon: A Joint Report and Statistical Survey* (Saskatoon: Steering Committee SCFLS Catholic Centre, 1960), n.p.; *This Is a Great Sacrament*, 335.
40 *Catholic Family Life Survey – City of Saskatoon: A Joint Report and Statistical Survey*, n.p.; Carter, "Report of the Family Life Survey of Sault Ste. Marie," n.p.
41 *This Is a Great Sacrament*, 350.
42 Ibid., 351–2.
43 Angus McLaren, *Impotence: A Cultural History*. (Chicago: University of Chicago Press, 2007), 106.
44 *This Is a Great Sacrament*, 327.
45 Ibid., 354.
46 Ibid., 326.
47 Ibid.
48 Ibid., 324.
49 "Your Marriage – 2. Your Husband," *Prairie Messenger*, 20 April 1950, 6.
50 *This Is a Great Sacrament*, 327.
51 Ibid., 114.
52 Ibid., 324.
53 Ibid., 325, emphasis added.
54 Most Reverend Robert J. Dwyer, "Sage and Sand – No Scientific Proof for God?" *Prairie Messenger*, 10 July 1958, 2.
55 Howard Fowler and Dr. H. Breault, "Special Interest Group Cana Conferences," in *The Christian Family Apostolate*, 165–7.
56 W.G.P., "So They Want Help," *Prairie Messenger*, 23 May 1946, 8.
57 Ibid.; "Pontiff Hails Large Family as Testimony to Vitality of Nations," *Prairie Messenger*, 13 February 1958, 1; "Pope Lauds Large Families," *Prairie Messenger*, 27 March 1958, 6; "Making Marriage Click – 'Too Many People,'" *Prairie Messenger*, 17 April 1958, 6; "Making Marriage Click – 'We'll Starve to Death,'" *Prairie Messenger*, 24 April 1958, 6; "Making Marriage Click – Is Birth Control the Answer?" *Prairie Messenger*, 8 May 1958, 6; "Making Marriage Click – Planning or Plotting Parenthood," *Prairie Messenger*, 19 June 1958, 6; "In Our Opinion ... Family 'Planners' Say God Forgot to Look Ahead," *Prairie Messenger*, 14 February 1962, 1; "The Family in Canada," Statement of the Canadian Hierarchy, November 1958; *This Is a Great Sacrament*, 151.
58 Father John J. O'Connor, "Rewards of Virtue in Family Life," *Prairie Messenger*, 14 February 1946, 6, reprinted from the *Wanderer*.
59 Interestingly, this made the Catholic Church one of the few groups raising concerns about the potential negative side effects of the Pill. Even

though they used this rhetoric to serve their own ends, there were health issues with the early forms of the Pill that were often superseded, both at the time and later, due to the public enthusiasm for such medications.

60 Margaret Marsh and Wanda Ronner, *The Fertility Doctor: John Rock and the Reproductive Revolution* (Baltimore: Johns Hopkins University Press, 2008), 57–8, 127.
61 "In Our Opinion ... Family 'Planners' Say God Forgot," 1.
62 *This Is a Great Sacrament*, 336, emphasis in original.
63 Ibid., 337.
64 Mitchinson, *The Nature of Their Bodies*, 61.
65 "In Our Opinion ... Family 'Planners' Say God Forgot," 1.
66 DeBlanc, "Making Marriage Click – Too Many People," 1.
67 "Something to Consider," *Prairie Messenger*, 26 September 1962, 8, reprinted from the *Catholic Herald*.
68 It should be noted that Koral Józef Wojtyla, who would become Pope John Paul II, was instrumental in the rulings of Vatican II and *Humanae Vitae*. Some Catholic historians credit his influence as key to the move towards conservatism prior to his elevation to the papacy. For more information on Vatican II, *Humanae Vitae*, and the general character of the international Catholic Church in the wake of World War II, see Gregory Baum, *Amazing Church: A Catholic Theologian Remembers a Half-Century of Change* (Ottawa: Novalis, St. Paul's University, 2005); John W. O'Malley, *What Happened at Vatican II* (Cambridge, MA: Harvard University Press, 2008); John T. Noonan Jr., *Contraception: A History of Its Treatment by the Catholic Theologians and Canonists* (Cambridge, MA: Harvard University Press, 1986); Susan A. Ross, "The Women's Movement and Theology in the Twentieth Century," in *The Twentieth Century: A Theological Overview*, ed. Gregory Baum, 186–203 (Ottawa: Novalis, St. Paul's University, 1999); Robert J. Schrieter, "The Impact of Vatican II," in *The Twentieth Century: A Theological Overview*, ed. Gregory Baum, 158–72 (Ottawa: Novalis, St. Paul's University, 1999).
69 According to Michael Gauvreau, most women in Quebec were focused on discourses that decentred parenthood, and *Humanae Vitae* was such a shock, so inconsistent with those belief systems, that it caused Quebecois women to abandon the Catholic Church in droves. Gauvreau, *Quebec Origins*, 245–6.
70 Unlike the Roman Catholic Church where (theoretically) power filters down from the supreme authority of the pope, the international Anglican Church's authority draws from a community of elite powers. Every ten years bishops from all over the world accept the archbishop of Canterbury's invitation to a conference, known as the Lambeth Conference, in England. Once there, these bishops discuss questions of contemporary

relevance, hear reports from committees formed to investigate those issues, and come to resolutions that are then published in the form of an encyclical to be accessed by the faithful. Though these resolutions are thus deemed the recommended course to follow, they do not technically have the weight of ecclesiastical law.

71 *The Lambeth Conference 1948 Encyclical Letter from the Bishops Together with the Resolutions and Reports* (London: SPCK, 1948), n.p.
72 Ibid., 97.
73 The British legal system had long allowed for divorce due to adultery as per the doctrinal acceptance of such by the Anglican Church. Prior to 1857, divorces in England could be granted to the select few men who could successfully petition Parliament for a divorce as well as successfully bringing civil charges against the man with whom his wife had committed adultery. The 1857 Matrimonial Causes Act made it much easier for men to divorce their wives for adultery and allowed women to seek a divorce, though the latter had to prove adultery and an additional cause such as cruelty or desertion. See Lesley A. Hall, *Sex, Gender and Social Change in Britain since 1880* (New York: St. Martin's Press, 2000); Jeffery Weeks, *Sex, Politics and Society: The Regulation of Sexuality Since 1800*, 2nd ed. (Essex: Longman House, 1989).
74 *Lambeth Conference 1948*, 10.
75 Ibid., 2.142–3.
76 Ibid., 2.144–5.
77 C.R. Fielding and H.R.S. Ryan, *Marriage in Church and State: An Introduction to the Canonical Regulation of Marriage in the Anglican Communion* (Toronto: Anglican Book Centre, 1965), n.p.
78 *The Lambeth Conference 1958 Encyclical Letter from the Bishops Along with Resolutions and Reports* (London: SPCK and Seabury Press, 1958), n.p.
79 UCAC, Accn. 83.052C f. 45–15, File of the Commission on Christian Marriage and Divorce, Leslie Hunter, "Divorce and the Remarriage of Divorced Persons," 195?, n.p.
80 UCAC, Accn. 83.052C f. 45–15, File of the Commission on Christian Marriage and Divorce, Dr. Patricia White, "'Marriage and Divorce' Statement for the Consideration of the Commission on Christian Marriage and Divorce," July 1948, 1; Archdeacon Kenneth C. Bolton, *Premarital Talks: A Counsellor's Approach to Couples About to Be Married* (Toronto: Anglican Church of Canada Joint Committee on Adult Religious Education, 1958), 14–16; "Canadian Family Life Status and Trends," *Bulletin of the Council for Social Service, The Church of England in Canada* 128 (2 September 1948): 10.
81 *The Hallowing of the Union*, 139.
82 Ibid.

83 *Lambeth Conference 1958*, 2.156.
84 W. Clark Ellzey, *Sex, Love, and Marriage* (New York: National Council of the Churches of Christ, 1954), 13–14. The United Church often made use of ecumenical publications such as these to supplement their very small amount of denominational literature. Ellzey made many contributions to *Christian Home* magazine.
85 Nancy Christie, "Sacred Sex: The United Church and the Privatization of the Family in Post-War Canada," in *Households of Faith: Family, Gender, and Community in Canada, 1760–1969*, ed. Nancy Christie (Montreal & Kingston: McGill-Queen's University Press, 2002), 349.
86 Reverend George Luxton, *Preparation for a Happy Marriage: A Companion to the Marriage Service in the Church of England in Canada* (Toronto: General Board of Religious Education, n.d.), 20.
87 UCAC, Accn. 83.051C f. 192–3, Dr. Richard Hosking, "Notes on Marriage Counselling Sessions Held at St. John Halifax and A.C.T.C.," 1.
88 Canon E.W. Scott, "The Person You Are Becoming," *Scope* 65 (April 1965): 5, 7.
89 Maxine Schweiker, "If You're a Working Mother, Be Prepared to Work Miracles," *Christian Home* (July 1961), n.p. Tina Block also notes a high level of ambiguity in United Church doctrine in her study of the First United Church and United Church doctrine in British Columbia. See Block, *The Secular Northwest*.
90 Emalene Sherman, "Be Glad You're a Housewife," *Christian Home* (July 1961): 33.
91 Anne C. Thomas, "Are You Faithful to Your Husband?" *Christian Home* (August 1962): 38.
92 Kay Hodell Chilcote, "When He Takes You for Granted," *Christian Home* (May 1965): 37.
93 Valerie J. Korinek, *Roughing It in the Suburbs: Reading* Chatelaine *Magazine in the Fifties and Sixties* (Toronto: University of Toronto Press, 2000).
94 Ibid., 358–63.
95 Ibid., 72, 100.
96 Ibid., 182–5.
97 Ibid., 276–7.
98 UCAC, Accn. 83.052C f. 45–15, File of the Commission on Christian Marriage and Divorce, Reverend Frank Morgan, "'Marriage and Divorce' Statement for the Consideration of the Commission on Christian Marriage and Divorce," July 1958, 1.
99 Bishop Hazen G. Werner, *The Marks of a Christian Home* (Nashville: Upper Room Christian Family Services, 1946), 14–15.
100 Fielding and Ryan, *Marriage in Church and State*, iv.
101 *Lambeth Conference 1958*, 115.

102 Evelyn Millis Duvall, "What Is Right with Today's Families," *Christian Home* (April 1966): 9.
103 See, in the Anglican discourse, *Lambeth Conference 1958*, 2.148–9; "Canadian Family Life Status and Trends," 3. For examples in the United Church discourse, see UCAC, Accn. 83.052C f. 45–15, File of the Commission on Christian Marriage and Divorce, letter to Mr. Fidler from Stanley B. Frost, 28 September 1959; UCAC, Accn. 82.086, box 1 f. 14, "Toward a Christian Understanding of Sex, Love, Marriage: A First Report of the Commission on Christian Marriage and Divorce, Approved by the Nineteenth General Council of the United Church of Canada, Edmonton Alberta September 1960," 2; UCAC, Accn. 83.052C f. 39–4, Hord "Report on Review and Revisions of Canadian Abortion Laws Needed," 5–6; UCAC, Accn. 83.052C f. 39–4, letter to the Honourable Lucien Cardin Minister of Justice from Secretary Board of Evangelism and Social Service, 7 March 1966; J. Termayn Copplestone, "If You Marry a Roman Catholic," *Christian Home* (May 1961): 44–6.
104 *Lambeth Conference 1958*, 2.146.
105 For example, though the Protestant churches were against permanent sterilization of married couples who had had all the children they wanted because they worried that in the case of widow(er)hood and remarriage more children might be desired, some authorities did support its use amongst the poor or "ignorant" populations, who could not be trusted to utilize contraceptives like the Pill effectively. See *Lambeth Conference 1958*, 2.148; "Toward a Christian Understanding of Sex, Love, Marriage," 2.
106 *The Hallowing of the Union*, 8.
107 See, for the Anglican Church, *The Hallowing of the Union*; Mrs. F.G.T. Dawson, "British War Wives," *Bulletin of the Council for Social Service* 119 (1945): 3–7; *Lambeth Conference 1948*; ACC, F. CSS G.S. 75–106, box 12, Marriage Commission Correspondence 1950–1962, "A Marriage Counselling Programme for the Church," A report on a three-day central Institute on Marriage Counselling conducted by the Joint Committee on Adult Religious Education of the Church of England, Toronto, 26–28 November 1951; Reverend Owen G. Barrow, "Sex Instruction in the Parish," *News and Notes for Clergy* 4 (26 February 1947): 2–8; *Lambeth Conference 1958*, 17–18; LAC, MG288 I 117, volume 73, Anglican Church of Canada Folder (1/2) 1954–1976, Graham Cotter, "Preparation of Marriage and Family Life: A Summary for The Canadian Conference on the Family," n.p.; C.R. Fielding and R.S. Ryan, *Marriage and Family Life 1: On Marriage and the Church (Canon and Commentary)* (Toronto: Anglican Book Centre, 1965); ACC SD20 F24.3, Marriage, Family and the Single State Folder, Charles R. Fielding, "Notes on Marriage, Family and the Single State in Preparation for Lambeth 1968," 13; Bolton, "Premarital Talks," 14; Maurice P.

Wilkinson, "Out of Wedlock," *The Bulletin* 193 (May 1966): 3–16. For the United Church, see LAC, MG 28 I10, volume 62, folder 492, Marriage – Counselling 1946–47, S.R. Laycock, "Premarital Counselling Clinic Organized by Saskatoon Church," 25 May 1946; Werner, "Marks of a Christian Home;" Ellzey, *Sex, Love, and Marriage*, n.p.; UCAC, Accn. 82.086 box 1 f. 14, "Toward a Christian Understanding of Sex, Love, Marriage: A First Report of the Commission on Christian Marriage and Divorce, Approved by the Nineteenth General Council of the United Church of Canada, Edmonton Alberta September 1960."

108 See LAC, MG 28 I10, volume 62, folder 492 Marriage – Counselling 1954–66, letter to Phyllis Burns, Secretary, Family and Child Welfare Division of the Welfare Council in Ottawa from the Office of the Board of Christian Education of the United Church of Canada in Toronto, 17 May 1954; UCAC, Accn. 83.052C, f. 45–15, File of the Commission on Christian Marriage and Divorce, A.V. Bentum, "Marriage and Divorce – A Brief on AID, 23 April 1959; Frederick Elkin, "Dimensions of the Problem of Unmarried Parenthood," *Bulletin* 193 (May 1966): 1–6. *Christian Home* contributors used this technique quite often. See Reverend Frank P. Fidler, "Marriage Preparation Begins in the Cradle," *Christian Home* (September 1960): 49; Allen J. Moore, "What's Happening to the North American Family?" *Christian Home* (May 1962): 4; Albert Dale Hagler, "Parents Can Help Divorced Teen-Agers," *Christian Home* (July 1964): 14; Mrs. Grier, "Vocation Homemaker," *Christian Home* (July 1964): 9.

109 Marion O. Robinson, *Give My Heart: The Dr. Marion Hilliard Story* (Garden City, NY: Doubleday & Company, 1964). According to Robinson, a close female friend inspired her conversion.

110 *The Hallowing of the Union*, 189.

111 For further information on Hilliard's column in *Chatelaine* see Korinek, *Roughing It in the Suburbs*, 272, 295–300, 306, 337, 370.

112 *Lambeth Conference 1958*, 2.142–3.

113 Children, of course, had limited ability to choose their religious affiliation, being most often raised in their parent's faith. However, by the time of marriage it could be argued that a degree of adult autonomy would have been achieved. And some children did assert their religious will. Diane West recounted to me that after having a conflict with her Anglican Sunday School teacher she demanded to be able to attend Sunday School at the United Church across the road. Her mother agreed as, according to Diane, all that mattered to her mother was that Diane attend some kind of Protestant service. Diane West, personal interview, 19 July 2010.

114 These changes would cause a schism in the international Anglican faith. Most recently at the 2016 General Synod gay marriage was again a divisive topic, mainly between northern and southern authorities. The official

acceptance of gay marriage only just failed to attain the votes needed to be uniformly allowed across the entire faith, leaving the issue once again in a grey area. The decision on gay marriage is supposed to be made in 2022. Many Anglican ministers in Canada currently do marry gay and lesbian couples in their churches.

4. Bringing Down Goliath: Oral Histories and the Engagement of Individual Bodies with the Ideal

1 For details about the interview recruitment process and information about the eighteen narrators, see Appendix.
2 I have adapted this from masculinity scholar R.W. Connell's term "patriarchal dividends." She describes this as the process by which all men, even if they do not engage in the more visible or harmful elements of patriarchy, get a benefit, both social and economic, simply for being male. In the same way, my narrators receive "dividends of normality," which are mainly social, by performing their day-to-day acceptance of postwar heterosexual normality. One of these dividends is the ability to create change within the dominant body politic from the inside without being seen to directly challenge its norms. For an explanation of patriarchal dividends see Connell, *Masculinities* (Berkley: University of California Press, 2005).
3 See Lynn Abrams, "Talking about Feminism: Reconciling Fragmented Narratives with the Feminist Research Frame," in *Beyond Women's Words: Feminisms and the Practices of Oral History in the Twenty-First Century*, ed. Katrina Srigley, Stacey Zembrzycki, and Franca Iacovetta (London: Routledge, 2018), 81–94; Kathryn Anderson and Dara C. Jack, "Learning to Listen: Interview Techniques and Analyses," in *Women's Words: The Feminist Practice of Oral History*, ed. Sherna Berger Gluck and Daphne Patai (New York: Routledge, 1991), 11–26; Katherine Borland, "'That's Not What I Said': Interpretive Conflict in Oral Narrative Research," in *Women's Words*, ed. Gluck and Patai, 63–75; Marie-Françoise Chenfrault-Duchet, "Narrative Structures, Social Models, and Symbolic Representation in the Life Story," in *Women's Words*, ed. Gluck and Patai, 77–92; Karen Dubinsky, "'Who Do you Think Did All the Cooking?' Baba in the Classroom," in *Changing Lives: Women in Northern Ontario*, ed. Margaret Kechnie and Marge Reitsma-Street (Toronto: Dundurn, 1996), 193–7; Franca Iacovetta, Katrina Srigley, and Stacey Zembrzycki, "Introduction," in *Beyond Women's Words*, ed. Srigley, Zembrzycki, and Iacovetta, 1–23; Nancy Janovicek, "Oral History and Ethical Practice: Towards Effective Policies and Procedures," *Journal of Academic Ethics* 4, no. 1 (2006): 157–74; Valerie J. Korinek, "Locating Lesbians, Finding 'Gay Women,' Writing Queer Histories: Reflections on Oral Histories, Identity, and Community

Memory," in *Beyond Women's Words*, ed. Srigley, Zembrzycki, and Iacovetta (London: Routledge, 2018), 126–36; Kristina Minister, "A Feminist Frame for the Oral History Interview," in *Women's Words*, ed. Gluck and Patai, 27–41; Joan Sangster, "Telling Our Stories: Feminist Debates and the Use of Oral History," *Women's History Review* 3, no. 1 (2006): 5–28; Penny Summerfield, "Talking about Feminism: Reconciling Fragmented Narratives with the Feminist Research Frame," in *Beyond Women's Words*, ed. Srigley, Zembrzycki, and Iacovetta, 78–80.

4 Elizabeth Lapovsky Kennedy and Madeline D. Davis, *Boots of Leather, Slippers of Gold: The History of a Lesbian Community* (New York: Routledge, 1993), 25.

5 Iacovetta, Srigley, and Zembrzycki, "Introduction," 3.

6 Summerfield, "Talking about Feminism," 78. Valerie J. Korinek also makes the important point that "slow scholarship" is a luxury usually afforded only to established scholars rather than graduate students or precariously employed historians. Korinek, "Locating Lesbians," 130.

7 Susan Zeiger noted this issue in her interviews with war brides. Zeiger, *Entangling Alliances: Foreign War Brides and American Soldiers in the Twentieth Century* (New York: New York University Press, 2010), 109–10. Other authors examining social movements have also noted the shared dominant narratives of activist groups. See for example Abrams, "Talking about Feminism," 83–4; Korinek, "Locating Lesbians," 127, 130–1.

8 Histories of war brides are dominated by commemorative works that were of limited use to this project. For some scholarly examinations of the war bride phenomenon in World War II and beyond, see Barbara G. Friedman, *From the Battlefront to the Bridal Suite: Media Coverage of British War Brides, 1943–1946* (Missouri: University of Missouri Press, 2007); Petra Goedde, "From Villains to Victims: Fraternization and Feminization of Germany, 1945–1947," *Diplomatic History* 23, no. 1 (1999): 1–20; Zeiger, *Entangling Alliances*.

9 Zeiger, *Entangling Alliances*, 109–10, 115.

10 The rituals surrounding the offering and taking of food in oral histories are not frivolous, and often the sharing of food holds symbolic meaning for narrators in terms of power and who has control over the environment. Every narrator offered me some kind of refreshment, usually tea, which I accepted, and often food, which I only refused during that short period of my first trimester for the aforementioned reasons.

11 Most of the narrators did assume that I was heterosexual before it was confirmed that I was, indeed, married to a man. I do not know whether the women who interviewed by telephone assumed I was white, though I suspect they visualized me as such. As for the in-person interviews, there was no discussion of my heritage, and my Caucasian appearance was

taken at face value. I mention this here because of discussions in chapter 2 and in the conclusion that discuss the ways that whiteness, national belonging, sexuality, and gender worked together.
12 These exceptions included instances where references to third parties were made and could not be included as part of ethical protocol.
13 Marjorie Taylor, personal interview, 17 October 2010; Florence Anderson, personal interview, 20 September 2010; Alice Hall, personal interview, 28 June 2010. Note that all oral history participants were given a pseudonym. Further details about each participant, including date they were married, can be found in the attached appendix.
14 For the ways that nostalgia shapes oral history, see for example Christopher Shaw and Malcolm Chase, "The Dimensions of Nostalgia," in *The Imagined Past: History and Nostalgia*, ed. Christopher Shaw and Malcolm Chase (Manchester: Manchester University Press, 1989), 1–17; David Lowenthal, "Nostalgia Tells It Like It Wasn't," in *The Imaged Past*, ed. Shaw and Chase, 18–32. For analysis of the ways in which putting a life history into narrative form changes its meaning, see Abrams, "Talking about Feminism," 81–94; Chenfrault-Duchet, "Narrative Structures, " 77–92; Korinek, "Locating Lesbians,'" 126–36.
15 Robert Rutherdale, "Fatherhood, Masculinity, and the Good Life during Canada's Baby Boom, 1945–1965," *Journal of Family History* 24, no. 3 (1999): 356.
16 Karen Rand, personal interview, 7 July 2010.
17 Fiona Shortt, personal interview, 5 July 2010.
18 Rand, interview, 7 July 2010.
19 Kate Fisher, *Birth Control, Sex, and Marriage in Britain 1918–1960* (Oxford: Oxford University Press, 2006).
20 Anderson, interview, 20 September 2010. Anderson recalls this situation falling into a grey area, as the rumour was that the sexual intercourse could have been consensual or not depending on who was telling the story. It is likely there was some coercion or intimidation occurring at the very least given the power differentials between adult male soldiers and underaged women.
21 Kennedy and Davis also discuss this in *Boots of Leather*, 24–5.
22 Shortt, interview, 5 July 2010.
23 Lois Adamson, personal interview, 19 March 2010.
24 Edith Small, personal interview, 19 September 2010.
25 Margaret Brown, personal interview, 27 June 2010. Edith Small gave a similar response, noting that feminism was okay as long as it did not go "too far." Small, interview, 19 September 2010.
26 *Suffragettes Who Have Never Been Kissed*, [print], Mary Evans Picture Library, London, 1909.

27 Of course, homophobia would weaken the second-wave feminist movement from within, as leaders, most famously Betty Friedan, cast lesbian feminists as the "lavender menace." Friedan and others argued that lesbian visibility within the movement would confuse the main issues of women's rights but were also clearly motivated by their own homophobia and concerns that the homophobia of other women would prevent them from joining a movement associated with lesbian activism. Many lesbian feminists have been rightly critical of how such divisions have been lost in the celebratory historical narrative of the second-wave movement.
28 Adamson, interview, 19 March 2010.
29 Ibid.
30 Zieger, *Entangling Alliances*, 140.
31 Hall, interview, 28 June 2010.
32 Ruth Bell, personal interview, 21 September 2010.
33 Rutherdale, "Fatherhood, Masculinity," 365.
34 Brown, interview, 27 June 2010; Jean Simpson, personal interview, 5 July 2010.
35 Shortt, interview, 5 July 2010.
36 Rand, interview, 7 July 2010.
37 Joyce Martin, personal interview, 4 October 2010.
38 Ibid.
39 Though Joyce backtracks and changes "mother" to "parent," the rest of her interview makes it clear that, in her mind, a woman would be best suited to such a role.
40 Taylor, interview, 17 October 2010. It would be years later, in the 1980s after her husband became very ill and required constant nursing from Marjorie, that they finally reconciled. They moved into an assisted living facility and, though they maintained separate bedrooms within their apartment, Marjorie says they became very close, finally talking about contentious issues that they had hitherto avoided. Whether this was an actual reconciliation where Marjorie's husband began to treat and value Marjorie as an equal, a power shift as Marjorie's husband became totally reliant on her, or the fact that Marjorie, in nursing her husband for six years, was returned to a more "normal" domestic role that her husband could accept, is impossible to tell.
41 Jessica Bateman, personal interview, 19 July 2010.
42 Ibid.
43 Mary Johnston, personal interview, 19 April 2010.
44 Simpson, interview, 5 July 2010.
45 Fisher, *Birth Control, Sex, and Marriage*, 26. Medical and religious authorities expressed concern about the lasting psychological harm that could

be caused by complete sexual ignorance. Further, both medical and religious authorities recognized the importance of controlling the new stream of sexual education discourse in order to maintain the correct balance between esoteric sexual knowledge and practical innocence prior to marriage.
46 In *Birth Control, Sex, and Marriage,* Fisher explains the paradox that most of her narrators left any birth control to their husbands, carefully cultivating a sense of ignorance around birth control to maintain an image of sexual naivete and purity despite the fact that they, as women, bore the consequences of (lack of) birth prevention tools. In contrast, almost all of my narrators took responsibility for birth control in their marriages, though usually in consultation with their husbands.
47 Small, interview, 19 September 2010.
48 Brown, interview, 27 June 2010.
49 Bell, interview, 21 September 2010. This was also echoed by fellow war bride Glenda Baker. Glenda Baker, personal interview, 20 September 2010.
50 Anderson, interview, 20 September 2010.
51 Rand, interview, 7 July 2010.
52 Friedman, *Battlefront to Bridal Suite,* 123; Zeiger, *Entangling Alliances,* 131.
53 King, interview, 20 September 2010.
54 Diane West, personal interview, 19 July 2010.
55 Taylor, interview, 17 October 2010.
56 Martin, interview, 4 October 2010.
57 Nancy Wilson, personal interview, 19 April 2010.
58 Hall, interview, 28 June 2010, emphasis added.
59 Michel Foucault, *The History of Sexuality: An Introduction, Volume 1,* trans. Robert Hurley (New York: Vintage Books), 4.
60 The importance and power of the image of scientific progress has been amply demonstrated throughout this book. For additional examples see Mary Louise Adams, *The Trouble with Normal: Postwar Youth and the Making of Heterosexuality* (Toronto: University of Toronto Press, 1997); Mona Gleason, *Normalizing the Ideal: Psychology, Schooling, and the Family in Postwar Canada* (Toronto: University Press, 1999); Valerie J. Korinek, *Roughing It in the Suburbs: Reading* Chatelaine *Magazine in the Fifties and Sixties* (Toronto: University of Toronto Press, 2000); Wendy Mitchinson, *Bodily Failure: Medical Views of Women, 1990–1950* (Toronto: University of Toronto Press, 2013); Cheryl Krasnick Warsh, *Prescribed Norms: Women and Health in Canada and the United States since 1800* (Toronto: University of Toronto Press, 2010).
61 Adamson, interview, 19 March 2010.
62 Rand, interview, 7 July 2010. To clarify, Karen's statement "I used to love it" did not express current regret but a recognition that her children were

grown and she was not a mother to them in the same way as she was when they were young.
63 Adamson, interview, 19 March 2010.
64 Hall, interview, 28 June 2010.
65 For a social history of daycare, see Lisa Pasolli, *Working Mothers and the Child Care Dilemma: A History of British Columbia's Social Policy* (Vancouver: UBC Press, 2015).
66 Martin, interview, 4 October 2010.
67 Small, interview, 19 September 2010.
68 Ibid. Nancy Wilson had a similar experience. She lost an ovary when it was removed during a cyst operation. It then took several years for her to get pregnant with her first child. This puzzled but did not unduly distress her. Wilson, interview, 19 April 2010.
69 Adamson, interview, 19 March 2010.
70 Wilson, interview, 19 April 2010.
71 See Nancy Ehrenreich, ed., *The Reproductive Rights Reader: Law, Medicine, and the Construction of Motherhood* (New York: New York University Press, 2008); Angus McLaren and Arlene Tigar McLaren, *The Bedroom and the State: The Changing Practices and Politics of Contraception and Abortion in Canada, 1880–1980* (Toronto: McClelland & Stewart, 1986); Dorothy E. Roberts, *Killing the Black Body: Race, Reproduction, and the Meaning of Liberty* (New York: Pantheon, 1997).
72 With the exception of Fiona Shortt, who though currently living in comfortable circumstances was facing some financial instability as a result of her divorce.
73 Baker, interview, 20 September 2010.
74 Taylor, interview, 17 October 2010.
75 Johnston, interview, 19 April 2010.
76 West, interview, 19 July 2010.
77 Ibid.
78 Shortt, interview, 5 July 2010.
79 Ibid.
80 Brown, interview, 19 July 2010.
81 Ibid.
82 Ibid.
83 It is possible that the men in those marriages also felt they were making sacrifices, and it would be interesting to see if they would frame those sacrifices within the gendered scripts of the day – for example, having to work long hours to provide for their families when they would rather be home with them. However, such an examination is beyond the scope of this research.
84 Baker, interview, 20 September 2010.

85 Adamson, interview, 19 March 2010; Hall, interview, 28 June 2010; King, interview, 20 September 2010.
86 Rand, interview, 7 July 2010.
87 Anderson, interview, 20 September 2010.
88 Fiona Shortt also conceptualized her modifications in this way, excusing her husband's behaviour by noting that he had been terribly abused by family members that he had been sent to as an evacuated child. Shortt, interview, 5 July 2010.
89 Rand, interview, 7 July 2010.
90 Wilson, interview, 19 April 2010.
91 Small, interview, 19 September 2010.
92 Taylor, interview, 17 October 2010.
93 King, interview, 20 September 2010.
94 Taylor, interview, 17 October 2010. This was also echoed by Mary Johnston. Johnston, interview, 19 April 2010.
95 Robert Rutherdale discusses this in his essay "New 'Faces' for Fathers: Memory, Life-Writing, and Fathers as Providers in the Postwar Consumer Era," in *Creating Postwar Canada, 1945–75*, ed. Magda Fahrni and Robert Rutherdale, 241–67 (Vancouver: UBC Press, 2008).
96 This normality was manifested most clearly by the having of children and simply staying together over the long term.
97 Adams, *The Trouble with Normal*, 26.
98 Jenny Ellison, *Being Fat: Women, Weight, and Feminist Activism in Canada* (Toronto: University of Toronto Press, 2020), 66–7.
99 Ibid., 26–7.
100 Simpson, interview, 5 July 2010.
101 According to several large-scale studies in the United States and Canada, the average amount of sexual activity for heterosexual couples is seven times a month, or slightly less than two times a week. See Amy Muise, "The Passion Paradox: The Ins and Outs of Sexual Frequency," *Psychology Today*, 8 June 2012. However, what is important about this exchange is not that Jean Simpson had more-frequent-than-average sexual contact with her husband but her reaction against being defined as not average and thus not "normal."
102 Bateman, interview, 19 July 2010.
103 Ibid.
104 Ibid.
105 Ibid.
106 Significantly, only Nancy Wilson, whose whole narrative was built around her concept of herself as an exceptional woman and self-professed "indigo" – a New Age term denoting a special person with a unique destiny on earth – was comfortable in proclaiming that her

personal sexual drive, as well as the frequency of sexual interaction with her husband, was uniquely high. Wilson, interview, 19 April 2010.
107 Foucault, *The History of Sexuality*, 4.
108 Shortt, interview, 5 July 2010; Johnston, interview, 19 April 2010.
109 West, interview, 19 July 2010.
110 Shortt, interview, 5 July 2010.
111 Small, interview, 5 July 2010.
112 Constance Backhouse, *Carnal Crimes: Sexual Assault Law in Canada, 1900–1975* (Toronto: Osgoode Society for Canadian Legal History, 2008), 112.
113 Ibid., 111.
114 Karen Dubinsky, *Improper Advances: Rape and Heterosexual Conflict in Ontario, 1880–1929* (Chicago: University of Chicago Press, 1993), 165.
115 Ibid.
116 Ibid., 8, 15–16, 164–5.
117 Jean Barman, "Aboriginal Women on the Streets of Victoria: Rethinking Transgressive Sexuality during the Colonial Encounter," in *Contact Zones: Aboriginal and Settler Women in Canada's Colonial Past*, ed. Katie Pickles and Myra Rutherdale (Vancouver: UBC Press, 2005), 205–27; Robin Jarvis Brownlie, "Intimate Surveillance: Indian Affairs, Colonization and the Regulation of Aboriginal Women's Sexuality," in *Contact Zones*, ed. Pickles and Rutherdale, 160–78; Constance Backhouse, *Carnal Crimes*, 227–62.
118 Karen Dubinsky, *The Second Greatest Disappointment: Honeymooning and Tourism at Niagara Falls* (Toronto: Between the Lines, 1999), 228.
119 The concept of the Coney Island mirror is borrowed from Susan M. Carini, "Love's Labors Almost Lost: Managing Crisis during the Reign of 'I Love Lucy,'" *Cinema Journal* 43, no.1 (2003): 44–62.
120 Hall, interview, 28 June 2010; Bell, interview, 21 September 2010.
121 Foucault, *The History of Sexuality*.

5. Conclusion: Making Good (Sex)

1 Michel Foucault, *The History of Sexuality: An Introduction, Volume 1*, trans. Robert Hurley (New York: Vintage Books, 1978), 135–59.
2 Valerie J. Korinek, *Roughing It in the Suburbs: Reading* Chatelaine *Magazine in the Fifties and Sixties* (Toronto: University of Toronto Press, 2000), 72–3.
3 Karen Dubinsky deconstructs the mythologizing of rural spaces as inherently sexually safe in her work. See Dubinsky, *Improper Advances: Rape and Heterosexual Conflict in Ontario, 1880–1929* (Chicago: University of Chicago Press, 1993).
4 Florence Anderson, personal interview, 20 September 2010.
5 Karen Rand, personal interview, 7 July 2010.

6 Verna King, personal interview, 20 September 2010.
7 Joyce Martin, personal interview, 4 October 2010.
8 Ibid.
9 Susan M. Carini, "Love's Labors Almost Lost: Managing Crisis during the Reign of 'I Love Lucy,'" *Cinema Journal* 43, no.1 (2003): 44–62.

Bibliography

Archives

Anglican Archives of Canada (AAC)
Library and Archives Canada, Ottawa (LAC)
United Church Archives of Canada (UCAC)

Interviews

All names are pseudonyms to protect the privacy of the individual interviewed.

Adamson, Lois. Interview by the author, 19 March 2010.
Anderson, Florence. Interview by the author, 20 September 2010.
Baker, Glenda. Interview by the author, 20 September 2010.
Bateman, Jessica. Interview by the author, 19 July 2010.
Bell, Ruth. Interview by the author, 21 September 2010.
Brown, Margaret. Interview by the author, 27 June 2010.
Carter, Evelyn. Interview by the author, 20 September 2010.
Hall, Alice. Interview by the author, 28 June 2010.
Johnston, Mary. Interview by the author, 19 April 2010.
King, Verna. Interview by the author, 20 September 2010.
Martin, Joyce. Interview by the author, 4 October 2010.
Rand, Karen. Interview by the author, 7 July 2010.
Shortt, Fiona. Interview by the author, 5 July 2010.
Simpson, Jean. Interview by the author, 5 July 2010.
Small, Edith. Interview by the author, 19 September 2010.
Taylor, Marjorie. Interview by the author, 17 October 2010.
West, Diane. Interview by the author, 19 July 2010.
Wilson, Nancy. Interview by the author, 19 April 2010.

Published Sources

Abrams, Lynn. "Talking about Feminism: Reconciling Fragmented Narratives with the Feminist Research Frame." In *Beyond Women's Words: Feminisms and the Practices of Oral History in the Twenty-First Century*, edited by Katrina Srigley, Stacey Zembrzycki, and Franca Iacovetta, 81–94. London: Routledge, 2018.

Adams, Mary Louise. *The Trouble with Normal: Postwar Youth and the Making of Heterosexuality*. Toronto: Toronto University Press, 1997.

Allyn, David. *The Sexual Revolution: An Unfettered History*. Boston: Little Brown and Company, 2000.

Anderson, Katheryn, and Dara C. Jack. "Learning to Listen: Interview Techniques and Analyses." In *Women's Words: The Feminist Practice of Oral History*, edited by Sherna Berger Gluck and Daphne Patai, 11–26. New York: Routledge, 1991.

Backhouse, Constance. *Carnal Crimes: Sexual Assault Law in Canada, 1900–1975*. Toronto: Osgoode Society for Canadian Legal History, 2008.

– *Petticoats and Prejudice: Women and the Law in Nineteenth-Century Canada*. Toronto: Osgoode Society by Women's Press, 1991.

Bailey, Beth L. *From Front Porch to Back Seat: Courtship in Twentieth-Century America*. Baltimore: Johns Hopkins University Press, 1988.

– *Sex in the Heartland*. Cambridge, MA: Harvard University Press, 1999.

Baillargeon, Denyse. *Babies for the Nation: The Medicalization of Motherhood in Quebec, 1910–1970*. Translated by Donald W. Wilson. Waterloo: Wilfred Laurier University Press, 2009.

Barman, Jean. "Aboriginal Women on the Streets of Victoria: Rethinking Transgressive Sexuality during the Colonial Encounter." In *Contact Zones: Aboriginal and Settler Women in Canada's Colonial Past*, edited by Katie Pickles and Myra Rutherdale, 205–27. Vancouver: UBC Press, 2005.

Bartky, Sandra. *Femininity and Domination: Studies in the Phenomenology of Oppression*. New York: Routledge, 1990.

Bates, Stephen. *A Church at War: Anglicans and Homosexuality*. London: I.B. Tauris, 2004.

Baum, Gregory. *Amazing Church: A Catholic Theologian Remembers a Half-Century of Change*. Ottawa: Novalis, St. Paul's University, 2005.

Bederman, Gail. *Manliness and Civilization: A Cultural History of Gender and Race in the United States*. Chicago: Chicago University Press, 1995.

Beemyn, Brett, ed. *Creating a Place for Ourselves: Lesbian, Gay, and Bisexual Community Histories*. New York: Routledge, 1997.

Bennett, John Sutton. *History of the Canadian Medical Association, 1954–1994*. Ottawa: CMA, 1996.

Berhrend-Martinez, Edward. "Manhood and the Neutered Body in Early Modern Spain." *Journal of Social History* 38, no. 4 (2005): 1073–93.
Berkus, Catherine A. *The Religious History of American Women: Reimagining the Past*. Chapel Hill: University of North Carolina Press, 2007.
Berry, J. Gerald. "The Christian Family Apostolate." In *The Christian Family Apostolate*, 64–7. Sudbury: Report of the Seventh Annual Session of the Catholic Social Life Conference, 1959.
Bibby, Rtheald W. *Fragmented Gods: The Poverty and Potential of Religion in Canada*. Toronto: Stoddart, 1990.
– *Restless Gods: The Renaissance of Religion in Canada*. Toronto: Stoddart, 2002.
Block, Tina. *The Secular Northwest: Religion and Irreligion in Everyday Postwar Life*. Vancouver: UBC Press, 2016.
Bolton, Kenneth C. *Premarital Talks: A Counsellor's Approach to Couples About to Be Married*. Toronto: Anglican Church of Canada Joint Committee on Adult Religious Education, 1958.
Borland, Katherine. "'That's Not What I Said': Interpretive Conflict in Oral Narrative Research." In *Women's Words: The Feminist Practice of Oral History*, edited by Sherna Berger Gluck and Daphne Patai, 63–75. New York: Routledge, 1991.
Boss, Sarah Jane. *Empress and Handmaid: On Nature and Gender in the Cult of Virgin Mary*. London: Cassell, 2000.
– ed. *Mary: The Complete Resource*. London: Continuum International, 2007.
Boston Women's Health Book Collective, ed. *Our Bodies, Ourselves: A Book by and for Women*. New York: Simon and Schuster, 1973.
Bouchard, Gerard. "La sexualité comme practique et rapport social chez les couples paysans du Saguenay (1860–1930)." *Revue d'histoire de l'Amerique française* 53, no. 2 (2000): 183–217.
Bourke, Joanna. *Dismembering the Male: Men's Bodies, Britain and the Great War*. Chicago: University of Chicago Press, 1996.
– *Fear: A Cultural History*. Emeryville, CA: Publishers Group West, 2006.
– "Sexual Violence, Marital Guidance, and Victorian Bodies: An Aesthesiology." *Victorian Studies* 50, no. 3 (2008): 419–36.
– *The Story of Pain: From Prayer to Painkillers*. Oxford: Oxford University Press, 2014.
Breines, Wini. *Young, White and Miserable: Growing Up Female in the Fifties*. Boston: Beacon, 1992.
Brookfield, Tarah. *Cold War Comforts: Canadian Women, Child Safety, and Global Insecurity*. Waterloo: Wilfred Laurier University Press, 2012.
Brown, Thomas E. "Dr. Ernest Jones, Psychoanalysis and the Canadian Medical Profession, 1908–1913." In *Medicine in Canada: Historical Perspectives*, edited by S.E.D. Shortt, 351–60. Montreal & Kingston: McGill-University Press, 1981.

Brownlie, Robin Jarvis. "Intimate Surveillance: Indian Affairs, Colonization, and the Regulation of Aboriginal Women's Sexuality." In *Contact Zones: Aboriginal and Settler Women in Canada's Colonial Past*, edited by Katie Pickles and Myra Rutherdale. 160–78. Vancouver: UBC Press, 2005.

Bulletin of the Council for Social Service, The Church of England in Canada. Brampton: Charter's, 1945–66.

Bunnik, Patricia R.J. "The Ecclesiastical Minister and Marriage: An Attempt at Clarification." *Social Compass* 12 (1965): 53–100.

Burnham, John C. *After Freud Left: A Century of Psychoanalysis in America.* Chicago: University of Chicago Press, 2012.

Burt, Sandra, Lorraine Code, and Lindsay Dorney, eds. *Changing Patterns: Women in Canada and Social Rights in America*. Toronto: McClelland & Stewart, 1988.

Butler, Judith. *Gender Trouble: Feminism and Subversion of Identity*. New York: Routledge, 1990.

Bynum, Caroline. *Holy Feast and Holy Fast: The Religious Significance of Food to Medieval Women*. Berkley: University of California Press, 1987.

– "Why All the Fuss about the Body? A Medievalist's Perspective." *Critical Inquiry* 22, no. 1 (1995): 1–33.

Canadian Medical Association Journal. Toronto: CMA, 1946–66.

Canadian Psychiatric Association Journal. Ottawa: Canadian Psychiatric Association, 1956–66.

Carey, John Jesse, ed. *The Sexuality Debate in North American Churches, 1988–1995: Controversies, Unresolved Issues, Future Prospects*. Lewiston: Mellen, 1995.

Carini, Susan M. "Love's Labors Almost Lost: Managing Crisis during the Reign of 'I Love Lucy.'" *Cinema Journal* 43, no.1 (2003): 44–62.

Carter, Alexander. "Report of the Family Life Survey of Sault Ste. Marie." In *The Christian Family Apostolate*, 83–93. Sudbury: Report of the Seventh Annual Session of the Catholic Social Life Conference, 1959.

Carter, Sarah. *The Importance of Being Monogamous: Marriage and Nation Building in Western Canada to 1915*. Edmonton: University of Alberta Press, 2008.

Catholic Family Life Survey – City of Saskatoon: A Joint Report and Statistical Survey. Saskatoon: Steering Committee SCFLS. Catholic Centre, 1960.

Celello, Kristin. *Making Marriage Work: A History of Marriage and Divorce in the Twentieth Century United States*. Chapel Hill: University of North Carolina Press, 2009.

Chang, M.Y. "The Crisis Is about Control: Consequences of the Priestly Decline in the US Catholic Church." *Sociology of Religion* 59, no.1 (1998): 1–5.

Chauncey, George. *Gay New York: Urban Culture and the Making of the Gay Male World, 1890–1940*. New York: Basic Books, 1994.

Chenfrault-Duchet, Marie-Françoise. "Narrative Structures, Social Models, and Symbolic Representation in the Life Story." In *Women's Words: The Feminist Practice of Oral History*, edited by Sherna Berger Gluck and Daphne Patai, 77–92. New York: Routledge, 1991.

Chenier, Elise. "Hidden from Historians: Preserving Lesbian Oral History in Canada." *Archivaria* 68 (Fall 2009): 247–69.

– "Rethinking Class in Lesbian Bar Culture: Living 'The Gay Life' in Toronto, 1955–1965." *Left History* 9, no. 2. (2004): 85–118.

– *Strangers in Our Midst: Sexual Deviancy in Postwar Ontario*. Toronto: University of Toronto Press, 2008.

Christian Family Apostolate, The. Report of the Seventh Annual Session of the Catholic Social Life Conference, Sudbury, 9–10 October 1959.

Christian Home. Toronto: United Church Publishing House, 1959–66.

Christie, Nancy. "Sacred Sex: The United Church and the Privatization of the Family in Post-War Canada." In *Households of Faith: Family, Gender, and Community in Canada, 1760–1969*, edited by Nancy Christie, 348–76. Montreal & Kingston: McGill-Queen's University Press, 2002.

Christie, Nancy, and Michael Gauvreau. *Christian Churches and Their Peoples, 1840–1965: A Social History of Religion in Canada*. Toronto: University of Toronto Press, 2010.

– *A Full-Orbed Christianity: The Protestant Churches and Social Welfare, 1900–1940*. Montreal & Kingston: McGill-Queen's University Press, 1996.

Clarke, Brian, and Stuart Macdonald. *Leaving Christianity: Changing Allegiances in Canada Since 1945*. Montreal & Kingston: McGill-Queen's University Press, 2017.

Cobble, Dorothy Sue. *The Other Women's Movement: Workplace Justice and Social Rights in America*. Princeton: Princeton University Press, 2004.

Collins, Marcus. *Modern Love: An Intimate History of Men and Women in the Twentieth Century*. London: Atlantic, 2003.

Colvin, Kelly Ricciardi. "'A Well-Made-Up Woman': Aesthetics and Conformity in Postwar France." *French Historical Studies* 38, no. 4 (2015): 691–718.

Comacchio, Cynthia. *Nations Are Built of Babies: Saving Ontario's Mothers and Children, 1900–1940*. Montreal & Kingston: McGill-Queen's University Press, 1993.

Connell, R.W. *Masculinities*. Berkley: University of California Press, 2005.

Conway, Jill. "Stereotypes of Femininity in a Theory of Sexual Evolution." In *Suffer and Be Still: Women in the Victorian Age*, edited by Martha Vicinus, 140–54. Bloomington: University of Indiana Press, 1972.

Cook, Ramsay. *The Regenerators: Social Criticism in Late Victorian English Canada*. 2nd ed. Toronto: University of Toronto Press, 1985.

Coontz, Stephanie. *Marriage, a History: From Obedience to Intimacy or How Love Conquered Marriage*. New York: Viking, 2005.

– *The Way We Never Were: American Families and the Nostalgia Trap*. New York: Basic Books, 1992.
Cott, Nancy. *Public Vows: A History of Marriage and the Nation*. Cambridge, MA: Harvard University Press, 2000.
Davidson, Reverend Canon W.H. *The Nature of Marriage*. Montreal: R.A. Regnault, 1946.
Dean, Carolyn J. *The Frail Social Body: Pornography, Homosexuality and Other Fantasies in Interwar France*. Berkley: University of California Press, 2000.
D'Emilio, John, and Estelle B. Freedman. *Intimate Matters: A History of Sexuality in America*. New York: Harper & Row, 1988.
Digby, Anne, and Jonathan Andrews. *Sex, Seclusion, Class, and Custody: Perspectives on Gender and Class in the History of British and Irish Psychiatry*. New York: Rodopi, 2005.
Dodd, Dianne. "Women's Involvement in the Canadian Birth Control Movement of the 1930s: The Hamilton Clinic." In *Delivering Motherhood: Maternal Ideologies and Practices in the 19th and 20th Centuries*, edited by Katherine Arnup, Andrée Lévesque, and Ruth Roach Pierson, 150–72. London: Routledge, 1990.
Dominion Bureau of Statistics. *1961 Census of Canada*. Ottawa: Dominion Bureau of Statistics, 1962.
Dominion Bureau of Statistics. *Ninth Census of Canada 1951*. Ottawa: Dominion Bureau of Statistics, 1953.
Dubinsky, Karen. *Improper Advances: Rape and Heterosexual Conflict in Ontario, 1880–1929*. Chicago: University of Chicago Press, 1993.
– *The Second Greatest Disappointment: Honeymooning and Tourism at Niagara Falls*. Toronto: Between the Lines, 1999.
– "'Who Do You Think Did All the Cooking?' Baba in the Classroom." In *Changing Lives: Women in Northern Ontario*, edited by Margaret Kechnie and Marge Reitsma-Street, 193–7, Toronto: Dundurn, 1996.
Duden, Barbara. "History Beneath the Skin." *Michigan Quarterly Review* 30, no. 1 (1991): 174–90.
Duder, Cameron. *Awfully Devoted Women: Lesbian Lives in Canada, 1900–65*. Vancouver: UBC Press, 2010.
Dumont, Micheline. "The Origins of the Movement in Quebec." Translated by Carol Cochrane. In *Challenging Times: The Women's Movements in Canada and the United States*, edited by Constance Backhouse and David H. Flaherty, 72–89. Montreal & Kingston: McGill-Queen's University Press, 1992.
Dyck, Erika. *Facing Eugenics: Reproduction, Sterilization and the Politics of Choice*. Toronto: University of Toronto Press, 2013.
– "Sterilization and Birth Control in the Shadow of Eugenics: Married, Middle-Class Women in Alberta, 1930s–1960s." *Canadian Bulletin of Medical History/Bulletin canadien d'historie de la medicine* 31, no. 1 (2004): 165–87.

Dyck, Erika, and Maureen Lux. *Challenging Choices: Canada's Population Control in the 1970s*. Montreal & Kingston: McGill-Queen's University Press, 2020.
Dyson, William A. "Husband-Wife Relationships." *Social Thought* 61, no. 2 (1960): 1–12.
Ehrenriech, Barbara, and Deirdre English. *Complaints and Disorders: The Sexual Politics of Sickness*. Old Westbury, NY: Feminist Press, 1973.
– *For Her Own Good: 150 Years of the Experts' Advice to Women*. Garden City, NY: Anchor Books, 1979.
Ehrenreich, Nancy, ed. *The Reproductive Rights Reader: Law, Medicine, and the Construction of Motherhood*. New York: New York University Press, 2008.
Ellison, Jenny. *Being Fat: Women, Weight, and Feminist Activism in Canada*. Toronto: University of Toronto Press, 2020.
Ellzey, W. Clark. *Sex, Love, and Marriage*. New York: Office of Publication and Distribution, National Council of the Churches of Christ, 1954.
Epp, Marlene, and Franca Iacovetta, eds. *Sisters or Strangers?: Immigrant, Ethnic, and Racialized Women in Canadian History*. 2nd ed. Toronto: University of Toronto Press, 2016.
Fahrni, Magda, and Robert Rutherdale, eds. *Creating Postwar Canada: Community, Diversity, and Dissent, 1945–75*. Vancouver: UBC Press, 2008.
"Family in Canada, The." Statement of the Canadian Hierarchy. In *The Christian Family Apostolate*, 48–53. Sudbury: Report of the Seventh Annual Session of the Catholic Social Life Conference, 1959.
Featherstone, Lisa. "'The One Single Primary Cause': Divorce, the Family and Heterosexual Pleasure in Postwar Australia." *Journal of Australian Studies* 37, no. 3 (2013): 349–63.
Fielding, C.R., and H.R.S. Ryan. *Marriage and Family Life 1: On Marriage and the Church (Canon and Commentary)*. Toronto: Anglican Book Centre, 1965.
– *Marriage in Church and State: An Introduction to the Canonical Regulation of Marriage in the Anglican Communion*. Toronto: Anglican Book Centre, 1965.
Fisher, Kate. *Birth Control, Sex, and Marriage in Britain, 1918–1960*. Oxford: Oxford University Press, 2006.
Fishman, Sarah. *From Vichy to the Sexual Revolution: Gender and Family Life in Postwar France*. Oxford: Oxford University Press, 2017.
Foucault, Michel. *Abnormal: Lectures at the Collège de France, 1974–1975*. Edited by Valerio Marcetti and Antonella Salmoni. Translated by Graham Burchell. New York: Picador, 1999.
– *The Archaeology of Knowledge and the Discourse of Language*. Translated by Sheridan Smith. New York: Pantheon Books, 1972.
– *The Birth of the Clinic: An Archeology of Medical Perception*. Translated by A.M. Sheridan. New York: Routledge, 1989.
– *Discipline and Punish: The Birth of Prison*. Translated by Alan Sheridan. New York: Vintage Books, 1995.

- *The History of Sexuality: An Introduction, Volume I.* Translated by Robert Hurley. New York: Vintage Books, 1990.
- *Power/Knowledge: Selected Interviews and Other Writings, 1972–1977.* Edited by Colin Gordon. Translated by Colin Gorden et. al. New York: Pantheon Books, 1980.

"Fourth Finger Left Hand." United Church Publishing House, Toronto, n.d.

Fowler, Howard, and H. Breault. "Special Interest Cana Conferences." In *The Christian Family Apostolate*, 165–7. Sudbury: Report of the Seventh Annual Session of the Catholic Social Life Conference, 1959.

Freeman, Susan K. *Sex Goes to School: Girls and Sex Education before the 1960s.* Urbana: University of Illinois Press, 2008.

Friedan, Betty. *The Feminine Mystique.* New York: W.W. Norton & Company, 1963.

Friedman, Barbara G. *From the Battlefront to the Bridal Suite: Media Coverage of British War Brides, 1943–1946.* Columbia: University of Missouri Press, 2007.

Gatens, Moira. *Imaginary Bodies: Ethics, Power, and Corporeality.* New York: Routledge, 1996.

Gauvreau, Michael. *The Catholic Origins of Quebec's Quiet Revolution, 1931–1970.* Montreal & Kingston: McGill-Queen's University Press, 2005.

Gentile, Patrizia, and Jane Nicholas eds. *Contesting Bodies and Nation in Canadian History.* Toronto: University of Toronto Press, 2013.

Gerhard, Jane. "Revisiting 'The Myth of the Vaginal Orgasm': The Female Orgasm in American Sexual Thought and Second Wave Feminism." *Feminist Studies* 26, no. 2 (2000): 449–76.

Gleason, Mona. *Normalizing the Ideal: Psychology, Schooling, and the Family in Postwar Canada.* Toronto: University of Toronto Press, 1999.

Goedde, Petra. "From Villains to Victims: Fraternization and Feminization of Germany, 1945–1947." *Diplomatic History* 23, no. 1 (1999): 1–20.

Gölz, Annalee. "Family Matters: The Canadian Family and the State in the Postwar Period." *Left History* 1, no. 2 (1993): 9–50.

Gordon, Linda. *The Moral Property of Women: A History of Birth Control Politics in America.* Urbana: University of Illinois Press, 2002.

- *Women's Body, Woman's Right: A Social History of Birth Control in America.* New York: Grossman, 1979.

Hale, Nathan G., Jr. *The Rise and Crisis of Psychoanalysis in the United States: Freud and the Americans 1917–1985.* Oxford: Oxford University Press, 1995.

Hall, Lesley A. *Sex, Gender and Social Change in Britain since 1880.* New York: St. Martin's Press, 2000.

Hallowing of the Union, The. Toronto: Diocesan Marriage Services, 196?.

Harris-Zsovan, Jane. *Eugenics and the Firewall: Canada's Nasty Little Secret.* Winnipeg: J.G. Shilingford, 2010.

Helps, Lisa. "Body, Power, Desire: Mapping Canadian Body History." *Journal of Canadian Studies/Revue d'études canadiennes* 41, no. 1 (2007): 126–50

Herzberg, David. *Happy Pills in America: From Miltown to Prozac*. Baltimore: Johns Hopkins University Press, 2009.

Hewitt, Nancy. *No Permanent Waves: Recasting Histories of U.S. Feminism*. New Brunswick: Rutgers University Press, 2004.

Hilliard, Marion. *A Woman Doctor Looks at Love and Life*. Toronto: Doubleday, 1957.

– *Women and Fatigue: A Women Doctor's Answer*. Garden City, NY: Doubleday, 1960.

Hubert, Ollivier, and Michael Gauvreau. "Introduction: Beyond Church History: Recent Developments in the History of Religion in Canada." In *The Churches and Social Order in Nineteenth- and Twentieth-Century Canada*, edited by Michael Gauvreau and Ollivier Hubert, 3–45. Montreal & Kingston: McGill-Queen's University Press, 2006.

Iacovetta, Franca. *Gatekeepers: Reshaping Immigrant Lives in Cold War Canada*. Toronto: Between the Lines, 2006.

Iacovetta, Franca, Katrina Srigley, and Stacey Zembrzycki. "Introduction." In *Beyond Women's Words: Feminisms and the Practices of Oral History in the Twenty-First Century*, edited by Katrina Srigley, Stacey Zembrzycki, and Franca Iacovetta, 1–23. London: Routledge, 2018.

Janovicek, Nancy. "Oral History and Ethical Practice: Towards Effective Policies and Procedures." *Journal of Academic Ethics* 4 (2006):157–74.

Katz, Jonathan Ned. *The Invention of Heterosexuality*. Chicago: University of Chicago Press, 1995.

– *Love Stories: Sex between Men before Homosexuality*. Chicago: Chicago University Press, 2001.

Kealey, Linda, and Joan Sangster, eds. *Beyond the Vote: Canadian Women and Politics*. Toronto: University of Toronto Press, 1989.

– "Introduction." In *Beyond the Vote: Canadian Women and Politics*, edited by Linda Kealey and Joan Sangster, 3–15. Toronto: University of Toronto Press, 1989.

Keehn, J.D. *Master Builders of Modern Psychology: From Freud to Skinner*. New York: New York University Press, 1996.

Kennedy, Elizabeth Lapovsky, and Madeline D. Davis. *Boots of Leather, Slippers of Gold: The History of a Lesbian Community*. New York: Routledge, 1993.

Keshen, Jeffry. *Saints, Sinners, and Soldiers: Canada's Second World War*. Vancouver: UBC Press, 2004.

Kinnear, Julia L. "The Professionalization of Canadian Nursing, 1934–32: Views in the *CN* and *CMAJ*." *Canadian Bulletin of Medical History/Bulletin canadien d'historie de la medicine* 11 (1994): 153–74.

Kinsman, Gary. *The Regulation of Desire: Sexuality in Canada.* Montreal: Black Rose Books, 1987.
Kinsman, Gary, and Patrizia Gentile. *The Canadian War on Queers: National Security as Sexual Regulation.* Vancouver: UBC Press, 2010.
Kline, Wendy. *Building a Better Race: Gender, Sexuality, and Eugenics from the Turn of the Century to the Baby Boom.* Berkeley: University of California Press, 2001.
Korinek, Valerie J. "'Don't Let Your Girlfriends Ruin Your Marriage': Lesbian Imagery in *Chatelaine* Magazine, 1950–1969." *Journal of Canadian Studies* 33, no. 3 (1998): 83–109.
– "Locating Lesbians, Finding 'Gay Women,' Writing Queer Histories: Reflections on Oral Histories, Identity and Community Memory." In *Beyond Women's Words: Feminisms and the Practices of Oral History in the Twenty-First Century*, edited by Katrina Srigley, Stacey Zembrzycki, and Franca Iacovetta, 126–36. London: Routledge, 2018.
– *Prairie Fairies: A History of Queer Communities and People in Western Canada, 1930–1985.* Toronto: University of Toronto Press, 2018.
– *Roughing It in the Suburbs: Reading* Chatelaine *in the Fifties and Sixties.* Toronto: University Press, 2000.
Ladd-Taylor, Molly. *Fixing the Poor: Eugenic Sterilization, and the Politics of Choice.* Baltimore: Johns Hopkins University Press, 2020.
Lambeth Conference 1948 Encyclical Letter from the Bishops Together with the Resolutions and Reports, The. London: SPCK, 1948.
Lambeth Conference 1958 Encyclical Letter from the Bishops Along with Resolutions and Reports, The. London: SPCK and Seabury Press, 1958.
Langhamer, Claire. "The Meanings of Home in Postwar Britain." *Journal of Contemporary History* 40, no. 2 (2005): 341–62.
Largent, Mark A. *Breeding Contempt: The History of Coerced Sterilization in the United States.* New Brunswick: Rutgers University Press, 2008.
Laqueur, Thomas. *Making Sex: Body and Gender from the Greeks to Freud.* Cambridge, MA: Harvard University Press, 1990.
Laughlin, Kathleen A., and Jacqueline L. Castledine. *Breaking the Wave: Women, Their Organizations, and Feminism, 1945–1985.* New York: Routledge, 2011.
Leahey, Thomas H. *A History of Modern Psychology.* Englewood Cliffs: Prentice-Hall, 1991.
Lenskyj, Helen. *Out of Bounds: Women, Sport and Sexuality.* Toronto: Women's Press, 1986.
Linteau, Paul-Andre, René Durocher, Jean-Claude Robert, and François Ricard. *Histoire du Québec contemporain: Le Québec depuis 1930.* Montreal: Boréal Express, 1989.
Lowenthal, David. "Nostalgia Tells It Like It Wasn't." In *The Imagined Past: History and Nostalgia*, edited by Christopher Shaw and Malcolm Chase, 18–32. Manchester: Manchester University Press, 1989.

Luxton, Reverend George. *Preparation for a Happy Marriage: A Companion to the Marriage Service in the Church of England in Canada.* Toronto: General Board of Religious Education, n.d.

MacDermot, H.E. *History of the Canadian Medical Association, 1888–1983.* Toronto: Murray Printing, n.d.

MacKinnon, Catharine A. *Women's Lives, Men's Laws.* Harvard: Harvard University Press, 2005.

Mansbridge, Jane, and Katherine Flaster. "The Cultural Politics of Everyday Discourse: The Case of 'Male Chauvinist.'" *Critical Sociology* 33 (2007): 627–60.

Marcus, Daniel. *The Fifties and Sixties in Contemporary Culture and Politics.* New Brunswick: Rutgers University Press, 2004.

Marrocco, Francis A. "A Diocesan Family Life Program." In *The Christian Family Apostolate*, 94–102. Sudbury: Report of the Seventh Annual Session of the Catholic Social Life Conference, 1959.

Marsh, Margaret, and Wanda Ronner. *The Fertility Doctor: John Rock and the Reproductive Revolution.* Baltimore: Johns Hopkins University Press, 2008.

Marshall, David B. *Secularizing the Faith: Canadian Protestant Clergy and the Crisis of Belief, 1850–1940.* Toronto: University of Toronto Press, 1992.

May, Elaine Tyler. *America and the Pill: A History of Promise, Peril, and Liberation.* New York: Basic Books, 2010.

– *Homeward Bound: American Families in the Cold War Era.* New York: Basic Books, 1998.

Maynard, Steven. "Through a Hole in the Lavatory Wall: Homosexual Subcultures, Police Surveillance, and the Dialectics of Discovery, Toronto, 1890–1930." *Journal of the History of Sexuality* 5, no. 2 (1994): 207–42.

McCann, Carole R. *Feminist Theory Reader: Local and Global Perspectives.* 3rd ed. New York: Routledge, 2013.

McLaren, Angus. *Impotence: A Cultural History.* Chicago: University of Chicago Press, 2007.

– *Our Own Master Race: Eugenics in Canada, 1885–1945.* Toronto: McClelland & Stewart, 1990.

– *Twentieth-Century Sexuality: A History.* Oxford: Blackwell, 1999.

McLaren, Angus, and Arlene Tigar McLaren. *The Bedroom and the State: The Changing Practices and Politics of Contraception and Abortion in Canada, 1880–1980.* Toronto: McClelland & Steward, 1986.

McPhail, Deborah. "What to Do with the 'Tubby Hubby'? 'Obesity' and the Crisis of Masculinity, and the Nuclear Family in Early Cold War Canada." *Antipode* 41, no. 5 (2009): 1021–50.

McPherson, Katheryn. *Bedside Matters: The Transformation of Canadian Nursing, 1900–1990.* Toronto: University of Toronto Press, 2003.

Meyerowitz, Joanne, ed. *Not June Cleaver: Woman and Gender in Postwar America, 1945–1960.* Philadelphia: Temple University Press, 1994.

Micale, Mark S. *Traumatic Pasts: History, Psychiatry and Trauma in the Modern Age*. Cambridge: Cambridge University Press, 2001.

Minister, Kristina. "A Feminist Frame for the Oral History Interview." In *Women's Words: The Feminist Practice of Oral History*, edited by Sherna Berger Gluck and Daphne Patai, 27–41. New York: Routledge, 1991.

Mitchinson, Wendy. *Bodily Failure: Medical Views of Women, 1900–1950*. Toronto: University of Toronto Press, 2013.

– *Fighting Fat: Canada, 1920–1980*. Toronto: University of Toronto Press, 2018.

– *Giving Birth in Canada, 1900–1950*. Toronto: University of Toronto Press, 2002.

– *The Nature of Their Bodies: Women and Their Doctors in Victorian Canada*. Toronto: University of Toronto Press, 1991.

Mol, Hans. *Faith and Fragility: Religion and Identity in Canada*. Burlington, ON: Trinity, 1985.

Mueller, Judith C. "Fallen Men: Representations of Male Impotence in Britain." *Studies in Eighteenth Century Culture* 28 (1999): 85–102.

Muise, Amy. "The Passion Paradox: The Ins and Outs of Sexual Frequency." *Psychology Today*, 8 June 2012. https://www.psychologytoday.com/us/blog/the-passion-paradox/201206/the-ins-and-outs-sexual-frequency.

Murphy, John. *Imagining the Fifties: Private Sentiment and Political Culture in Menzies' Australia*. Kensington: UNSW Press, 2000.

New Oxford Annotated Bible. 3rd ed. Edited by Michael D. Coogan. Oxford: Oxford University Press, 2001.

News and Notes for Clergy. 1946–66.

Nicholas, Jane. *Canadian Carnival Freaks and the Extraordinary Body, 1900–1970s*. Toronto: University of Toronto Press, 2018.

– *The Modern Girl: Feminine Modernities, the Body, and Commodities in the 1920s*. Toronto: University of Toronto Press, 2015.

Noonan, John T., Jr. *Contraception: A History of Its Treatment by the Catholic Theologians and Canonists*. Cambridge, MA: Harvard University Press, 1986.

O'Malley, John W. *What Happened at Vatican II*. Cambridge, MA: Harvard University Press, 2008.

Orsi, Robert. "Everyday Miracles: The Study of Lived Religion." In *Lived Religion in America: Toward a History of Practice*, edited by David D. Hall, 3–21. Princeton: Princeton University, 1997.

Owram, Doug. *Born at the Right Time: A History of the Baby-Boom Generation*. Toronto: University of Toronto Press, 1996.

Parr, Joy. "Notes for a More Sensuous History of Twentieth-Century Canada: The Timely, the Tacit, and the Material Body." *Canadian Historical Review* 82, no. 4 (2001): 719–45.

Pasolli, Lisa. *Working Mothers and the Child Care Dilemma: A History of British Columbia's Social Policy*. Vancouver: UBC Press, 2015.

Peiss, Kathy, *Cheap Amusements: Working Women and Leisure in Turn-of-the-Century New York*. Philadelphia: Temple University Press, 1986.

Perry, Adele. *On the Edge of Empire: Gender, Race and the Making of British Columbia, 1849–1871*. Toronto: University of Toronto Press, 2001.

Pickren, Wade E., and Donald A. Dewsbury, eds. *Evolving Perspectives on the History of Psychology*. Washington, DC: American Psychological Association, 2002.

Pierson, Ruth Roach. *Canadian Women and the Second World War*. Ottawa: Historical Association Booklet, 1983.

– *"They're Still Women After All": The Second World War and Canadian Womanhood*. Toronto: McClelland & Stewart, 1986.

Prairie Messenger. Muenster, SK: Order of St. Benedict, 1946–66.

Purvis, Trevor, and Alan Hunt. "Discourse, Ideology, Discourse, Ideology, Discourse, Ideology ..." *British Journal of Sociology* 44, no. 3 (1993): 473–99.

Reis, Elizabeth. *Bodies in Doubt: An American History of Intersex*. Baltimore: Johns Hopkins University Press, 2009.

Roberts, Dorothy. *Killing the Black Body: Race, Reproduction, and the Meaning of Liberty*. New York: Random House, 1997.

Robinson, Marion O. *Give My Heart: The Dr. Marion Hilliard Story*. Garden City, NY: Doubleday & Company, 1964.

Roediger, David R. *Working towards Whiteness: How America's Immigrants Became White: The Strange Journey from Ellis Island to the Suburbs*. New York: Basic Books, 2005.

Ross, Susan A. "The Women's Movement and Theology in the Twentieth Century." In *The Twentieth Century: A Theological Overview*, edited by Gregory Baum, 186–203. Ottawa: Novalis, St. Paul's University, 1999.

Routhier, Gilles. "Governance of the Catholic Church in Quebec: An Expression of the Distinct Society?" In *The Churches and Social Order in Nineteenth- and Twentieth-Century Canada*, edited by Michael Gauvreau and Ollivier Hubert, 292–314. Montreal & Kingston: McGill-Queen's University Press, 2006.

Rutherdale, Robert. "Fatherhood, Masculinity, and the Good Life during Canada's Baby Boom, 1945–1965." *Journal of Family History* 24, no. 3 (1999): 351–73.

– "'I'm a Lousy Father': Alcoholic Fathers in Postwar Canada and the Myths of Masculine Crises." In *Making Men, Making History: Canadian Masculinities across Time and Place*, edited by Peter Gossage and Robert Rutherdale, 409–26. Vancouver: UBC Press, 2018.

– "New 'Faces' for Fathers: Memory, Life-Writing, and Fathers as Providers in the Postwar Consumer Era." In *Creating Postwar Canada: 1945–75*, edited by Magda Fahrni and Robert Rutherdale, 241–67. Vancouver: UBC Press, 2008.

– "Three Faces of Fatherhood as a Masculine Category: Tyrants, Teachers, and Workaholics as 'Responsible Family Men' during Canada's Baby Boom." In

What Is Masculinity? Historical Dynamics from Antiquity to the Contemporary World, edited by John A. Arnold and Sean Brady, 323–46. Basingstoke: Palgrave Macmillan, 2013.

Sampson, Amy. "Eugenics in the Community: Alberta's Sexual Sterilization Act, 1928–1972." *Canadian Bulletin of Medical History/Bulletin canadien d'historie de la medicine* 31, no. 1 (2014): 143–63.

Sangster, Joan. "Creating Popular Histories: Re-interpreting 'Second Wave' Canadian Feminism." *Dialectical Anthropology* 39 (2015): 381–404.

– "Incarcerating 'Bad Girls': The Regulation of Sexuality through the Female Refuges Act in Ontario, 1920–1945." *Journal of the History of Sexuality* 7, no. 4 (1991): 471–504.

– "Radical Ruptures: Feminism, Labor and the Left in the Long Sixties in Canada." *American Review of Canadian Studies* 40, no. 1 (2010): 1–21.

– *Regulating Girls and Women: Sexuality, Family and the Law, 1920–1960.* Oxford: Oxford University Press, 2001.

– "Telling Our Stories: Feminist Debates and the Use of Oral History." *Women's History Review* 3, no.1 (2006): 5–28.

Scarry, Elaine. *The Body in Pain: The Making and Unmaking of the World.* Oxford: Oxford University Press, 1985.

Schiebinger, Londa. *Nature's Body: Gender in the Making of Modern Science.* New Brunswick: Rutgers University Press, 2013.

– "Skeletons in the Closet: The First Illustrations of the Female Skeleton in Eighteen-Century Anatomy." In *Feminism and the Body*, edited by Londa Schiebinger, 25–57. Oxford: Oxford University Press, 2000.

Schoenherr, Richard A. *Goodbye Father: The Celibate Male Priesthood and the Future of the Catholic Church.* Oxford: Oxford University Press, 2002.

Schrieter, Robert J. "The Impact of Vatican II." In *The Twentieth Century: A Theological Overview*, edited by Gregory Baum, 158–72. Ottawa: Novalis, St. Paul's University, 1999.

Scott, Canon E.W. "The Person You Are Becoming." *Scope* 65 (1965): 3–10.

Scott, Joan W. "The Evidence of Experience." *Critical Inquiry* 17, no. 4 (1991): 773–97.

Semple, Neil. *The Lord's Dominion: The History of Canadian Methodism.* Montreal & Kingston: McGill-Queen's University Press, 1996.

Sethna, Christabelle. "The Evolution of the *Birth Control Handbook*: From Student Peer-Education Manual to Feminist Self-empowerment Text, 1968–1975." *Canadian Bulletin of Medical History/Bulletin canadien d'historie de la medicine* 23, no. 1 (2006): 89–118.

– "The University of Toronto Health Service, Oral Contraception, and Student Demand for Birth Control, 1960–1970." *Historical Studies in Education* 17, no. 2 (2005): 265–92.

Sethna, Christabelle, and Gayle Davis, eds. *Abortion across Borders: Transnational Travel and Access to Abortion Services*. Baltimore: Johns Hopkins University Press, 2019.

Shantz, Mary-Ann. "Centring the Suburb, Focusing on the Family: Calgary's Anglican and Alliance Churches, 1945–1969." *Social History/Histoire sociale* 42, no. 84 (2009): 423–46.

Shaw, Christopher, and Malcolm Chase. "The Dimensions of Nostalgia." In *The Imagined Past: History and Nostalgia*, edited by Christopher Shaw and Malcolm Chase, 1–17. Manchester: Manchester University Press, 1989.

Siena, Kevin. "'Pliable Bodies': The Moral Biology of Health and Disease." In *A Cultural History of the Body in the Age of Enlightenment*, edited by Carole Reeves, 35–52. Oxford: Berg, 2010.

Smith, Susan L. *Sick and Tired of Being Sick and Tired: Black Women's Health Activism in America, 1890–1950*. Philadelphia: University of Pennsylvania Press, 1995.

Smith-Rosenburg, Carroll. *Disorderly Conduct: Visions of Gender in Victorian America*. New York: Alfred A. Knopf, 1985.

Sontag, Susan. *AIDS and Its Metaphors*. London: Penguin, 1989.

Stanley, Heather. "Primal Urge/National Force: Sex, Sexuality, and National History." In *Reading Canadian Women's and Gender History*, edited by Nancy Janovicek and Carmen Nielson, 225–77. Toronto: University of Toronto Press, 2019.

Stein, Melissa N. *Measuring Manhood: Race and the Science of Masculinity, 1803–1934*. Minneapolis: University of Minnesota Press, 2015.

Stepan, Nancy, *The Idea of Race in Science: Great Britain, 1800–1960*. London: Macmillan, 1982.

– "Race, Gender, Science and Citizenship." *Gender & History* 10, no. 1 (1998): 26–52.

Stephen, Jennifer A. "Balancing Equality for the Post-War Woman: Demobilizing Canada's Women Workers after World War Two." *Atlantis* 31, no. 1 (2007): 125–35.

Stettner, Shannon, ed. *Without Apology: Writings on Abortion in Canada*. Edmonton: Athabasca University Press, 2016.

Stoler, Ann. *Carnal Knowledge and Imperial Power: Race and the Intimate in the Colonial World*. Berkley: University of California Press, 2002.

Strange, Caroline. *Toronto's Girl Problem: The Perils and Pleasures of the City, 1880–1930*. Toronto: University of Toronto Press, 1995.

Strong-Boag, Veronica. "Canada's Wage-Earning Wives and the Construction of the Middle Class, 1945–60." *Journal of Canadian Studies* 29, no. 3 (1994): 5–25.

– "Home Dreams: Women and the Suburban Experiment in Canada, 1945–1960." *Canadian Historical Review* 72, no. 4 (1991): 471–502.

- *The New Day Recalled: Lives of Girls and Women in English Canada, 1919–1939.* Toronto: Copp Clark Pitman, 1988.
- "Pulling in Double Harness or Hauling a Double Load: Women, Work and Feminism on the Canadian Prairie." In *The Prairie West: Historical Readings.* 2nd ed. Edited by R. Douglas Francis and Howard Palmer, 401–23. Edmonton: Pica Pica, 1992.

Suffragettes Who Have Never Been Kissed. [Print]. Mary Evans Picture Library, London, 1909.

Summerfield, Penny. "Talking about Feminism: Reconciling Fragmented Narratives with the Feminist Research Frame." In *Beyond Women's Words: Feminisms and the Practices of Oral History in the Twenty-First Century,* edited by Katrina Srigley, Stacey Zembrzycki, and Franca Iacovetta, 81–94. London: Routledge, 2018.

Sutherland, Neil. "When You Listen to the Winds of Childhood, How Much Can You Believe?" *Curriculum Inquiry* 22, no. 3 (1992): 235–56.

This Is a Great Sacrament. Ottawa: Le Droit, 196?.

Tone, Andrea. *The Age of Anxiety: A History of America's Turbulent Affair with Tranquilizers.* New York: Basic Books, 2009.

- *Devices and Desires: A History of Contraceptives in America.* New York: Hill and Wang, 2001.

Toward a Christian Understanding of Sex Love and Marriage. Edmonton: National General Council of the United Church of Canada, 1960.

Valverde, Mariana. *The Age of Light, Soap and Water.* Toronto: McClelland & Stewart, 1991.

- "Building Anti-Delinquent Communities: Morality, Gender, and Generation in the City." In *A Diversity of Women: Ontario, 1945–1980,* edited by Joy Parr, 19–45. Toronto: Toronto University Press, 1995.

Vicinus, Martha. *Intimate Friends: Women Who Loved Women, 1778–1928.* Chicago: Chicago University Press, 2004.

Vickers, Jill McCalla. "Feminist Approaches to Women in Politics." In *Beyond the Vote: Canadian Women and Politics,* edited by Linda Keeley and Joan Sangster, 16–36. Toronto: University of Toronto Press, 1986.

Vipond, Mary. *The Mass Media in Canada.* Toronto: J. Lorimer, 1989.

Walker, Gillian. "Eunuchs for the Kingdom of Heaven: Constructing the Celibate Priest." *Studies in Gender and Sexuality* 5, no. 2 (2004): 233–57.

Walkowitz, Judith R. *City of Dreadful Delight: Narratives of Sexual Danger in Late-Victorian London.* Chicago: University of Chicago Press, 1992.

Warner, Marina. *Alone of All Her Sex: The Myth and Cult of the Virgin Mary.* New York: Random House, 1976.

Warner, Tom. *Never Going Back: A History of Queer Activism in Canada.* Toronto: University of Toronto Press, 2002.

Warsh, Cheryl Krasnick. *Prescribed Norms: Women and Health in Canada and the United States since 1800.* Toronto: University of Toronto Press, 2010.

Weeks, Jeffery. *Sex, Politics and Society: The Regulation of Sexuality since 1800.* 2nd ed. Essex: Longman House, 1989.

Weiner, Marli F., with Mazie Hough. *Sex, Sickness, and Slavery: Defining Illness in the Antebellum South.* Urbana: University of Illinois Press, 2012.

Weiss, Jessica. *To Have and to Hold: Marriage, the Baby Boom and Social Change.* Chicago: University of Chicago Press, 2000.

Wells, Andrew. "Confusion Embodied: Epistemologies of Sex and Race in *Memoirs of a Woman of Pleasure* (1748–49) and the *Histoire naturelle* (1749–1804)." In *Bodies, Sex and Desire from the Renaissance to the Present*, edited by Kate Fisher and Sarah Toulalan, 49–69. London: Palgrave Macmillan, 2011.

Werner, Bishop Hazen G. *The Marks of a Christian Home.* Nashville: The Upper Room Christian Family Services Series, 1946.

Young, Brian. *A Short History of Quebec.* 2nd ed. Toronto: Copp Clark, 1993.

Zieger, Susan. *Entangling Alliances: Foreign War Brides and American Soldiers in the Twentieth Century.* New York: New York University Press, 2010.

Index

Page numbers in italics refer to illustrations.

abortion, 37–8, 81, 117–18, 135, 139, 166n51, 167n55. *See also* birth control; sterilization
activism, 8, 136, 139–40, 159n26. *See also* feminism
Adams, Mary Louise, 8–9, 123
Adamson, Lois (pseudonym): about, 145–6; birth control and, 112, 114; emotional management and, 119; gender roles and, 95, 96, 97; motherhood and, 108
adoption, 36, 57
advertising, 26–7, *27, 28,* 29, *30, 31*
alternative readings, 139
American Methodist Church, 54
Anderson, Florence (pseudonym): about, 146; denominational scarcity and, 141; husband's alcoholism, 119; on sexual danger during WWII, 94, 182n20; sexual innocence and, 103–4
Anglican Church: about, 12–13; on birth control, 79–81; on divorce, 68–70; educational efforts on marriage and sex, 54–5; on extra- and premarital sex, 73–4; gay marriage and, 179n114; on gender roles, 51, 74–5, 77–8, 98; *The Hallowing of the Union* marriage manual, 54, 72, 81; indirect governance by, 138–9; on infidelity, 127; on marriage, sex, and one-flesh body, 47–8, 50–1, 68, 70–1, 72–3, 77–8, 84–5; medical science and, 78–9, 82–3; organizational structure of, 53, 175n70; psychoanalysis and, 82
anti-nausea (anti-morning sickness) medication, 25, 26–7, *27, 28,* 165n40
artificial insemination by donor (AID), 35–7, 167nn62–3
assault, sexual, 92–4, 128–34
average, 123–4. *See also* normality

baby boom era, 8
Backhouse, Carol, 132–3, 134
Baillargeon, Denyse, 16
Baker, Glenda (pseudonym): about, 146; birth control and, 114; child loss, 113; emotional management and, 118–19; sexual innocence and, 184n49
Barclay, L.T., 32–3

Barman, Jean, 134
Bartky, Sandra, 5
Bateman, Jessica (pseudonym): about, 147; gender roles and personal sacrifice, 100–1, 120; infidelity and, 101, 127; married sex and, 125–6
"bedroom": euphemism for married sexuality, 15; medical assumptions about, 15, 138
Bell, Ruth (pseudonym): about, 147; gender roles and, 97–8, 134–5, 140; sexual innocence and, 103
Bellergal (medication), 29, *31*
Berry, J. Gerald, 59
birth control: Anglican and United churches on, 79–81; class and, 113; diaphragm, 105; intrauterine devices (IUDs), 34–5, 113; lived experiences of, 112, 114–15, 139; medical discourse on, 33–5; Pill, 34, 35, 65–6, 113, 115, 139, 174n59, 178n105; rhythm method, 66–7, 112, 114, 115, 173n25; Roman Catholic Church and, 50, 55–6, 64–7, 114–15, 174n59; scholarship on, 166n51; sexual innocence and responsibility for, 102, 184n46. *See also* abortion; sterilization
Block, Tina, 177n89
bodies, 10–11, 47, 140. *See also* lived experiences; mother body; one-flesh body
Bonamine (medication), 26–7, *27*, 165n40
Bond, Ian K., 45, 170n96
Boston Women's Health Book Collective (*Our Bodies, Ourselves*), 3, 170n97
Bouchard, Gérard, 5
Breault, H., 64

Brown, Margaret (pseudonym): abortion, 117–18, 135, 139; about, 147–8; birth control and, 114; on feminism, 95–6; gender roles and, 96, 97; sexual innocence and, 103
Brownlie, Robin Jarvis, 134
Bruser, M., 23

Canada, postwar social and moral concerns, 4, 137, 155n3
Canadian Medical Association Journal (CMAJ): about, 12; advertising, 26–7, *27*, *28*, *30*, *31*; artificial insemination by donor (AID) and, 36, 167n63; birth control and, 33–5; circulation and growth, 17, 160n6; editorial perspective of, 17–18; femininity and, 21–2, 33; homosexuality and, 44, 170n94; intersexuality and, 32, 165n45; methodological approach to, 17; mother body and, 45; older female patients and, 38, *39*; pregnancy and, 25–6; psychoanalysis and, 20, 21; public trust and, 22, 162n24; scholarship on, 160n5; self-reflection by doctors in, 22, 163n25; sterilization and, 38–9; white vs. ethnic and racialized bodies in, 18–19. *See also* medical discourse
Canadian Psychiatric Association Journal (CPAJ), 21, 162n20
capital, social, 126, 133–4, 142
Cappon, Daniel, 25
Carini, Susan M., 134
Carter, Evelyn (pseudonym), 148
Castro de la Mata, R., 40–3, 98
Catholic Action: Service de Préperation au Mariage (SPM), 57, 173n25
Catholic Church. *See* Roman Catholic Church

Catholic Herald (newspaper), 57, 68
Chatelaine (magazine), 29, 77, 82, 164n29
Chenier, El, 9, 21, 161n11, 162n21, 170n96
Chilcote, Kay Hodell ("When He Takes You for Granted") 76–7
children: adoption of, 36, 57; Anglican and United churches on procreation, 50–1, 68, 70–1, 81; baby boom era and, 8; divorce and, 69; religious affiliation and, 179n113; Roman Catholic Church on procreation, 50, 55–6, 65, 68; societal normalization of, 107. *See also* birth control; motherhood; pregnancy
Christian Home, The (magazine), 54, 75–7, 98, 177n84
Christianity and Christian discourse: about, 11–12, 12–13, 85, 170n2; church marriages, 49, 171n8; concerns about postwar family, 51–2; denominational affiliation and choice, 49, 84, 171n7, 179n113; denominational scarcity in rural spaces, 141; indirect governance and influence, 49–50, 138–9; medical science and, 60–1, 64, 78–9, 82–4, 123; scholarship on, 48; sex and sexuality in, 47. *See also* Anglican Church; one-flesh body; Roman Catholic Church; United Church of Canada
Clarke, Brian, 171n7
class, and birth control, 113
Cold War era, 58, 137
Commachio, Cynthia, 16
Coney Island funhouse mirrors, 134, 143
Connell, R.W., 180n2
contraceptives. *See* birth control
Coontz, Stephanie, 4

danger, sexual, 92–4, 128–34
Davies, Madeline D., 89
Dean, Carolyn J., 11
DeBlanc (Catholic priest), 67
Demerson, Velma, 133
deviance, sexual, 44, 45, 170n96
diaphragm, 105
disciplinary power, 137–8
displacement, 19, 23, 164n30
divorce, 68–70, 71–2, 176n73
double day, 42, 75, 76, 98–100
Dubinsky, Karen, 5, 133, 134, 187n3
Duden, Barbara, 11
Duder, Cameron, 9
Duvall, Evelyn Millis, 80
Dwyer, Robert J., 64
Dyck, Erika, 40
dyspareunia, 22–3

Ellison, Jenny, 123
Ellzey, W. Clark, 177n84
embodied history, 10, 158n17
emotional management, 118–20, 140
endometriosis, 23, 164n27
Epp, Marlene, 8
ethnic and racialized peoples, 8, 18–19, 134, 160n9, 168n72
eugenics, 19, 40
extramarital sex, 56, 73–4, 165n37

family, and mother body, 40–3
family planning. *See* birth control
Farrar, C.B., 20
femininity, 21–2, 33, 166n50
feminism: ambivalence towards, 95–6, 134–5, 182n25; "feminist men," 102; second-wave, 32, 33, 95–6, 114, 159n26, 183n27. *See also* activism
fertility. *See* birth control; children; pregnancy
Fielding, C.R., 79

finances, family, 96
Fisher, Kate, 93, 102, 184n46
Fortin, J.N., 24
Foucar, H.O., 19–20
Foucault, Michel: on disciplinary power, 10, 137–8; on hegemony, 6, 136; on heterosexuality and homosexuality, 9; on organized systems of knowledge, 5; on sexual repression, 107, 126, 128
Fowler, Howard, 64
Friedan, Betty, 32, 82, 95, 183n27

Gatens, Moira, 11
Gauvreau, Michel, 57, 173n25, 175n69
gay marriage, 179n114. *See also* homosexuality
gender roles: acceptance of/security within, 95–7; Anglican and United churches on, 51, 74–8, 98; deviance from, 100–2; double day and, 42, 75, 76, 98–100; "feminist men" and, 102; husbands as "boss," 97–8; lived experiences of, 94–102, 134–5; medical discourse on, 15–16, 22–5, 40–3, 138; Roman Catholic Church on, 51, 59–60, 98; vs. sex as indicator of marital success, 121–3, 142–3, 186n96; in triad with sex and sexuality, 7
Gentile, Patrizia, 9, 10
Gleason, Mona (*Normalizing the Ideal*), 8–9
governance, indirect, 138–9
Gringas, G., 40–3, 98

Hall, Alice (pseudonym): about, 148; emotional management and, 119; gender roles and, 97–8, 134–5, 140; motherhood and, 108–10; sexual innocence and, 106

Hallowing of the Union, The (Anglican marriage manual), 54, 72, 81
Harrison, C.P., 37
hermaphroditism, 32–3, 165–6n45
Hilliard, Marion, 29–30, 32, 82–3, 109, 179n109
history: embodied, 10, 158n17; oral, 88–9, 181n10
homosexuality: Anglican Church and gay marriage, 179n114; heterosexuality and, 9; homophobia in second-wave feminism, 183n27; lack of privacy, 137, 156n5; pathologization of in medical discourse, 6, 44–5, 170n91, 170n94
Humanae Vitae, 68, 175nn68–9
husbands: abortion and, 37–8; birth control and, 34–5; as "boss" within family, 97–8; emotional management and, 118–20, 140, 142; failure of and mother body, 40–3, 134–5; as "feminist men," 102; gender role adherence and marital success, 122, 142; Roman Catholic Church on sexual role of, 61–4
Hutchinson, Harry C., 45, 170n96

Iacovetta, Franca, 8
Indigenous peoples, 18, 40, 134, 171n8
indirect governance, 138–9
infertility, 10, 35–7, 57, 110–12, 185n68
infidelity, 101, 125, 126–8
innocence, sexual, 102–5, 106
intersexuality, 32–3, 165n45
intrauterine devices (IUDs), 34–5, 113
intrauterine insemination (IUI), 167n62. *See also* artificial insemination by donor (AID)
in vitro fertilization, 167n61

John Paul II (pope), 68, 175n68
Johnston, Mary (pseudonym): about, 149; birth control and, 114, 115, 139; "feminist" husband of, 102; married sex and, 186n94; personal sacrifice by, 119–20
Jones, Robert O., 21
journals, medical, 18. See also *Canadian Medical Association Journal*

Kalz, F., 24
Kinch, R.A.H., 15
King, Verna (pseudonym): about, 149; emotional management and, 119; married sex and, 121–2; medical access and, 141–2; sexual innocence and, 104–5
Kinsman, Gary, 9
knowledge: organized systems of, 5; sexual, 105–7, 140–1, 183n45
Korinek, Valerie J., 9, 77, 90, 181n6; *Roughing It in the Suburbs*, 8

Lapovsky, Elizabeth, 89
Laycock, Samuel, 44, 52, 170n91
Lenskyj, Helen, 160n4
LGBTQ2+ communities. See homosexuality
lived experiences: about, 13, 87–8, 134–6; gender roles, 94–102, 134–5; infidelity, 126–8; of interview participants, 89–90, 145, 182n13; married sex, 120–6, 135; motherhood, 107–15; and narrative structures and social vocabularies, 91–2; personal sacrifice and managing inequalities, 115–20, 135; sexual danger, 92–4, 128–34; sexual innocence and knowledge, 102–7; social relationship between interviewer and interviewees, 90–1, 181nn10–11; whole-life perspective, 94
Luxton, George, 74

Macdonald, Stuart, 171n7
MacFarlane, Dr., 23
marriage: in church, 49, 171n8; conflation with motherhood, 15–16; and homosexuality and other sexual deviance, 44–5; infidelity, 101, 125, 126–8; postwar perceptions of, 4–5; romanticization of, 52. See also gender roles; one-flesh body; sex
Marrocco, Francis A., 51–2
Martin, Joyce (pseudonym): about, 149–50; double day and gender roles, 99–100, 183n39; infertility and, 110; medical access and, 142; personal sacrifice by, 119–20; sexual knowledge and, 106
masculinity: failure of and mother body, 40–3, 134–5; "feminist men," 102; gender role adherence and marital success, 122, 142; husbands as "boss" within family, 97–8; pathologization of homosexuality and, 6, 44–5, 170n91, 170n94; social vocabularies and, 92. See also husbands
May, Elaine Tyler (*Homeward Bound*), 7–8
McEwan, Donald C., 29
McLaren, Angus, 62
McNair, F.E., 43
McPhail, Deborah, 164n34
McPherson, Katheryn, 160n4
medical discourse: about, 11, 12, 16–17, 45–6; on abortion, 37–8, 167n55; Anglican and

medical discourse (*continued*)
  United churches and, 78–9,
  82–3; on birth control, 33–5; on
  doctors' families, 22, 43, 163n25,
  169nn88–9; eugenics and, 19; on
  femininity, 21–2, 33; and gender
  and race, 18–19, 160n9; on gender
  roles, 15–16, 22–5, 40–3, 138; on
  homosexuality, 6, 44–5, 170n91,
  170n94; indirect governance
  by, 138; infertility and artificial
  insemination by donor (AID),
  35–7, 167nn62–3; on infidelity,
  127; on intersexuality, 32–3; on
  married sex, 33, 120; medical
  journals, 18; on menopause, 27–30,
  30, *31*; normality and, 123; on
  pregnancy and anti-nausea (anti-
  morning sickness) medication,
  25–7, *27*, *28*; psychoanalysis and,
  19–21, 162n21; on psychosexual
  development, 25, 107; Roman
  Catholic Church and, 60–1, 64,
  84; vs. rural spaces, 141–2; on
  sexual knowledge, 183n45; on
  sterilization, 38–40; subversion
  of, 32. See also *Canadian Medical
  Association Journal*; mother body
memory making, 93
men. *See* homosexuality; husbands;
  masculinity
menopause, 27–30, *30*, *31*, 32
mental illness, maternal, 113–14
Meyerowitz, Joanne (*Not June
  Cleaver*), 8
miscarriages, 111, 113, 117, 135, 140
Mitchinson, Wendy, 16, 18, 21, 26,
  164n34, 166n51
moral relativity, 84
Morgan, Frank, 78
Mornidine (medication), 26–7, *28*,
  165n40

mother body: about, 6, 16–17,
  45–6; anti-nausea (anti-morning
  sickness) medication and, 26–7,
  27, *28*; communal nature of and
  familial ownership of fertility,
  33–40; femininity and, 33; and
  homosexuality and other sexual
  deviance, 44–5, 170n96; masculine
  failures and, 40–3; medical
  control over, 138; menopause and,
  27–30, *30*, *31*, 32; psychoanalytical
  approach to gender norms and, 22–
  5, 164n34. *See also* medical discourse
motherhood: adoption and, 36, 57;
  as antidote to boredom, 108–9; as
  choice, 109–10; conflation with
  marriage, 15–16; emotional
  management and personal
  sacrifice, 115–18, 135, 140; lived
  experiences of, 107–15; mental
  illness and, 113–14; pride in, 107–8;
  professional veneer and status of,
  173n30; Roman Catholic exaltation
  of, 57–9; societal normalization
  of, 107; spiritual, 57. *See also* birth
  control; children; pregnancy
Muir, Leilani, 40

natural law, 50, 79–80
Nicholas, Jane, 10
normality: baby boom era and,
  8–9; dividends of, 134, 180n2;
  gender role adherence and, 122–3,
  142, 186n96; intersexuality and,
  32–3; married sex and desire to be
  average, 123–6, 135, 138, 186n101;
  policing of, 5–6
nostalgia and nostalgia trap, 4, 91, 106

O'Connor, John J., 65
one-flesh body: about, 47–8, 83–5;
  Anglican and United churches

on, 50–1, 70–1, 72–3, 77–9; birth control and, 65, 79–80; and education about marriage and sex, 53–5; and extra- and premarital sex, 73; gender roles and, 51, 56–7; vs. medical science, 83; Roman Catholic Church on, 50, 55–7. *See also* Anglican Church; Roman Catholic Church; United Church of Canada
oral history, 88–9, 181n10. *See also* lived experiences
orgasm, 56, 62, 173n25
Our Bodies, Ourselves (Boston Women's Health Book Collective), 3, 7, 170n97
Owram, Doug (*Born at the Right Time*), 8

patriarchy: Anglican and United churches and, 51, 74; husbands as "boss," 97–8; medical discourse and, 41; patriarchal dividends, 180n2; Roman Catholic Church and, 51, 58
Paul VI (pope), 68, 84
Pfizer, 26–7, 27
Pill (birth control), 34, 35, 65–6, 113, 115, 139, 174n59, 178n105
Pius XII (pope), 58
Prairie Messenger (Catholic newspaper), 52, 53, 63, 65, 67, 68
pregnancy: anti-nausea (anti-morning sickness) medication, 25, 26–7, 27, 28, 165n40; in *CMAJ*, 25–6; infertility and, 10, 35–7, 57, 110–12, 185n68; medical discourse on excessive nausea during, 7, 138; miscarriage, 111, 113, 117, 135, 140; psychosexual development and, 25, 107. *See also* birth control; children; motherhood

premarital sex, 73–4. *See also* extramarital sex
premenstrual tension syndrome (PTS), 24–5
Preuter, Gordon W., 25
Primarin (medication), 29
privacy, 5, 137, 156n5
procreation: Anglican and United churches on, 50–1, 68, 70–1, 81; Roman Catholic Church on, 50, 55–6, 65, 68. *See also* children; motherhood; pregnancy
Protestant churches. *See* Anglican Church; United Church of Canada
pseudohermaphroditism, 32–3, 165n45
psychoanalysis, 16–17, 19–21, 22–5, 82, 162n21, 164n30. *See also* medical discourse

Quebecois women, 175n69
queer communities. *See* homosexuality

racialized and ethnic peoples, 8, 18–19, 134, 160n9, 168n72
Rand, Karen (pseudonym): about, 150; denominational scarcity and, 141; double day and, 98–9; husband's alcoholism, 119; married sex and, 120; motherhood and, 108, 184n62; perspective of, 94; on sexual danger during WWII, 92, 93–4; sexual innocence and, 104
repression, sexual, 107, 126, 128
reproductive systems, as sites of danger, 23–4, 164n31
rhythm method, 66–7, 112, 114, 115, 173n25
Robinson, Elsie, 52
Robinson, Marion O., 179n109

Rock, John, 65–6
Roman Catholic Church:
  about, 12–13; anglophones
  vs. francophones, 48–9, 57,
  173n25; birth control and, 50,
  55–6, 64–7, 114–15, 174n59; on
  celibacy vs. marital sex, 55;
  changing discourses within,
  67–8; educational efforts on
  marriage and sex, 53, 54–5,
  173n25; on gender roles, 51,
  59–60, 98; *Humanae Vitae*, 68,
  175nn68–9; indirect governance
  by, 138–9; on infidelity, 126–7; on
  marriage, sex, procreation, and
  one-flesh body, 47–8, 50, 55–7,
  79; medical science and, 60–1,
  64, 84; organizational structure
  of, 53, 172n19; on orgasm, 56, 62;
  Quebecois women and, 175n69;
  on sexual roles within marriage,
  61–4; on spiritual motherhood, 57;
  This Is a Great Sacrament marriage
  manual, 54, 55, 56, 59–60, 62, 66;
  on women's value as mothers/
  wives, 57–9
romance, 52, 121
Ross, Becki L., 9
Roth, Martin, 21
Routhier, Gilles, 49
rural spaces, 46, 77, 106, 140–2,
  187n3
Rutherdale, Robert, 43, 92, 98
Ryan, H.R.S., 79

sacrifice, personal, 115–18, 135, 140,
  185n83, 186n88
Sangster, Joan, 8, 159n26
scholarship, slow, 89, 181n6
Schweiker, Maxine ("If You're a
  Working Mother, Be Prepared to
  Work Miracles"), 75

science, medical, 60–1, 64, 78–9,
  82–3, 84, 123. *See also* medical
  discourse
Scott, W.E., 74–5
Searle & Co., 26–7, *28*
second-wave feminism, 32, 33,
  95–6, 114, 159n26, 183n27. *See also*
  feminism
security, sense of, 96
self-regulation, 137–8
Sethna, Christabelle, 35
sex: "bedroom" as euphemism for,
  15; Christian churches on one-
  flesh body and, 47–8, 50–1, 55–7,
  72–4, 83–5; extra- and premarital,
  56, 73–4, 165n37; vs. gender roles
  as indicator of marital success,
  121–3, 142–3, 186n96; "good
  sex," 143–4; indirect governance
  of, 138–9; infidelity and, 101,
  125, 126–8; lived experiences of
  married sex, 120–6, 135; medical
  discourse on, 33, 120; normality
  and desire to be average, 123–6,
  135, 138, 186n101; as pleasurable
  and romantic, 120–1; policing of,
  5–6; postwar perceptions of, 4–5;
  psychoanalysis and, 19–20, 22, 25;
  Roman Catholic Church on sexual
  roles, 61–4; self-regulation and,
  137–8; sexual danger, 92–4, 128–
  34; sexual deviance, 45, 170n96;
  sexual innocence, 102–5, 106;
  sexual knowledge, 105–7, 140–1,
  183n45; sexual repression, 107,
  126, 128; in triad with sexuality
  and gender, 7
Shantz, Mary-Ann, 172n11
Sherman, Emalene ("Be Glad You're
  a Housewife"), 75–6
Shortt, Fiona (pseudonym): about,
  150–1; birth control and, 114;

financial difficulties, 185n72; gender roles and, 98; married sex and, 122; maternal mental illness and, 114; personal sacrifice by, 116–17, 135, 140, 186n88; perspective of, 94; sexual assault and, 92–4, 129–30, 132, 133, 134

Simpson, Jean (pseudonym): about, 151; birth control and, 112, 113; "feminist" husband of, 102; married sex and, 124–5, 186n101; sexual information from mother, 105

Skully, H.J., 165n37

Small, Edith (pseudonym): about, 151–2; on feminism, 95, 182n25; fertility challenges and miscarriage, 110–11; gender roles and, 96, 97; on married sex, 120–1; sexual assault and, 130–2, 134; sexual innocence and, 103

social capital, 126, 133–4, 142

Sousa-Poza, J., 37

spiritual motherhood, 57

Stephen, Jennifer A. ("Balancing Equality for the Post-War Woman"), 8

sterilization, 38–40, 81, 178n105. *See also* abortion; birth control

Straker, M., 25

Strong-Boag, Veronica, 164n29; "Home Dreams," 8

Summerfield, Penny, 89, 90

Tace (medication), 29, *30*

Tallin, G.P.R., 36

Taylor, Marjorie (pseudonym): about, 152; gender roles and, 100; married sex and, 121; maternal mental illness and, 114; reconciliation with husband, 183n40; sexual knowledge and, 105–6

This Is a Great Sacrament (Catholic marriage manual), 54, 55, 56, 59–60, 62, 66

Thomas, Anne C. ("Are You Faithful to Your Husband?"), 76

Trudeau, Pierre, 11

United Church of Canada: about, 12–13; on birth control, 79–81; *The Christian Home* magazine, 54, 75–7, 98, 177n84; on divorce, 71–2; doctrinal ambiguity, 177n89; education about marriage and sex, 54–5, 177n84; on gender roles, 51, 74, 75–8; indirect governance by, 138–9; on infidelity, 127–8; on marriage, sex, and one-flesh body, 47–8, 50–1, 68, 71, 72–3, 77–8, 84–5; medical science and, 78–9, 82–3; psychoanalysis and, 82

vaginal reconstruction, 32–3, 166n48

Victorian era, 16, 50, 56–7, 60–2, 67, 107

Viner, N., 20

war brides, 89–90, 104–5, 141, 181n8

Warsh, Cheryl Krasnick, 16, 21

Watters, W.W., 37

Wellman, Marvin, 44–5

Werner, Hazen G., 78

West, Diane (pseudonym): about, 152–3; birth control and, 112, 113; infidelity and, 127–8; personal sacrifice by, 115–16; religious affiliation as child, 179n113; sexual information from mother, 105

whiteness, 8, 18–19, 134, 181n11

Wilson, Nancy (pseudonym): about, 153; birth control and, 112, 113; fertility challenges, 185n68; married sex and, 120, 186n106;

Wilson, Nancy (*continued*)
    personal sacrifice by, 119–20;
    sexual knowledge and, 106
Wittkower, E.D., 24, 40–3, 98
women: activism, 8, 136, 139–40, 159n26; 1950s images of, 3–4; normality and, 5–6, 8–9, 123; pathologization of femininity, 21–2, 33; Quebecois, 175n69; reproductive systems as sites of danger, 23–4, 164n31; research approach to, 6–7, 8–14; scholarship on, 7–8, 163n26; triad of sex, sexuality, and gender, 7. *See also* feminism; gender roles; lived experiences; marriage; medical discourse; mother body; motherhood; one-flesh body; sex

Zarfas, D.E., 38
Zeiger, Susan, 181n7

STUDIES IN GENDER AND HISTORY

General Editors: Franca Iacovetta and Karen Dubinsky

1 Suzanne Morton, *Ideal Surroundings: Domestic Life in a Working-Class Suburb in the 1920s*
2 Joan Sangster, *Earning Respect: The Lives of Working Women in Small-Town Ontario, 1920–1960*
3 Carolyn Strange, *Toronto's Girl Problem: The Perils and Pleasures of the City, 1880–1930*
4 Sara Z. Burke, *Seeking the Highest Good: Social Service and Gender at the University of Toronto, 1888–1937*
5 Lynne Marks, *Revivals and Roller Rinks: Religion, Leisure, and Identity in Late-Nineteenth-Century Small-Town Ontario*
6 Cecilia Morgan, *Public Men and Virtuous Women: The Gendered Languages of Religion and Politics in Upper Canada, 1791–1850*
7 Mary Louise Adams, *The Trouble with Normal: Postwar Youth and the Making of Heterosexuality*
8 Linda Kealey, *Enlisting Women for the Cause: Women, Labour, and the Left in Canada, 1890–1920*
9 Christina Burr, *Spreading the Light: Work and Labour Reform in Late-Nineteenth-Century Toronto*
10 Mona Gleason, *Normalizing the Ideal: Psychology, Schooling, and the Family in Postwar Canada*
11 Deborah Gorham, *Vera Brittain: A Feminist Life*
12 Marlene Epp, *Women without Men: Mennonite Refugees of the Second World War*
13 Shirley Tillotson, *The Public at Play: Gender and the Politics of Recreation in Postwar Ontario*
14 Veronica Strong-Boag and Carole Gerson, *Paddling Her Own Canoe: The Times and Texts of E. Pauline Johnson (Tekahionwake)*
15 Stephen Heathorn, *For Home, Country, and Race: Constructing Gender, Class, and Englishness in the Elementary School, 1880–1914*
16 Valerie J. Korinek, *Roughing It in the Suburbs: Reading* Chatelaine *Magazine in the Fifties and Sixties*
17 Adele Perry, *On the Edge of Empire: Gender, Race, and the Making of British Columbia, 1849–1871*
18 Robert A. Campbell, *Sit Down and Drink Your Beer: Regulating Vancouver's Beer Parlours, 1925–1954*
19 Wendy Mitchinson, *Giving Birth in Canada, 1900–1950*

20 Roberta Hamilton, *Setting the Agenda: Jean Royce and the Shaping of Queen's University*
21 Donna Gabaccia and Franca Iacovetta, eds., *Women, Gender, and Transnational Lives: Italian Workers of the World*
22 Linda Reeder, *Widows in White: Migration and the Transformation of Rural Women, Sicily, 1880–1920*
23 Terry Crowley, *Marriage of Minds: Isabel and Oscar Skelton Reinventing Canada*
24 Marlene Epp, Franca Iacovetta, and Frances Swyripa, eds., *Sisters or Strangers? Immigrant, Ethnic, and Racialized Women in Canadian History*
25 John G. Reid, *Viola Florence Barnes, 1885–1979: A Historian's Biography*
26 Catherine Carstairs, *Jailed for Possession: Illegal Drug Use Regulation and Power in Canada, 1920–1961*
27 Magda Fahrni, *Household Politics: Montreal Families and Postwar Reconstruction*
28 Tamara Myers, *Caught: Montreal Girls and the Law, 1869–1945*
29 Jennifer A. Stephen, *Pick One Intelligent Girl: Employability, Domesticity, and the Gendering of Canada's Welfare State, 1939–1947*
30 Lisa Chilton, *Agents of Empire: British Female Migration to Canada and Australia, 1860s–1930*
31 Esyllt W. Jones, *Influenza 1918: Disease, Death, and Struggle in Winnipeg*
32 Elise Chenier, *Strangers in Our Midst: Sexual Deviancy in Postwar Ontario*
33 Lara Campbell, *Respectable Citizens: Gender, Family, and Unemployment in the Great Depression, Ontario, 1929–1939*
34 Katrina Srigley, *Breadwinning Daughters: Young Working Women in a Depression-Era city, 1929–1939*
35 Maureen Moynagh with Nancy Forestell, eds., *Documenting First Wave Feminisms, Volume 1: Transnational Collaborations and Crosscurrents*
36 Mona Oikawa, *Cartographies of Violence: Women, Memory, and the Subject(s) of the "Internment"*
37 Karen Flynn, *Moving beyond Borders: A History of Black Canadian and Caribbean Women in the Diaspora*
38 Karen Balcom, *The Traffic in Babies: Cross-Border Adoption and Baby-Selling between the United States and Canada, 1930–1972*
39 Nancy M. Forestell with Maureen Moynagh, eds., *Documenting First Wave Feminisms, Volume II: Canada – National and Transnational Contexts*

40 Patrizia Gentile and Jane Nicholas, eds., *Contesting Bodies and Nation in Canadian History*
41 Suzanne Morton, *Wisdom, Justice and Charity: Canadian Social Welfare through the Life of Jane B. Wisdom, 1884–1975*
42 Jane Nicholas, *The Modern Girl: Feminine Modernities, the Body, and Commodities in the 1920s*
43 Pauline A. Phipps, *Constance Maynard's Passions: Religion, Sexuality, and an English Educational Pioneer, 1849–1935*
44 Marlene Epp and Franca Iacovetta, eds., *Sisters or Strangers? Immigrant, Ethnic, and Racialized Women in Canadian History*, Second Edition
45 Rhonda L. Hinther, *Perogies and Politics: Canada's Ukrainian Left, 1891–1991*
46 Valerie J. Korinek, *Prairie Fairies: A History of Queer Communities and People in Western Canada, 1930–1985*
47 Julie Guard, *Radical Housewives: Price Wars and Food Politics in Mid-Twentieth Canada*
48 Nancy Janovicek and Carmen Nielson, eds., *Reading Canadian Women's and Gender History*
49 L.K. Bertram, *The Viking Immigrants: Icelandic North Americans*
50 Donica Belisle, *Purchasing Power: Women and the Rise of Canadian Consumer Culture*
51 Allyson D. Stevenson, *Intimate Integration: A History of the Sixties Scoop and the Colonization of Indigenous Kinship*
52 Nadia Jones-Gailani, *Transnational Identity and Memory Making in the Lives of Iraqi Women in Diaspora*
53 Franca Iacovetta, *Before Official Multiculturalism: Women's Pluralism in Toronto, 1950s–1970s*
54 Heather Stanley, *Sex and the Married Girl: Heterosexual Marriage and the Body in Postwar Canada*

www.ingramcontent.com/pod-product-compliance
Lightning Source LLC
Chambersburg PA
CBHW030316080526
44584CB00012B/587